Wisdom Seekers

The Rise of the New Spirituality

Wisdom Seekers

The Rise of the New Spirituality

Dr Nevill Drury

BOOKS

Winchester, UK
Washington, USA

First published by O-Books, 2011
O-Books is an imprint of John Hunt Publishing Ltd., Laurel House, Station Approach,
Alresford, Hants, SO24 9JH, UK
office1@o-books.net
www.o-books.com

For distributor details and how to order please visit the 'Ordering' section on our website.

ISBN: 978 1 84694 512 0

Design: Tom Davies

Printed in the UK by CPI Antony Rowe
Printed in the USA by Offset Paperback Mfrs, Inc

We operate a distinctive and ethical publishing philosophy in all
areas of our business, from our global network of authors to
production and worldwide distribution.

CONTENTS

Introduction   1

1: Wisdom from the East, Wisdom from the West   6
2: Pioneers of the Psyche   44
3: Towards the Transpersonal   68
4: Esalen, Gestalt and Encounter   81
5: The Psychedelic Years   94
6: Maps for Inner Space   117
7: The Holistic Perspective   137
8: Mystics and Metaphysicians   151
9: Spirit, Myth and Cosmos   174
10: Science and Spirituality   199
11: The Challenge of Death   218
12: The Future of the New Age   243

Notes   254
Bibliography   276
Index   297

The central ideal within New Age teachings is not just revolutionary in the best sense, but arguably necessary for a world long plagued and divided by rigid religious dogma and blind prejudice. The New Age, in the best sense of what it represents, has long been in need of a chronicler and interpreter who can explain its essence without resorting to a tone of superior academic scorn or shallow, gullible cheerleading. In Nevill Drury, an accomplished author of dozens of works on the great wisdom traditions, the New Age has found its scribe and interpreter. In this comprehensive book he lucidly explains the nuts and bolts of the movement, warts and all — delving into its host of colourful characters, all the way from Blavatsky and Gurdjieff to Sun Bear, Elisabeth Kubler-Ross and Robert Monroe — without losing sight of the genuine spark of heart and wisdom behind it. This is a thoroughly researched, eminently readable and highly recommended book.

P.T. Mistlberger, author

Nevill Drury has written a wonderfully accessible and carefully researched review of the major historical and intellectual sources of the New Age. It is rich with detail, entertaining anecdotes, and thoughtful analysis.

Dr Douglas Ezzy, Associate Professor of Sociology, University of Tasmania

Nevill Drury's in-depth overview of the New Age movement is about as good as it gets. Readers will emerge from this text not merely informed as to the movement's extraordinarily varied developmental history, they will also emerge with a deepened appreciation of New Age ideas, aims and values in relation to the sacred, mythic dimension of life. Drury's approach replaces facile scrutiny with astute penetration of what it means to be awake and aware. This is, in other words, a book to be read more than once.
Douglas Lockhart, author

Does not disappoint, with a plethora of incisive comments and fresh analysis of the origin, present status, and possible future of the 'New Age' or 'New Spirituality'. Nevill Drury has again brought a world of unique insights to us and this makes a must-have addition to the library.
Dr Jonn Mumford (Swami Anandakapila Saraswati), author

Thoroughly researched, provides an in-depth understanding of the evolution of the New Age movement in a nutshell.
Bronwen and Frans Stiene, authors

Introduction

The New Age movement may well reflect the future face of Western religion – a fusion of experiential and transformative spiritual practices grounded in the perennial wisdom traditions of both East and West. In a welcome contrast to fundamentalist extremism, the New Age argues for a spirituality without borders or confining dogmas, for an essentially tolerant approach to religious belief which does not exclude outsiders on the basis of doctrinal difference. The New Age is also actively seeking a paradigm which embraces the insights of scientific understanding whilst recognizing that at a fundamental level the foundations of life remain a mystery. The New Age urges us to explore the sacred paths of connectedness that link all aspects of humanity, Nature and Cosmos. At the same time the New Age also supports the view that there are many authentic paths to self-realization, that no religion holds a unique and exclusive key to spiritual enlightenment.

This, then, is the focus of the New Age – a movement which clearly seeks the middle ground between institutional Western religion and the secular, often skeptical, materialism of the modern age. It is a movement, fast gathering momentum internationally, which supports an experiential and transformative approach to human spiritual development and which challenges the rigidity of religious fundamentalism wherever it is found.

Nevertheless, the New Age is not without its critics. Many of these critics have strong Christian affiliations and possibly sense a genuine threat from a movement that denies the concept of an exclusive path to spiritual salvation. Some of these critics have dismissed the New Age as a form of consumerist spirituality – as an uncritical and eclectic fusion of metaphysical ideas without any clear direction. Others have labeled the New Age as narcissistic and hedonistic. We will explore these criticisms later in this book.

Much of the inspiration driving the New Age derives from ancient and perennial wisdom teachings – from the Vedas, from Yoga and Tibetan Buddhism, from Sufism and indigenous spirituality. At the same time the New Age movement is also a creative fusion of metaphysics, self-help psychology and holistic approaches to self-awareness. To this extent, the New Age is both old and new, both ancient and contemporary.

Nevertheless, it also seems clear to me that there are deep and significant currents propelling and sustaining the New Age movement which are unique to the contemporary context. These contemporary philosophical and spiritual currents are leading rapidly towards the emergence of a new holistic paradigm – a paradigm which encompasses both spirituality and science and which is much broader in its scope than the cosmologies of the past. It is only by considering the nature of this transformational thrust that we can assess the true impact and likely legacy of the New Age movement. Exploring the nature and origin of the currents of thought which inform and sustain the New Age, and which provide it with its special impetus, is a central concern in the present book.

I am sure that most intelligent Christians would take umbrage in having their religious beliefs viewed solely through the lens of the commercial style of evangelism that emanates from the heartland of American fundamentalism. And so it is with the New Age movement, which has been similarly accused of promoting commercial forms of spirituality. In presenting this overview of the New Age as a whole, I deal not only with the movement's quirky eccentricities and shortcomings – including its commercial aspects – but also with its undoubted strengths and originality. These strengths include its emphasis on the spiritual potential innate within each individual human being, its recognition of the universal aspects of the religious experience, its openness to fusing new discoveries in science with insights from both Eastern and Western spiritual traditions, and its willingness to embrace an essentially holistic view of humanity and the world at large.

How we perceive the New Age depends very much on our definition. In terms of popular usage such expressions as 'the human potential movement', the 'personal growth movement' and the umbrella term of the 'New Age' itself, are all to some extent interchangeable and point in the same direction. However they also require some clarification. Historically the New Age movement builds on a concept promoted during the late 19th century by the Theosophists[1] – the idea that there is a universal wisdom tradition that embraces the spiritual teachings of both East and West. However, the New Age also draws substantially on the self-help aspects of 20th century psychology – especially the psychology of personal self-realization and integration advocated by pioneering thinkers like Carl Jung and Abraham Maslow. Meanwhile, the term 'transpersonal' – which refers to states of awareness beyond the human ego – is an expression that has been used by Jungian and humanistic psychologists alike,[2] just as the expressions 'personal growth' and 'human potential' were originally associated with the rise of humanistic psychology in the 1960s. The Esalen Institute in Big Sur, California – the archetypal source-model for all experiential 'personal growth' centers – was founded on the very idea of fusing self-help psychology with the perennial wisdom traditions, and the Esalen experience has helped define the New Age movement as we encounter it around the world today.

It is also important to emphasize that, contrary to the popular media-image promoted by its detractors, the New Age is not just about hedonistic self-help and sensory indulgence. Some first-rate thinkers – including Aldous Huxley, Krishnamurti and Joseph Campbell – have presented their perspectives at Esalen, and similar qualitative thinking continues to feed into the New Age from a deeper source. This deeper source is the international transpersonal movement – a progressive group of psychologists, physicists, biologists, anthropologists, philosophers, spiritual scholars and social theorists whose ideas have helped clarify the quest for a new paradigm: a worldview which embraces both science and spirituality. Among these prominent thinkers are such figures as Stanislav Grof, Ken Wilber, Jean Houston, Fritjof Capra, Rupert Sheldrake, Ralph Metzner, Kenneth Ring, Jean Shinoda Bolen, Danah Zohar, Charles Tart, James Fadiman and Frances Vaughan – all of whom have solid academic credentials. The view I am presenting in the present book is that the best ideas emanating from the transpersonal movement gradually find their way through to the New Age, albeit in a more popular and accessible form. These ideas then help shape the New Age movement as it moves forward with the passage of time.

On one level the New Age movement can be seen as an eclectic blend of self-help modalities and spiritual practices – as a diverse mix of metaphysical ideas and body/mind therapies. However, many of the most progressive ideas feeding through to the New Age from the transpersonal movement are at the cutting edge of contemporary thought and demand our attention. For this reason, the New Age movement deserves much more than a passing glance. I also believe that the history of the New Age is really quite fascinating. I have nominated four key precursors of the New Age – Emanuel Swedenborg, Franz Anton Mesmer, Madame Helena Blavatsky and George Ivanovitch Gurdjieff – as the starting point for this overview, for it seems to me that these historical figures embody much of what the New Age now sets out to achieve. They are, however, only a starting point, and there have been many twists and turns along the way. As we will see, the unfolding story of the New Age takes us through the rise of 20th century psychology, through the often reckless period of experimentation with mind-expanding psychedelic drugs in the 1960s, to the increasing fascination with Eastern gurus, the subsequent pursuit of non-drug practices like yoga and meditation, and the exploration of universal maps of consciousness.

Essentially the New Age focuses on the perennial quest for wisdom and understanding – for spiritual and philosophical perspectives that will help transform humanity and the world as a whole. New Agers are willing to absorb these wisdom teachings wherever they can find them, whether from an Indian guru, a renegade Christian priest, an itinerant Buddhist monk, an experiential psychotherapist, or a Native American shaman. They are eager to explore their own inner potentials with a view to becoming part of a broader process of social transformation. Their journey is one which points finally towards wholeness and totality of being, for devotees of the New Age are wisdom seekers in quest of a new paradigm. Their essential quest – one that I also happen to share and endorse – is for a holistic worldview that offers both insight and hope for the challenging times that lie ahead. In the chapters which follow we will explore the fascinating rise of the international New Age movement and its enthusiastic pursuit of the new spiritual paradigm.

Chapter I

Wisdom from the East, Wisdom from the West

It is often said that many key precepts of the New Age have been with us for some time, that there is nothing especially new about the New Age. While I think this is basically true, it is also apparent that the New Age is a fusion of ideas and influences unique to its own era. In drawing on both Eastern and Western spiritual and metaphysical traditions and then infusing this mix with further influences from self-help and motivational psychology, holistic health, parapsychology, consciousness research and quantum physics, the New Age has emerged with characteristics that are all its own. Nevertheless, amidst the far-ranging, eclectic influences that have impacted on the New Age movement as we know it today, it is certainly possible to identify a number of key precursors – specific individuals from earlier periods in history whose outlook has contributed to, and helped shape, contemporary New Age perspectives. Among these early pioneers are such figures as Emanuel Swedenborg, Franz Anton Mesmer, Madame Helena Blavatsky and George Ivanovitch Gurdjieff.

Swedenborg is of interest to us in the context of the New Age because he began his professional life as a distinguished scientist and only later, after a series of transformative experiences which began when he was 55 years old, did he become a mystic. His attempt to describe the visionary world of the afterlife in a completely dispassionate way, based entirely on his own personal experiences, parallels and anticipates the transpersonal approach to near-death studies described later in this book.

Among the other major New Age precursors, Mesmer is a controversial figure, and is frequently depicted as a charlatan and opportunist. However, whatever one may think of his unorthodox healing methods, he did reintroduce a vitalist conception of the human organism to the medical practices of his day. His concept of 'animal magnetism' – which we would nowadays refer to as 'life-force' or *ch'i* – has clear parallels with the healing energy utilized in many contemporary New Age forms of spiritual healing, where it is assumed that the practitioner becomes a vehicle for a vital healing force that can be transmitted directly to the patient. Even though the concept of animal magnetism did not endure, and it was later recognized that trance states did not involve a transfer of vital energy from the mesmerist to the patient, Mesmer and his disciples nevertheless contributed directly to the rise of modern hypnotherapy.

Like Mesmer, the 19th century Theosophist Madame Blavatsky similarly combined trickery and a capacity for preposterous claims with genuine visionary insight. Although she was eventually caught out deceiving her followers with her claim that she could manifest spirit-messages from Tibetan Masters resident on the inner planes, Madame Blavatsky was ahead of her time in other respects. She held the view, now widely embraced in the New Age movement, that no spiritual tradition can ever lay claim to an exclusive hold on truth or revelation and that many different religious and metaphysical philosophies – from both East and West – represent authentic paths to spiritual transcendence. In fostering an awareness of the universal truths underlying all the major religious traditions she anticipated thinkers like Aldous Huxley, Alan Watts, Joseph Campbell and Ken Wilber – all of whom in turn would also influence New Age perspectives.

Madame Blavatsky also supported the idea that we should seek a synthesis of science and spirituality in order to comprehend the nature of the universe in which we live. In our own era, at a time when many fundamentalist Christians are still hostage to retrogressive concepts like Creationism, this remains a lesson worth heeding. As Madame Blavatsky sought to explain through her voluminous metaphysical writings, a religious doctrine can only hope to endure if it reflects the full spectrum of human experience and complements the current scientific understanding of the world in which we live. What Madame Blavatsky understood to be true and authentic science remains a matter of debate – she was fiercely hostile to Darwin's approach to evolution, for example, and held an eccentric view of human development – but the principle itself remains valid. The concept of fusing science and spirituality has since become a hallmark of the transpersonal perspective which in turn has strongly influenced contemporary New Age belief.

Finally, among the major historical precursors of the New Age, George Ivanovitch Gurdjieff emerges as a prototypical Western guru, albeit from an earlier era. In urging his followers to 'wake up' from their habitual behavior – conditioning which he believed made them act like robots or machines – Gurdjieff was more like an 1960s encounter therapist than a late 19th century mystic. He was eminently practical, extremely focused and disciplined, and he saw through the veneer of external appearances. Had he lived in California during the 1960s and 1970s he would no doubt have embraced bodywork and Gestalt therapy and put in numerous appearances at the Esalen Institute – he was certainly as fierce and demanding as Fritz Perls and he had a clear vision of what he wanted to achieve.

These days Gurdjieff's theory of universal numbers may seem a little abstruse and his concept of the three traditional paths to enlightenment – those of the fakir, the monk and the yogi – comes across as rather simplistic, even if he did propose his own 'fourth way' as an alternative. And few in the New Age nowadays would accept his view that humans are simply machines whose actions, thoughts and feelings are the result of external influences.

Nevertheless, the very fact that Gurdjieff was able to attract a band of dedicated followers in Russia and then travel with them through the Caucasus Mountains and on to Constantinople, Berlin and Paris, provides us with the image of an inspirational visionary who clearly had a message to deliver. Gurdjieff is the most direct and practical of the New Age precursors profiled here, and perhaps the least mystical. His uncompromising approach to human self-development anticipates the approach of the experiential workshops and confrontational encounter groups that would emerge in the American counterculture during the 1960s.

Emanuel Swedenborg (1688–1772)

Emanuel Swedenborg, whose surname was originally Swedberg, was born in Stockholm on 29 January 1688 – the third of nine children. Emanuel's father was a court chaplain and professor of theology at the University of Uppsala, and was highly regarded by his peers. Emanuel lived in Uppsala during his formative years but when his father was appointed Archbishop of Skara he went to live with his brother-in-law, Eric Benzelius, who was thirteen years his senior.

At this stage of his life Emanuel was still a young university student, and his inclinations were clearly oriented towards science rather than theology. After graduating from the University of Uppsala in 1710 he pursued his interest in metallurgy and engineering and in 1716 was appointed special assessor to the Royal College of Mines by King Charles XII of Sweden. In 1719, when he was 31 years old, Emanuel's family was ennobled and the family name changed from Swedberg to Swedenborg. Emanuel was now entitled to take his place in the Swedish House of Nobles.

Nevertheless, his position with the Swedish Board of Mines would remain the only professional appointment of his career. So absorbed was he with his research into mining engineering that Swedenborg declined an opportunity to follow his father and become a professor at the University of Uppsala. Fascinated by science in all its forms he would go on to produce experimental drawings for a flying machine and to explore the properties of light. In due course his numerous scientific publications included works on mathematics, chemistry, astronomy, magnetism and psychology, as well as human anatomy. He wrote learned tracts on the pituitary gland and the cerebral cortex as well as on cerebrospinal fluid, and was the first person to discover the function of the cerebellum. In 1734 he also proposed the 'nebular hypothesis' to account for the formation of the planets – anticipating the theories of Immanuel Kant and the French astronomer, Marquis de Laplace.

In 1744 Swedenborg produced a work titled *On the Infinite and Final Cause of Creation* in which he explored the relationship between the soul and the body. At this stage he was still very much a scientist, but he was drawing ever closer to the deep involvement in spiritual matters that would characterize the latter years of his life. Swedenborg would soon be transformed by a series of powerful dreams and visions that would compel him to pursue his mystical interests to the exclusion of everything else.

Swedenborg recorded in his diaries that in late 1744 he began to experience a number of vivid dreams. These dreams highlighted his sinfulness and his intellectual pride and had a profoundly humbling effect on him. Then, in 1745, he had a decisive vision while he was eating his dinner at an inn in London. Swedenborg claimed that during this visionary episode he met the Lord God himself and that he was subsequently instructed to document his experiences of the spiritual realms and to produce an account of the true meaning of the Christian scriptures: 'Towards the close of the meal I noticed a sort of dimness before my eyes; this became denser, and I then saw the floor covered with horrid crawling reptiles ... I was amazed, for

I was perfectly conscious, and my thoughts were clear.' Swedenborg now noticed a man sitting in the corner of the room who said to him, 'Eat not so much.' The darkness intensified and then finally cleared. He now found he was alone in the room. Swedenborg continues his account:

> Such an unexpected terror hastened my return home … I went home, and during the same night the same man revealed himself to me again, but I was not frightened now. He then said that he was the Lord God, the Creator of the world, and the Redeemer, and that he had chosen me to explain to men the spiritual sense of the Scripture and that He Himself would explain to me what I should write on this subject; that same night were opened to me so that I became thoroughly convinced of their reality, the worlds of spirits, heaven and hell, and I recognized there many acquaintances of every condition in life. From that day I gave up the study of all worldly science, and labored in spiritual things.[1]

Swedenborg's life would now be totally dedicated to pursuing the source of his revelations. In 1747, at the age of 59, he resigned his position with the Royal College of Mines and accepted a half-pension in order to dedicate what remained of his life to exploring the realms of spirits and angels. Swedenborg was well aware that many would view his quest with scepticism and disbelief, but he did not allow this to become an obstacle. 'Many will say that it is all a phantasy …' he wrote in his three-volume work *Arcana Coelestia*. 'But by all this I am not deterred, for I have seen, I have heard, I have felt.'[2]

Swedenborg believed he could bring the same vigor and discipline to describing the spiritual realms that he had applied earlier in the natural sciences. For him his new spiritual quest simply involved factual observation within an unfamiliar domain – the visionary exploration of a world rarely glimpsed by mortal eyes. Swedenborg seems to have used some form of meditative trance to enter these visionary states of consciousness and would, on occasion, startle his servants by engaging in conversations with spirit-beings who were visible only to him. He was clearly living and operating in two different worlds.

In his voluminous mystical works Swedenborg describes a universe in which everything emanates from the One God, or Creator, who sustains the universe through the spiritual sun – the primal source of love and knowledge. According to Swedenborg, the spiritual hierarchy is as follows:

Swedenborg's Spiritual Hierarchy
The Lord (One God)

The three levels of Heaven:
Celestial Heaven
Spiritual Heaven
Natural Heaven
[These three levels of Heaven have their three equivalent Hells]

World of spirits

Humanity on Earth

The world of Nature

Above humanity and the natural world in the hierarchy we enter the realm of spirits – this is the world accessed at death – and above them in turn are the three levels of Heaven (each of which has an equivalent Hell). According to Swedenborg, all of the angels and spirit-beings residing in these heavens were once persons who had lived in the world but they were now functioning in realms appropriate to their level of spiritual realization and development.

In Swedenborg's cosmology all forms in the natural world come into existence through impulses from the spiritual realm. God's spiritual sun of love and wisdom, for example, has its counterpart in the natural sun, whose light and warmth sustain Nature. Essentially the cosmos operates through a spiritual hierarchy of cause and effect. Swedenborg refers to the symbolic relationship between spiritual and natural forms as 'correspondences': the hierarchy of beings in the different heavens represent different orders of spiritual existence and act in 'correspondence' with each other. According to Swedenborg, the Lord acts through his celestial angels, who in turn correspond on a lower level to spiritual angels, who in turn correspond to angels in the third natural heaven, who in turn correspond to the world of humanity below. Swedenborg also maintained that in many ancient cultures in the Middle East a knowledge of these sacred correspondences provided the basis for various forms of ceremonial worship, for example the burnt offerings and sacrifices employed by the Israelites. He also believed that ancient Egyptian hieroglyphics were based on these correspondences and represented a type of sacred visionary script. According to Swedenborg the principle of correspondences influenced 'many kingdoms ... particularly in the Land of Canaan, Egypt, Assyria, Chaldaea, Syria, Arabia and in Tyre, Sidan and Nineveh. It was thence communicated to Greece, but it was there changed into fable.'[3]

In Swedenborg's cosmology the concept of exercising 'free will' is a comparatively narrow option for any human being because within the greater scheme of things all individuals are subject to the interactions of good and evil spirits who tower above them in the cosmic hierarchy and who represent positive and negative causality in the universe. Each human being is a type of meeting ground for these great hierarchies. As American psychologist and Swedenborg scholar Wilson Van Dusen has expressed it, 'In effect, good and its opposite evil rule through this hierarchy of beings down to man who stands in the free space between them.'[4]

This means that while, as sentient human beings, we each may feel that we are exercising our own free will in our everyday lives, in reality we are nothing other than minor players on God's stage. For Swedenborg, 'good' people can be recognized through their willingness to work in harmony with the natural world, thereby accepting this shared destiny of souls, whereas 'evil' people remain isolated and self-centered, and through arrogance and pride take full credit for their personal achievements, not realizing that they have been guided by the realm of good and evil spirits. Swedenborg maintained that most people have two good spirits and two evil spirits in permanent attendance.[5] In modern parlance we might be inclined to view these spirits more as forces or polarities within the subconscious mind. However, the real message that Swedenborg was conveying was that every human being is subject to potent forces beyond the scope of normal ego-based awareness. Such is the power of the spiritual hierarchy operating in the manifest universe.

Swedenborg claimed that angels had taken him through the process of death on several occasions and he was able to observe in great detail what took place in the afterlife. He maintained that Heaven and Hell both exist but 'they are states rather than places'. After passing through the process of death, all human beings become discarnate spirits and then, after being greeted by friends and family who have preceded them in death, they are drawn towards the good or evil realms that correspond to the true inner nature of their soul. According to Swedenborg, death is nothing other than a state of transition in which we continue to perceive and interact with other beings just as we did when we were alive. Many people do not even realize that they have died![6]

Swedenborg says that in seeking passage to Heaven the apparently 'good' acts we perform in life are not in themselves sufficient; it is the character of the inner person that is really significant. Referring to the process of afterlife transition he writes:

> Almost all of them desire to know whether they shall come into heaven, and many believe that they shall, because they led a moral and civil life in the world, not reflecting that both the wicked and the good lead a similar life outwardly, doing good to others in the same manner, going to churches, hearing sermons, and praying; and not knowing at all that outward deeds and outwards acts of worship are of no avail, but the internal states from which the external acts proceed.[7]

In other words it is the state of our soul – our true inner nature – that really counts. We will all enter the Heaven or Hell we deserve. Indeed, we are even living in these realms now, for the polarities of good and evil continue to hold sway over our everyday lives on Earth.

Interestingly, although Swedenborg was strongly Christian himself he had a universal view of religion and believed that many different spiritual traditions had their own valid interpretation of 'truth'. Swedenborg claimed to have heard from the angels themselves that 'churches which are in a variety of goods and truths are like so many jewels in a king's crown'.[8]

He also wrote that 'varieties in matters of doctrine and worship are like the varieties of the senses'[9] and maintained that 'the church of the Lord consists of all those, whosoever they are, who are in truths derived from good'.[10] As Wilson Van Dusen has thoughtfully observed, 'Swedenborg was speaking of the heart of religion that transcends the boundaries of creeds, nations, cultures, times, people. All who act in the good that they know will be saved.'[11]

Franz Anton Mesmer (1734–1815)

Franz Anton Mesmer is of considerable interest as one of the major precursors of the New Age movement. Quite apart from his role in the development of what would later become hypnotherapy, Mesmer advocated a vitalist approach to healing through the transmission of 'animal magnetism' to his patients. As mentioned earlier, Mesmer's core concept of transferring healing energy to one's patients continues to flourish in a number of energy-based forms of spiritual healing. And although Mesmer could not have anticipated the findings of 20th century quantum physics he similarly emphasized the interconnectedness of all the heavenly bodies and natural life-forms in the universe, a holistic concept now widely embraced by New Age devotees keen to explore the apparent parallels between mysticism and the New Physics.[12]

Franz Anton Mesmer was born in Iznang, Germany, near the shores of Lake Constance, and originally intended to enter the Church. However, he was drawn to mathematics and science and decided to study medicine at the University of Vienna. Here he absorbed the prevailing scientific view that a magnetic fluid permeates all aspects of life.

The concept of 'magnetism' as a form of vital force was an idea of long standing – Paracelsus and Van Helmont shared a similar belief in a subtle fluid pervading the universe. Like Paracelsus before him, Mesmer was fascinated by the influence of the heavenly bodies on individual health and well-being and in his dissertation at the University of Vienna – *De Planetarum Influxu* ('On the Influence of the Planets'), written in 1766 – Mesmer wrote that the sun, moon and stars not only influenced each other in a way similar to the movement of the tides but that they also 'affect in similar manner all organized bodies through the medium of a subtle fluid, which pervades the universe and associates all things together in mutual intercourse and harmony'. For Mesmer this natural flow of energy equated with health and vitality. Blocking the flow of energy in the body would lead to disease and ill-health.

Mesmer's thesis attracted the attention of a Jesuit priest named Father Maximilian Hehl, who was court astrologer to Empress Maria Theresa and also a professor of astronomy at the University of Vienna. Professor Hehl believed in the impact of planetary magnetism on physical health and used magnets to 'correct' imbalances in the human organism.

After Mesmer graduated from the University of Vienna he adopted Professor Hehl's approach and began to use magnetism in his medical treatments. His first patient, Fraulein Oesterline, was an epileptic. Mesmer attached three magnets to her stomachs and both legs and was greatly encouraged when she claimed that the painful subtle energies she had been experiencing were now subsiding to the lower part of her body. Her convulsive symptoms disappeared after six hours.

However Mesmer soon discovered that Hehl's magnets were not essential for treating his patients. Mesmer found that he could produce equally effective cures by transmitting healing energy to his patients through touch, by pointing his forefinger or making passes over his patients with his hands, or by using iron rods or wands which he had personally 'magnetized'. Mesmer referred to this healing force as 'animal magnetism' and considered it an innate human quality – a quite different proposition from the 'mineral magnetism' utilized through Professor Hehl's magnets. Mesmer noted that during his treatments some of his patients lost control of their limbs while others went into convulsions, began speaking in strange voices or sank into states of catalepsy or coma. However he seems to have taken the view that these unusual symptoms were all part of the healing process.

Not surprisingly Mesmer soon fell out of favor with Professor Hehl and the Viennese medical profession. In 1778 Mesmer moved to Paris, and quickly gained a new audience. Soon large numbers of patients began coming to him for cures.

Many of Mesmer's patients were wealthy aristocrats and he took great care to create an ambience that would impress them. Mesmer's consulting rooms were lit with soft light and were decorated with paintings, mirrors, clocks and crystal objects. A chamber orchestra played soft music as he and his assistants moved among the patients, waving their wands in order to stroke and 'magnetize' the patients. Mesmer himself wore a shirt of leather, lined with silk, to prevent his personal 'magnetic fluid' from escaping from his body.

Mesmer's reputation as an unconventional but successful healer spread rapidly. In fact, so many patients wanted to come to visit Mesmer that soon he had to develop a method for treating them collectively. In order to do this he created a device called a *baquet* – a round wooden bath tub that he filled with magnetized water and iron filings. A number of iron rod conductors protruded from the tub and the patients were asked to hold these rods while also being bound by a moistened cord in a continuous circle to close 'the force'. Mesmer claimed that magnetism from the tub would transfer to the patients, thereby alleviating their various illnesses.

When Mesmer first came to Paris his first convert was Charles D'Eslon – physician to Comte d'Artois, the brother of Louis XVI. In September 1780, impressed by what he regarded as an exciting and revolutionary approach to healing, D'Eslon asked the Faculty of Medicine to investigate Mesmer's methods. However the proposal was rejected and D'Eslon was threatened that his name would be struck off the rolls at the end of the year if he did not recant.

As one might expect, Mesmer's unconventional successes continued to attract hostility from the Medical Academy. Finally, in 1784, a Royal Commission was set up by Louis XVI to investigate Mesmer and his claims of 'animal magnetism'. The Commission was chaired by Benjamin Franklin – who at the time was United States Ambassador to France – and also included the distinguished chemist Antoine Lavoisier; Dr J-I. Guillotin, a physician better known as the inventor of the execution device that still bears his name; Jean-Sylvain Bailly, an astronomer and a future mayor of Paris; and the highly regarded botanist Laurent Jussieu. Mesmer declined any direct involvement but the committee was able to investigate Mesmer's colleague Charles D'Eslon and the controversial *baquet* in operation. By this time D'Eslon had developed a technique for inducing states of trance in some of the patients. Here is Jean-Sylvain Bailly's account of what he observed:

> The sick persons, arranged in great numbers, and in several rows around the baquet, received the magnetism by means of the iron rods, which conveyed it to them from the baquet by the cords wound around their bodies, by the thumb which connected them with their neighbours and by the sounds of a pianoforte, or an agreeable voice, diffusing magnetism in the air. The patients were also directly magnetised by means of the finger and wand of the magnetiser, moved slowly before their faces, above or behind their heads, or on the diseased parts. The magnetiser acts also by fixing his eyes on the subjects; by the application of his hands on the region of the solar plexus, an application which sometimes continues for hours. Meanwhile the patients present a very varied picture. Some are calm, tranquil and experience no effect. Others cough and spit, feel pains, heat or perspiration. Others, again, are convulsed.[13]

The investigating committee did not dispute that many of the patients gained great benefits from the unconventional treatment. However, the committee was able to establish that when the patients were blindfolded and unable to tell whether or not they had been 'magnetized', nothing specific happened one way or the other. The investigating committee therefore decided that it was the patients' own imaginations which had produced the healing benefits and they also found no evidence to support 'animal magnetism' or the presence of a magnetic fluid. More specifically, the committee recommended that members of the Faculty of Medicine who adopted Mesmer's approach to healing should be expelled from professional practice.

Although Mesmer and his colleagues continued to practice magnetic healing in Paris, the report of the Royal Commission had the effect of temporarily diminishing its appeal. Nevertheless, a strong and influential ally would soon emerge to rescue the cause. This person was Armand Chastenet, Marquis de Puységur, a former artillery officer who had studied with Mesmer and who was just beginning to explore the healing benefits of animal magnetism.

Puységur was not a trained physician but was a former president of the Lyon Medical Society. He began demonstrating his own animal magnetism cures in Busancy in 1784, the year the Royal Commission rejected the concept out of hand. Puységur did not employ a baquet but instead magnetized a tree, fastened cords around it and invited patients to tie themselves to it.

Puységur also discovered he could induce a state of trance in some of his patients simply by making 'passes' over them and lulling them into what he called 'magnetic sleep'. Puységur found that this form of trance was able to eliminate convulsions and, perhaps not surprisingly, he attributed this phenomenon to animal magnetism.

One of his patients, a young 23-year-old peasant named Victor, appeared to fall asleep in his arms. However this was not conventional sleep but something quite different. While in this state, Victor began to talk aloud but on waking remembered nothing. Puységur was also amazed to discover that while in a state of trance Victor would do what he was told to do through words or signs and that he also seemed to respond to unspoken commands. Puységur thought that perhaps Victor was clair-voyant, and similarly attributed the phenomenon to animal magnetism. However this was a breakthrough of a quite different order. As the noted parapsychologist Dr Nandor Fodor has observed, this represented the discovery of the somnambulic state.[14]

Despite the respite provided by Puységur, Mesmer's fortunes began to decline and were not helped when one of his strongest supporters, Antoine Court de Gebelin, best known for his now discredited theory that the Tarot was of Egyptian origin, died while sitting in a baquet. Mesmer continued with his practice in Paris until 1789 when the French Revolution forced him to leave France. Mesmer went to Karlsruhe, and then to Vienna in 1793. He was accused of being a French spy and was jailed for two months. After his release he returned to Lake Constance. He died in 1815.

Fate was nevertheless kind to Mesmer and his followers. When Napoleon came to the French throne it was no longer politically dangerous to dabble in mesmerism, and interest in the theories of Mesmer and Puységur was revived by a young curator at the Paris Jardin des Plantes named Jean Philippe Deleuze (1753–1835). In 1812, after four years of research, Deleuze published his *Histoire Critique du Magnétisme Animal*, in which he sought to establish the reality of the mesmerism and to describe how subjects behaved once they had entered a somnam-bulistic state. Deleuze was intrigued that patients could respond to the mesmerist's verbal or visual instructions while in a state of somnambulistic trance.

Mesmer and his followers, D'Eslon and Puységur, claimed that a fluid or force radiated from the mesmerist to the subject and induced these states of trance but this view was disputed by Alexandre Bertrand, a young French physician who had been attracted to the study of animal magnetism through the work of Deleuze. Bertrand made a study of induced trance and published two important works, *Traité du Somnambulisme* (1823) and *Du Magnétisme Animal en France* (1826). Bertrand believed that the cures resulting from treatment in trance states did not derive from animal magnetism or magnetic fluid but from the suggestions of the practitioner acting on the imagination of the patient, whose suggestibility was increased while in a state of trance.

Meanwhile, another influential voice would now enter the debate – that of a Portugese priest, Abbé J.C. Faria. During the years while Napoleon was in exile in St Helena, Abbé Faria had begun giving public demonstrations in Paris in which he would put subjects into a state of somnambulistic trance and then take apparent control of them. He did not make passes over his subjects as Mesmer had done but instead asked them quietly and firmly to 'sleep'.

Faria's approach did not endear him to the mesmerists. Faria did not believe in the existence of magnetic fluid and in 1813, just as the members of the Royal Commission had done in 1784, Faria ascribed the magnetic phenomenon to the imagination. Nevertheless the debate over the therapeutic value of Mesmer's animal magnetism would have long-lasting consequences. By focusing on the power of suggestion enhanced during trance states, Abbé Faria and Dr Alexandre Bertrand laid the basis for the subsequent rise of hypnotherapy.

Madame Helena Petrovna Blavatsky (1831–1891)

Widely regarded as one of the leading founders of modern occultism, Madame Helena Blavatsky was born in 1831 in Ekaterinoslav in the Ukraine. She was the daughter of Colonel Peter von Hahn and a cousin of Count Sergei Yulievich Witte who served as the Tsarist prime minister of Russia from 1905 to 1906. Helena's mother was Helena Fadeyev, a well-known novelist and herself the daughter of Princess Elena Dolgorukov, but she died when Helena was 11.

Young Helena grew up on large estates near the Volga.

Although she received no formal schooling she learned several languages from her grandmother and became highly proficient in them. She was also a gifted artist and pianist, and something of a tomboy – she liked to ride horses that had not yet been fully broken in. Just before her seventeenth birthday she married a widower then in his forties, Nikifor Blavatsky, Vice-Governor of the Province of Erivan in Armenia. After just a few months, and without consummating the marriage, she abandoned her husband to lead the life of a bohemian.

According to Count Witte, who published his memoirs many years later,[15] Helena pursued a range of varied and exotic activities after leaving her marriage. These included riding horses in a circus in Constantinople, giving piano lessons in London and Paris, managing an artificial flower factory in Tiflis, and wandering around Europe with an opera singer. Helena's travels also took her to Egypt. When the American artist Albert Leighton Rawson met her in Cairo in 1850–51 she was dressed as an Arab, smoking hashish and taking lessons from a snake charmer named Sheik Yusuf ben Makerzi.[16]

In 1873, aged 42, Helena Petrovna Blavatsky arrived penniless in New York from Paris, having traveled steerage across the Atlantic. She was now very overweight and a relentless chain-smoker. Helena found accommodation in a tenement house for working women and would later claim that she had been urged by her spiritual Masters to come to America to explore spiritualism.

Around this time, two brothers named William and Horatio Eddy were holding séances in Chittenden, Vermont and claiming to materialize discarnate beings who had once lived on Earth. These discarnate spirits included soldiers from the Civil War and a number of drowned sailors and Indian squaws. The séances were being held in a room that was dimly lit, and the audience was kept at a safe distance from the spirit-manifestations by a wooden barrier. As one might expect, the claimed materializations attracted both intrigue and skeptical disbelief.

In 1874 the New York *Daily Graphic* dispatched one of its feature writers, Colonel Henry Steel Olcott, to report on the Eddy brothers. Colonel Olcott (1832–1907) had been a Union officer in the American Civil War. He had also been a farmer in Ohio, and later became a successful lawyer in New York as well as working as a journalist. He had a lifelong interest in spiritualism and psychic phenomena and as a youth had experimented with mesmerism.

When Olcott's articles on the Chittenden seances were published in the *Daily Graphic* they caused something of a sensation.[17] Madame Blavatsky was one of the many enthusiastic readers who devoured these articles, and she decided she must immediately visit the Eddy farm in Vermont. Fortunately it had now been turned into a hotel to accommodate the anticipated rush of visitors.

As Colonel Olcott would later recount, when he first caught a glimpse of Madame Blavatsky at the Eddy residence he was amazed by her appearance. She had frizzy blonde hair and large blue eyes, and was wearing a scarlet Garibaldi blouse – a sign of her unconventional and ostentatious tendencies. She was speaking loudly to another woman in French.

After dinner, when Madame Blavatsky went outside to roll a cigarette, Colonel Olcott came forward and offered to light it for her. The evening of 17 September 1874 would mark one of the most significant meetings in the history of modern metaphysics. As they began talking, Olcott became intrigued when Madame Blavatsky told him she was a Russian aristocrat and a spiritual medium in her own right. Not only was she thoroughly familiar with what was taking place at the Eddy farm but some of the discarnate beings had now begun speaking to her in Russian!

Back in New York Colonel Olcott arranged to interview Madame Blavatsky for the *Daily Graphic*. She claimed to have spent three nights in the Pyramid of Cheops and said she had also witnessed the well-known English psychic Daniel Dunglas Home, levitating out of an elevated window in London. Olcott described her in the *Daily Graphic* as 'handsome, with [a] full voluptuous figure, large eyes, well-formed nose and rich sensuous mouth and chin'.

Soon Madame Blavatsky and Colonel Olcott began to see quite a lot of each other. Olcott had already become estranged from his devout church-going wife and within a year had moved into Madame Blavatsky's apartment in New York City, taking care to point out to his friends that he was sharing her premises but not her bedroom.[18] Soon their apartment on West 47th Street became known as the 'Lamasery' and it served as a meeting place for mystical seekers, esotericists and bohemians, with a seemingly endless succession of parties and lectures. Madame Blavatsky was now claiming regular psychic contact with spirit guides who were almost god-like. She referred to them as Brothers or Masters – they were similar to the beings known in India as Mahatmas. Madame Blavatsky claimed she had even met her personal guide, Master Morya, face to face at the Great Exhibition in London in 1851, although she had known him on the inner planes for many years.

One evening the Colonel suggested it would be a good idea to make the meetings at the Lamasery more formal by establishing a society that could provide some sense of an overriding structure. Madame Blavatsky seconded the idea and searched for a name for the new society. She came up with the word Theosophy, meaning 'divine wisdom' and in this way the Theosophical Society was born. Colonel Olcott was appointed president of the newly formed Theosophical Society and gave his inaugural address on 17 November 1875. Madame Blavatsky, meanwhile, was appointed corresponding secretary and would work primarily as a channel for the spiritual Masters who would guide the new organization. The preamble to the by-laws of the Theosophical Society made it clear that the aim of its members was to 'obtain knowledge of the nature and attributes of the Supreme Power, and of the higher spirits by the aid of physical processes'[19] – a well-focused and practical approach to occultism and metaphysics. Early members of the New York branch of the Theosophical Society included the celebrated inventor Thomas A. Edison and General Abner Doubleday, generally acknowledged as the founder of the game of baseball.

It was now incumbent on HPB – as she liked to be known – to produce an authoritative book on the nature and origins of the divine wisdom itself. Such a volume would serve as a guiding credo for the new organization. This task would take her two years and resulted in *Isis Unveiled*, published in New York in 1877.

Isis Unveiled encompassed Neoplatonism, Pythagoreanism, Alchemy, Masonic symbolism, Hinduism and Zoroastrianism. It commended the pioneering work of Mesmer and included references to the ancient Egyptians, the Chaldeans, and the Kabbalah. It also compared the lives of Krishna, Buddha and Jesus. Although in one sense the book was a text in praise of western Gnosis – esoteric spiritual knowledge of the sort that had become heretical with the rise of institutionalized Christianity – *Isis Unveiled* pointed finally to the East for its ultimate source of inspiration, asserting that the wisdom of the West's profoundest mind was but a compendium of 'the abstruse systems of old India' which were thousands of years older.[20]

In *Isis Unveiled* HPB alluded to the existence of a brotherhood of adepts who continued to transmit the secret science of the ancients to those worthy to receive it. HPB claimed to be in touch personally with the Tibetan section of this group and maintained that two Masters from the Great White Brotherhood – Master Morya and Master Koot Hoomi – had trained her for her unique role in history. As someone with a highly developed mind, awakened intuition and far-ranging psychic powers, she had been chosen by the Masters as a special agent through whom the wisdom of the East could be channeled through to the West.

Nevertheless, despite the blessing of the Masters, HPB's vision of expanding Theosophy in the West could easily have faltered soon after its birth. Within a comparatively short space of time, HPB concluded that the United States did not provide a suitable environment in which to foster the new spiritual movement – its values were too materialistic. Instead she was drawn to India, home of the Mahatmas and the universal wisdom tradition, and she invited the Colonel to come with her.

Colonel Olcott and Madame Blavatsky embarked for India via London on 19 December 1878. In January 1879 they established the London branch of the Theosophical Society which would later attract such notable figures as William Butler Yeats, the Gnostic scholar G.R.S. Mead, and Oscar and Constance Wilde, and by mid-February they had arrived in Bombay.

Here they were met by the local representative of a Hindu reformist organization named the Arya Samaj, or Society of Men of Good Will, with whom Colonel Olcott had already been in contact.

Led by a figure named Dayananda Sarasvati, whom Madame Blavatsky soon declared to be an incarnation from the Great White Brotherhood, the Arya Samaj had been founded in 1875 to reform Hinduism on the basis of the Vedas. It also included the young Mohandas Gandhi among its followers. Olcott and HPB's initial approach was to align the Theosophical Society with the Arya Samaj – it had, after all, provided them with an opening to India – but Olcott would later come to view it as too conservative, and not sufficiently 'universal' in its approach. Increasingly Olcott and HPB would find themselves drawn more to Buddhism than Hinduism, but for the moment they were spiritually and psychologically willing to embrace all things Indian. They soon became so pro-Indian that they were perceived locally as being both anti-British and anti-European.

In October 1879 Olcott and HPB sank much of their capital

into publishing a magazine called *The Theosophist* – a journal devoted to oriental philosophy, art, literature and occultism. The tone of *The Theosophist* was distinctly pro-Indian and equally anti-Christian, stating plainly that Theosophy was an 'ancient Wisdom-Religion dating back to Ammonius Saccas and Plotinus of the Neoplatonic School at Alexandria, and far beyond, as far back as the sacred Indian Vedas. It consisted of mystical and esoteric knowledge – brutally suppressed in the Christian era – about the single Supreme Essence, Unknown and Unknowable'.[21] *The Theosophist* sold surprisingly well and helped Colonel Olcott and Madame Blavatsky make many new friends. However, the activities of the Theosophists did not go unnoticed by the local Christian missions, who viewed the newcomers with intense suspicion.

In 1882 the Colonel and HPB paid £600 sterling to acquire Huddlestone's Gardens, a spacious mansion located on the banks of the Adyar River, 8 miles south of Madras. Set in 28 acres of lush tropical land, the Adyar complex remains the world headquarters of the Theosophical Society to this day. From his base at Adyar the Colonel would soon embark on a program of intense proselytizing activity, attracting many new converts to the Theosophical cause. In 1883 he established a connection with Ceylon (now Sri Lanka), promoting Theosophy while also assisting with reforms in education and agriculture for which he is still remembered.[22]

Meanwhile, HPB and Olcott continued to maintain that they were in regular contact with the Masters. Olcott said he used to meet Koot Hoomi from time to time as he traveled around India – the Master would pause to give Olcott advice on a particular matter and would then vanish into thin air. For her part, Madame Blavatsky remained deeply engaged with the Great White Brotherhood and now regarded spiritualism as a pale alternative to the universal wisdom-tradition which stretched back to ancient times. As Theosophical scholar Jill Roe has written:

Blavatsky stressed particularly the superior possibilities of Theosophy as compared with spiritualism, now proven not only narrow, but dangerous to its practitioners, amateur manipulators of powerful unseen forces. The findings of spiritualism could be comprehended only if they were recognized as but feeble repetitions of what had already been seen and studied in former epochs, indicated by a formidable collection of references to ascetics, mystics, theurgists, prophets, ecstatics, astrologers, 'magicians' and 'sorcerers' in times past.[23]

Delighted with the progress made in establishing Theosophy in India, Madame Blavatsky decided to return to Europe in 1884, staying first in France as a guest of Lady Caithness, and then traveling on to England. Olcott was also coming to London on behalf of the Buddhists of Ceylon. However, while HPB was in England a scandal broke that could well have doomed the Theosophical movement, both in India and abroad.

HPB had left the Adyar headquarters in the care of a colleague whom she had first met in Cairo, Madame Emma Coulomb, and her husband Alexis. However, the Coulombs had become involved in an internal quarrel at Adyar during HPB's absence and were about to change sides. In league with a group of Christian missionaries in Madras who were strongly opposed to Theosophy and all it stood for, the Coulombs revealed that the carpentry in Madame Blavatsky's rooms at Adyar had been altered to assist her mediumistic performances and materializations. In an article published in the *Madras Christian College Magazine* in September 1884, which focused on a series of letters sent to her by Madame Blavatsky, Madame Coulomb described how she herself had been involved in a fraudulent collaboration to produce 'marvellous phenomena', helping to drop forged letters from the Mahatmas through a slit in the rafters while her husband donned robes and did Koot Hoomi impersonations.

In response, the scholarly British Psychical Research Society – highly regarded for its systematic investigations of paranormal phenomena – suggested they should conduct an inquiry into the matter. With Madame Blavatsky's blessing, the Society dispatched Richard Hodgson, a young Australian lawyer and a protégé of Professor Henry Sidgwick, to investigate the situation. At Adyar, following an examination of the premises, Hodgson was able to confirm Madame Coulomb's claim that sliding panels had been created and that there was a hidden door linking the so-called 'shrine room', where many alleged miracles occurred, with Madame Blavatsky's bedroom. These secret entrances made possible a variety of deceptions including claimed spirit-manifestations of flowers and the mysterious transmission of messages from Tibetan masters. Hodgson was not impressed, and the conclusions of the Psychical Research Society regarding the claims of 'marvellous phenomena' and Madame Blavatsky herself were nothing less than damning:

> For our own part we regard her neither as the mouth-piece of hidden seers, nor as a mere vulgar adventuress; we think she has achieved a title to permanent remembrance as one of the most accomplished, ingenious, and interesting imposters in history.[24]

This could well have signaled the demise of Theosophy and its co-founder. However, whether or not Madame Blavatsky was a fraudulent medium and something of a trickster – which she undoubtedly was – Theosophy nevertheless introduced a number of significant concepts into the metaphysical arena. Several of these ideas have persisted to the present day, greatly impacting on the contemporary New Age movement.

A sympathetic statement published in an Australian religious newspaper in 1890 provides a concise overview of the early Theosophical perspective:

The Theosophical Society, whose headquarters are in New York and Madras, is now, it appears, a large body. Its aim is the foundation of a universal brotherhood, and the study specifically of the religions and science of the East. Theosophy presupposes that beneath all the creeds and religions there lies a *secret doctrine*, which has been corrupted and lost sight of amid the materialism and unspiritualness [sic] of the religionists and the world. To restore to men this hidden treasure, and unite them on the basis of a universal religion (or Divine Wisdom) is the object of the theosophist. There are also, it is asserted, certain *psychic powers* in human nature, which have been allowed, through non-cultivation, to die out in most people, or which, in the hands of the ignorant or unscrupulous, have been abused and perverted to the ends of sorcery and the black arts. These powers a section of theosophists seek to cultivate and to use for the good of their fellow-men. Mesmerism and hypnotism they affirm are only re-discoveries of certain natural powers, and anticipations of a power possessed by man far beyond what modern science even dreams of.[25]

As this article makes clear, Madame Blavatsky and her Theosophical colleagues promoted a concept which continues to resurface in various guises – of secret teachings and mystical insights, long forgotten in the mists of antiquity, which nevertheless become available to humanity from time to time through initiated seers and adepts. Madame Blavatsky clearly considered herself a spokesperson for this ancient wisdom tradition and seems to have regarded the Masters as members of an occult hierarchy ruling the world from the inner planes, assisting devotees with their spiritual progress back to the Godhead.

Theosophy also drew attention to the psychic potential of human nature – a theme that would similarly prove enduring. Like Theosophy, the New Age movement continues to be concerned with new paradigms of consciousness, and with the exploration of the psychic and spiritual potentials in all human beings.

Brief mention is also made in the newspaper article of the fundamental Theosophical idea that one can only obtain spiritual truth by embracing both religion and science. Indeed, although she was personally opposed to the evolutionary biological determinism of Charles Darwin, Madame Blavatsky believed that the fundamental truths of religion and science could be fused to produce a grand synthesis – a concept developed in detail in her magnum opus, *The Secret Doctrine*. From the Theosophical perspective such an approach extended well beyond the limitations of conventional religious doctrines. The idea of integrating science and spirituality would also be taken up by the New Age movement many decades later.

However, perhaps the most significant element in the Theosophical vision is a concept that would later come to be known as the 'perennial philosophy' – the idea of universal themes uniting the world's major spiritual traditions. For many years the Theosophical Society has sought to explore and promote the study of comparative religion and it can rightly be considered the first institutional supporter of Eastern spirituality in the West. As the well-known authority on Buddhism, Christmas Humphreys, wrote in 1977:

The original objects of the Theosophical Society were not as now. At that time the main purpose was the study of spiritualistic phenomena, while the present first and most important object, 'to form a nucleus of the universal brotherhood of humanity', only appeared at the virtual refounding of the Society in India in 1879. [In its first object] it failed. It succeeded, nevertheless, in its second object, the study of comparative religion, and the present Western interest in the study of religions, in an attempt to find the spiritual truths at

32

the heart of all of them, comes largely from the pioneer work of the Theosophical Society.[26]

It is only fair to point out, however, that the Theosophists were not alone in pointing to the universal aspects of the religious experience. This idea was also promoted by the Indian spiritual teacher Vivekananda, who first visited the United States in 1893 as a delegate to the Parliament of Religions in Chicago.

Vivekananda (1862–1902) was the leading disciple of the great Hindu mystic Ramakrishna (1836–1886), who was widely regarded in India as a saint. Ramakrishna taught Vedanta, a philosophy which draws on the Vedas, the non-dualistic philosophy of Shankara, and the yoga of Patanjali. According to Vedanta, God is both transcendent and immanent. The transcendent aspect of God is Brahman – absolute existence, knowledge and bliss beyond space, time and form. The immanent aspect of God is Atman, who dwells within man as his real Self or soul. Nevertheless, in truth, Brahman and Atman are one.

Vivekananda first met Ramakrishna in 1881, when he was only 18 years old. Significantly, Ramakrishna was not only an exponent of Vedantist non-dualism but had also explored Christian and Islamic approaches to meditation and prayer and he believed they were all paths to the same experience of God. Ramakrishna therefore impressed upon his young disciple the idea that all of the major religions of the world are essentially aspects of the same universal truth.[27] When Vivekananda came to the United States in 1893 this was the message he conveyed to his audience. In his address to the Parliament of Religions in Chicago, Vivekananda explained that each and every religion had its own appointed time and place. All religions belonged to a universal and eternal tradition and he did not believe religious unity would ever come about through the triumph of one religion over another.[28]

Nevertheless, despite embracing a universalist approach to world religions Vivekananda was not inclined to support the cause of Theosophy, which he referred to as the 'Indian grafting of American Spiritualism – with only a few Sanskrit words taking the place of spiritualistic jargon'. Although Vivekananda avoided direct public criticism of Theosophy during his two national tours of the United States – these tours extended from 1893 to 1895 and resumed when he visited America again in 1899–1900 – he clearly had little interest in the popular forms of occultism and psychic phenomena that had attracted many to Theosophy. 'We are fools indeed,' he told his audience, 'to give up God for legends of ghosts or flying hobgoblins.' Vivekananda would later write scornfully that 'the Hindus have enough of religious teaching and teachers amidst themselves ... and they do not stand in need of dead ghosts of Russians and Americans.'[29]

As religious scholar Hal Bridges has noted, Vivekananda's national lecture tours 'electrified large audiences with his bold oratory'[30] and soon after his first visit to the United States the Vedanta Society was established in New York. By 1904 there were also branches in San Francisco and Los Angeles and in due course centers for the study of Vedanta would also be established in several other American cities like Boston, St Louis, Chicago and Seattle.[31]

The distinguished psychologist and philosopher William James was greatly impressed by Vivekananda's presentation of Vedanta, and made frequent reference to it in his groundbreaking work *The Varieties of Religious Experience*. Vedanta would also transform the lives of the well-known British intellectuals Aldous Huxley, Gerald Heard and Christopher Isherwood, all of whom made their pilgrimage to the United States in the late 1930s. Many believe that it was Gerald Heard who converted Huxley from being a novelist to being a mystic[32] and after moving to Los Angeles in 1937 both Heard and Huxley were attracted to the Vedanta teachings of Swami Prabhavananda, head of the local branch of the Ramakrishna Order. Heard and Huxley were also early visitors to the Esalen Institute when it was established in Big Sur, California in the early 1960s.[33] And in something of a departure from Vedantist tradition, Huxley would also become a pioneer of the American psychedelic revolution – an early advocate of the spiritual significance of mescaline with its potential to open the mystical 'doors of perception'. We will explore these developments in a later chapter.

George Ivanovitch Gurdjieff (1872?–1949)

The exact date of Gurdjieff's birth is unknown. Gurdjieff maintained that he was born in 1866, but according to his sister the year was 1877. His biographer J.G. Bennett, meanwhile, gave the year as 1872. Nevertheless it is generally agreed that Gurdjieff was born in Alexandropol near the Russo-Turkish border. The son of a Greek father and an Armenian mother, he was brought up in a very patriarchal world and spent his early years in the village of Kars.

Kars was located in a region of considerable cultural and religious ferment and Gurdjieff would have been subject to Christian, Armenian, Assyrian, Islamic and Zoroastrian influences while he was growing up. While he was still in his teens or early twenties, Gurdjieff and a group of friends who called themselves 'the Seekers of Truth' wandered through regions of Central Asia and the Mediterranean and also visited more distant locations like Ethiopia, Mecca, the Gobi Desert and Tibet. Gurdjieff wrote in his first book, *The Herald of Coming Good*, published in 1934, that he was driven at this time by a yearning for 'secret knowledge'. In Central Asia Gurdjieff observed the dance practices of Sufi dervishes, and when he visited monasteries and lamasaries he paid close attention to the techniques of rhythmic breathing and mental prayer that were part of the monks' religious practice. According to one of his many biographers, Louis Pauwels, Gurdjieff was also influenced by the

Vajrayana Buddhist tradition in Tibet and worked for a time as a tutor to the Dalai Lama.[34]

Having explored an extensive range of transformative techniques and spiritual philosophies and then sifted out what he found useful, Gurdjieff began to hold study groups in the Russian cities of St Petersburg and Moscow, in 1914–15. It was here that he met the man who would become one of his leading disciples, Peter D. Ouspensky. Ouspensky would later write of his encounter with Gurdjieff: 'I realized that I had met with a completely new system of thought surpassing all I had known before. This system threw quite a new light on psychology and explained what I could not understand before in esoteric ideas.'[35]

Ouspensky was a member of the Russian intelligentsia. He was also a Theosophist and had visited Adyar just prior to meeting Gurdjieff. For his part Gurdjieff was opposed to Theosophists and occultists in general, regarding such groups as 'breeding grounds of delusion'. Gurdjieff's approach was much more grounded and practical although it did appear to draw on various mystical traditions and the sacred symbolism of numbers. Gurdjieff called his technique 'self-remembering' and said his approach would help people to 'wake up' and thereby assist their spiritual development. Gurdjieff never revealed the specific sources of his esoteric knowledge but he stated that his principal goal was to waken humankind from its complacency and to help people become aware of their limitations. It was only through 'conscious labors and intentional suffering' that humanity could evolve.

In 1917 Gurdjieff decided to move his study groups away from Moscow and St Petersburg in order to escape the Russian Revolution. Together with a small band of students which included Ouspensky and his wife, Gurdjieff traveled by foot across the mountains to Essentuki in the Caucasus. Within a few months, however, Gurdjieff and his followers were forced to flee the turmoil created by the war between the Red and White

Russian Armies and Gurdjieff now moved his group to Tbilisi in Georgia, which was not under threat from the Bolsheviks. Here he established the imposingly named Institute for the Harmonious Development of Man as a center for his educational program, which focused on developing and integrating the physical, emotional and intellectual aspects of human awareness. However, the Institute attracted little public interest and was soon disbanded. Gurdjieff and his followers now moved on to Constantinople and later to Berlin, but their final destination would be France. In 1922 Gurdjieff acquired a large chateau 40 miles outside Paris in the Forest of Fontainebleau. The Prieuré des Basses Loges, known simply as the Prieuré or Priory, would now become the new home of the Institute for the Harmonious Development of Man.

By the time Gurdjieff and his disciples decided to move to Fontainebleau, Ouspensky had already left Constantinople and had moved on to London – deciding that although he admired Gurdjieff's teachings he could no longer accommodate the Master's autocratic style. Nevertheless, although Ouspensky had now formally parted company with Gurdjieff, he gave a series of lectures on Gurdjieff's teachings in Britain and encouraged many potential followers to go to the Priory and explore Gurdjieff's approach first hand. Another former Theosophist, A.P. Orage, stirred up similar interest in Gurdjieff's ideas and practices in New York.[36]

At his Institute at Fontainebleau Gurdjieff formalized the activities that would come to be known as 'the Work'. And it was work of a very specific kind, for his followers soon found themselves engaged in hard physical labor – working vigorously through the day on a variety of practical chores in the house or gardens. When he was giving lectures Gurdjieff liked to keep his classes small and intimate and conveyed an impression to his followers that they were partaking of something precious and elusive. Gurdjieff also liked secrecy: he forbade his followers to talk about the Work to outsiders and after meetings they were told to disperse quickly and quietly, like conspirators in a secret cabal. At night they were involved in sacred dances known as 'Movements', which were based in part on Gurdjieff's observation of Sufi dervishes in Central Asia. These dances were intended to help his followers rid themselves of any preconceived conditioning and thereby enhance self-awareness. And because 'self-remembering' involved cultivating a state of 'perpetual watchfulness and readiness' Gurdjieff would sometimes go into the dormitory and clap his hands at four in the morning to awaken his followers and keep them 'alert'. It was a vigorous and somewhat relentless night-and-day regime at the Priory – definitely not for the faint-hearted.

In 1924 Gurdjieff visited the United States for the first time, and a group of around 40 of his followers gave demonstrations of the sacred Movements. Gurdjieff also provided displays of trick and genuine paranormal phenomena and asked his audience to distinguish between the two. Gurdjieff made it clear that he was not engaging in acts of magic based on fear or exploitation – the only true magic involved what he called 'doing'. One of Gurdjieff's favourite expressions was: 'Only he who can *be* can do.' His own particular form of magic was grounded in conscious self-transformation.

Gurdjieff was intrigued by the fact that most human beings seem to have almost limitless potential and yet for the most part suffer from an ongoing form of sleep-sickness. They need to wake up but instead they act like robots entrenched in habits and routine behavior – and this robs them of their freedom. As Gurdjieff once proclaimed: 'Man is a machine. All his deeds, actions, words, thoughts, feelings, convictions, opinions and habits are the result of external influences. Out of himself a man cannot produce a single thought, a single action.'[37] In times past, Plato had evoked the image of shadows flickering on the wall of a cave, which man mistook for reality. However for Gurdjieff reality was much starker than that. Basically, said Gurdjieff, man is in prison: 'All you can wish for, if you are a sensible man, is to escape.'

Given that Gurdjieff had such a pessimistic view of the human predicament, what sort of person was he in everyday life? According to a range of accounts from people who visited the Priory, Gurdjieff could quickly lose his temper but he was also capable of great kindness and warmth, and would often roar with laughter. He was a heavy smoker and consumed vast quantities of vodka. He was also apparently highly sexed. When Gurdjieff's wife died at the Priory, he promptly took a mistress and also slept with other willing female disciples. However, there was a very confronting side to his makeup as well. Gurdjieff was resolute in paring back the masks behind which people would hide and as one writer has expressed it: 'Beneath the exacting benevolence of Gurdjieff's gaze everyone was naked.'[38] He also made people pay as much as they could afford when they came to the Priory because he subscribed to the view – later championed by American self-help organizations like Erhard Seminars Training (est) – that people only value what has cost them effort or sacrifice. Gurdjieff believed we devalue anything we obtain too easily.

In 1933 Gurdjieff sold the Priory and moved to Paris. Although he continued to travel widely, Gurdjieff retained his base in Paris until his death in 1949.

While still at the Priory Gurdjieff had begun to draw his teachings together in a major work titled *All and Everything*, in which he sought to cover every aspect of human life. Here he reiterated his central message that man has a unique role in the cosmos but is asleep and needs to wake up. Only when he awakens into consciousness can his spiritual evolution begin. *All and Everything*, better known as *Beelzebub's Tales to his Grandson*, was published in 1950, a year after Gurdjieff's death. It was soon followed by Ouspensky's *In Search of the Miraculous*, a publication financed by English disciples who had joined the Paris group after the death of Ouspensky in 1947. The two works clearly complemented each other – the second helped clarify the first and in this way 'opened up the teaching'. Gurdjieff's *Meetings with Remarkable Men*, which was intended as a sequel to *All and Everything*, was published in 1960, and a third, fragmentary work titled *Life is Real Only Then, When 'I Am'* was released in the early 1970s.

Summarizing Gurdjieff's key ideas is a difficult task because his writing is often abstruse and complex. Nevertheless, certain key themes emerge.

Gurdjieff taught that we are all capable of obtaining the enlightened state he referred to as 'objective consciousness' but most of us do not know this because we are 'prisoners' in our everyday lives. Essentially Gurdjieff regarded the Work as a method of self-development that could help individuals liberate themselves from the heavy burden imposed on humanity by the universe itself. Gurdjieff's view of the universe is reflected in his notion of good and evil, which is explained in Ouspensky's book *In Search of the Miraculous*:

A permanent idea of good and evil can be formed in man only in connection with a permanent aim and permanent understanding. If a man understands that he is asleep and if he wishes to awake, then everything that helps him to awake will be *good* and everything that hinders him, everything that prolongs his sleep, will be *evil*. ... But this is only so for those who want to awake ... Those who do not understand that they are asleep ... cannot have understanding of good and evil.[39]

Gurdjieff also maintained that the universe was governed by two cosmic laws – the Law of Three and the Law of Seven:

The Law of Three was based on three forces: active, passive and neutral. These forces could be found everywhere in the universe and nothing could occur without all three being present. Gurdjieff maintained that human beings have three bodies: carnal, emotional and spiritual. If people were prepared to work on themselves they could raise themselves from being carnal to being truly spiritual.

Gurdjieff based the Law of Seven on Pythagoras' theories of harmonics and the concept of seven stages of development. According to Gurdjieff, once the thread of occurrences (initiated by the Law of Three) had begun to take place in any given situation, the Law of Seven would then begin to operate. Gurdjieff believed there is an orderly discontinuity in every progression of events. This is characterized by what Gurdjieff called the 'law of shock' where additional energetic input from humanity and other living things would inevitably disturb an otherwise natural flow of events. To demonstrate this principle, Gurdjieff made use of a mystical diagram known as an enneagram, which is probably derived from the Sufi tradition. The enneagram is a circle whose circumference is divided by nine points, yielding an uneven six-sided figure and a triangle. The enneagram represents the whole universe and encompasses both the Law of Three and the Law of Seven. Man is created in an incomplete form and has the potential to evolve to a higher octave. Points 3, 6 and 9 on the enneagram represent 'shock points' that allow this spiritual development to take place.[40]

Gurdjieff also believed that prior to the introduction of the Work there had been three fundamental approaches to spiritual enlightenment, each associated with three different types of man. These three types of man he referred to as 'instinctive man', 'emotional man' and 'thinking man'.

- Instinctive man is primitive and sensual and is drawn to religious rites and ceremonies. He is represented by the Fakir.
- Emotional man is sentimental and is drawn to religions

involving faith and love. However he is also inclined to persecute heretics. He is represented by the Monk.

• Thinking man is intellectual and is drawn to religions characterized by proofs and arguments. He is represented by the Yogi.

Traditionally, if they are to attain enlightenment, the fakir, monk and yogi are all obliged to renounce the world, give up their families, and devote their entire energy and commitment to their own personal development. Also, in a very real sense, each of these individuals needs to 'die' to his past in order to achieve enlightenment at some point in the future. Gurdjieff, however, proposed what he called the Fourth Way – the Way of the Sly or Cunning Man – which required that the individual spiritual seeker should be 'in the world but not of it'. In pursuing the Fourth Way, one could ground oneself in everyday experience, and there was no need to renounce one's family in order to achieve a spiritual breakthrough. The Fourth Way also offered opportunities that were lacking in the other spiritual paths:

> The fakir undergoes tremendous physical torture and recon-ditioning to suppress his body to his will, but has no outlet for the emotional or the intellectual. The monk possesses great faith and gives himself to his emotional commitment to God, but suffers pains of the body and intellectual starvation. The yogi studies and ponders the mysteries of life, but has no emotional or physical expression. But in the Fourth Way, people do not need to suffer physical, emotional or intel-lectual tortures, but merely start from their own life experi-ences. They work on themselves as they are, trying to harmonize all paths and using every cunning trick they know to keep themselves 'awake'.[41]

Gurdjieff's influence on the New Age movement has been considerable and is reflected in what the American counterculture historian Theodore Roszak has called 'therapy by ordeal' – encounter groups, Transactional Analysis, Erhard Seminars Training (est) and other techniques of practical self-transformation which tend to focus primarily on the mechanistic aspects of human nature. The Arica Institute, founded by Oscar Ichazo in New York in 1971, has also been strongly influenced by Gurdjieff. One can argue, I think, that Gurdjieff was one of the first gurus of spiritual self-help in the West. The path of self-transformation he proposed was vigorous, and his personal sense of focus and self-discipline unstinting. Gurdjieff used to say, 'Man must live till he dies', by which he meant that man should consciously labor and voluntarily suffer in order to achieve true spiritual growth – and he not only believed it but he put it into practice. Gurdjieff was very much a precursor of the confrontational, take-no-prisoners approach adopted by the founder of Gestalt therapy, Fritz Perls, whom we shall meet in a later chapter. In many ways Gurdjieff was years ahead of his time.

Chapter 2

Pioneers of the Psyche

At the very heart of the New Age movement is a widely held view that we must explore human consciousness itself if we are to gain any useful insights into the true nature of everyday reality. For this reason the New Age has drawn strongly on applied, experiential psychology as well as embracing a wide range of metaphysical and mystical beliefs. In order to understand contemporary New Age philosophies we therefore need to consider the ideas of several key pioneers of modern psychology, including such figures as William James, Sigmund Freud, Carl Jung, Alfred Adler and Wilhelm Reich. Whether or not these towering figures of Western thought would have approved of the New Age movement is entirely another question. The fact is that, willingly or not, their ideas and perspectives have been absorbed into the spectrum of New Age beliefs and have since acquired a separate momentum of their own.

William James (1842–1910)

William James is one of the founding figures of American psychology and helped pioneer the study of consciousness prior to the advent of Freudian psychoanalysis and the rise of behaviorism. James' interests were far-ranging and encompassed all aspects of human perception. He taught anatomy, psychology and philosophy at Harvard University, explored the consequences of pragmatism as an aspect of personal belief, and was interested in altered states of consciousness – from religious and drug-induced ecstasy through to mediumistic and psychic phenomena. His best-known publications include *The Principles of Psychology, The Varieties of Religious Experience* and *Pragmatism –*

all of them influential and major works.

James defined psychology in 1892 in a way that still sounds completely modern, referring to it simply as 'the description and explanation of states of consciousness'.[1] For William James, individual consciousness was characterized by a process of continuous thought and could not be considered separate or discrete in any way. It was more appropriate, he believed, to regard everyday human awareness as part of a much broader spectrum of universal consciousness. 'Our normal waking consciousness,' he wrote, 'is but one special type of consciousness whilst all about it, parted from it by the filmiest of screens, there lie potential forms of consciousness entirely different.'[2]

Influenced by Eastern mysticism – while also maintaining that he wasn't himself a mystic[3] – William James wrote that 'there is a continuum of cosmic consciousness, against which our individuality builds but accidental fences, and into which our several minds plunge as into a mother-sea or reservoir',[4] a view reminiscent of Vedanta. Indeed, William James was greatly impressed by the published addresses of Swami Vivekananda and included several references to them in *The Varieties of Religious Experience*.

James was especially interested in applying the systematic techniques of scientific observation to the visionary realm of the paranormal and he was convinced that psychical research could bridge the gulf between what he described as 'impersonal science and personal reality'.[5] But James was also aware that such a marriage of ideas would require a major change of attitude among his scientific peers. In his essay 'What Psychical Research Has Accomplished' James drew a clear distinction between science and personal experience and he went on to note that personal experiences of premonitions, apparitions, dreams and visions were invariably highly significant to those who experienced them. And yet despite the importance of these experiences to the people concerned, one could not expect such paranormal phenomena to be investigated impartially because science itself remained 'callously indifferent to their experiences'.[6]

However, it is not only in relation to the visionary realms of the paranormal that one finds a resonance between William James and mystical New Age thinking. As a pragmatist, James emphasized the importance of personal self-improvement, which is also a distinctive aspect of the contemporary New Age credo. James believed that all individuals had an innate ability to modify or adapt their behavior, thereby 'evolving' to new levels of personal attainment. He also felt that a positive attitude was vital for mental health – a viewpoint now considered axiomatic in holistic health practices – and he believed, like Sigmund Freud and Wilhelm Reich after him, that blocking emotional energy could result in illness.

Maintaining a self-help perspective, William James believed that exercising the individual will was essential for personal growth, and he described the human will as 'the pivotal point from which meaningful action can occur'.[7] Will, as an expression of mental perception, enabled the human mind to 'engender truth upon reality' and could thereby have a meaningful impact on the world at large. For this reason William James believed that all human beings should learn to develop their willpower. 'Willing orients consciousness,' he wrote, 'so that a desired action can unfold of its own accord.'[8]

The emotional aspects of human consciousness, on the other hand, held a somewhat less exalted position in James' psychological schema. He believed it was important to retain a balance between expressing passionate feelings and retaining an almost clinical sense of detachment. James quoted Hannah Smith, who said of the emotions: 'They are not the indicators of your spiritual state but are merely the indicators of your temperament or of your present physical condition.'[9] James was well aware that emotional expressions could become excessive, or obsessive. An excess of love, for example, could manifest as possessiveness; an excess of loyalty could become fanaticism; an excess of concern could become sentimentality. Such apparent virtues, he believed, 'diminished' a person when expressed in an extreme form.

While on this particular point James parted company from the more hedonistic aspects of the New Age movement – personified, for example, by Bhagwan Shree Rajneesh's ashram practices in Oregon during the 1980s – William James nevertheless anticipated the New Age in several other ways. He distinguished three aspects of the self – the material self (physical body/home/family) from the social self (social roles and recognition) and the spiritual self (inner being) – thereby foreshadowing the much later emphasis in transpersonal psychology on the spiritual dimensions of human well-being. For William James the reality of one's inner self was paramount and the body was an expressive tool of the indwelling consciousness, rather than the source of stimulation itself.[10] He also supported a practice that New Age devotees would call 'imaging' or 'creative visualization' – the technique of focusing on specific mental images in order to train and develop the will.

So, for a variety of reasons we can consider William James an important forerunner of the New Age movement. While 20th century scientific psychology would become increasingly more reductionist and would endeavor to explain the subtleties of human perception and brain functioning in terms of basic biological activity, James believed that consciousness itself posed a mystery. For William James human consciousness provided a potential opening to broader and often unfamiliar domains of existence and causality:

The whole drift of my education goes to persuade me that the world of our present consciousness is only one of many worlds of consciousness that exist, and that those other worlds must contain experiences which have a meaning for our life also; and that although in the main their experiences and those of this world keep discrete, yet the two become continuous at certain points and higher energies filter in.[11]

Sigmund Freud (1856–1939)

These days it has become rather fashionable to denigrate Sigmund Freud for seeking to explain the complex and multi-faceted aspects of human personality primarily in sexual terms. While there is some truth in the assessment itself – Freud always stuck to his original position that sexuality in its various aspects is the central problem underlying psychological adjustment – his contribution to modern thought is much more far-reaching in its scope.

It is easy to forget that Freud was the first person in the history of Western psychology to emphasize the importance of the unconscious mind, to systematize the study of dreams, and to distinguish certain elementary instincts. And while Freudian psychotherapy sometimes seems heavily laden with analytical concepts, it is important to remember that Freud did not dwell on repressed sexuality and other aspects of neurosis purely for their own sake. In Freud's view, the essential task of the therapist, in aiding the process of self-knowledge and personal growth, was to help the patient recover and reintegrate material from the unconscious mind – and in so doing to counter psychosis and neurosis. Carl Jung once said of Freud that his 'greatest achievement probably consisted in taking neurotic patients seriously and entering into their peculiar individual psychology. He had the courage to let the case material speak for itself, and in this way was able to penetrate into the real psychology of his patients ... By evaluating dreams as the most important source of information concerning the unconscious processes, he gave back to mankind a tool that had seemed irretrievably lost.'[12]

In the Freudian approach the idea of self-knowledge entails

discovering who one truly *is*. As Ilham Dilman, a noted interpreter of Freud, has observed, the process of Freudian psychotherapy involves 'not only the shedding of screens, but also the integration of what is old, and the assimilation of what is new'.[13]

Like William James, Freud believed that the starting point in the study of psychology was consciousness itself, although in his view the conscious mind could only be regarded as a small part of the whole. Freud was especially interested in what he termed the 'pre-conscious' mind which included the immediate memories readily accessible to consciousness, and the 'unconscious' mind – that vast pool of non-conscious material which included instincts and repressed memories.

Early on, Freud considered erotic and physically gratifying sexual instincts and aggressive, destructive instincts to be the two main impulses of human life. He later changed his emphasis, drawing a contrast between life-supporting and life-denying instincts as the unresolved polarities in human nature. Freud conceived of a conscious ego welling up from a formless, unorganized *id* – representing a kind of 'reservoir of energy for the whole personality'.[14] The life-instinct, or *libido*, he equated primarily with sexual energy: a support for the ego in its quest to pursue pleasure and self-preservation. Freud also formulated his idea of the superego as a censor to the ego, inhibiting unwelcome thoughts and providing a sense of morality or conscience. In this sense the superego was a restrictive overseer of voluntary actions.

According to Freud, the unconscious contents of the mind only remained unconscious at the expense of a considerable amount of libidinal energy and he believed that the dramatic release of pent-up energies invariably provided a sense of 'explosive satisfaction'. In making this important observation, Freud would subsequently influence not only Wilhelm Reich but also future generations of contemporary New Age bodywork practitioners – for whom the body's musculature would come to be seen as a repository of stored tension and sexual repression. Freud's insight also made possible the subsequent rise of modern cathartic mind/body modalities like Bioenergetics. In Bioenergetics, an approach developed by Dr Alexander Lowen, individuals learn to move through their barriers of blocked emotion and are encouraged to release these pent-up energies within a supportive setting. We will discuss these therapies in more detail later in this book.

Freud emphasized that libidinal energy could be re-channeled from essentially sexual or aggressive goals towards artistic, intellectual or cultural pursuits. However he also believed that human beings are not the rational animals they think they are. Instead, he regarded them as creatures driven by powerful emotional forces that were unconscious in origin – and he noted that the restriction of these forces would invariably lead to neurosis, suffering and pain. Freud believed in a world where, ideally, the rational ego could rise up and overcome the irrational id – he once famously declared, 'Where id is, there let ego be.'[15] Freud also felt that there were no psychological accidents in human behavior. Our choice of friends, locations, favorite foods, recreational pastimes – all of these are linked to unconscious memories, and in turn provide clues towards a rationale of our conscious lives. According to Freud, the essential task was to further self-knowledge by probing as far as possible into the contents of the unconscious mind, and he developed psycho-analysis specifically with this purpose in mind. Freud's intention was to 'liberate previously inaccessible unconscious materials so that they may be dealt with consciously'.[16] In this way people could be freed from the suffering they perpetually bring upon themselves.

The related idea that we cause our own suffering, and, by extension, that we are primarily to blame for the diseases we inflict upon ourselves, is also very much a New Age belief. In a manner which blends Freud's basic concept with the Hindu teaching of karma, it has become fashionable in New Age circles to emphasize that we all 'create our own reality' and that we should then 'take the responsibility' to liberate ourselves from the shortcomings we have unconsciously chosen. Admittedly, this is Freud simplified to the point of cliché, but it nevertheless allows us to see how the New Age movement draws on psychological concepts and adapts them to its own ends.

We are reminded in this context that the practical goal of psychoanalysis is to strengthen the ego and to eliminate the unconscious blocks which cause self-destructive behavior. The Freudian idea of personal growth is to reclaim one's life-energy from the grips of the unconscious. As Ilham Dilman puts it, 'A neurotic who has been cured has really become a different person, although at bottom of course he remains the same – that is, he has become his best self, what he would have been under the most favourable conditions.' The analyst aims to bring about the change by 'making conscious the unconscious, removing repressions [and] filling in the gaps in memory'.[17]

According to Freud, one of the most important ways of exploring unconscious energies was through an analysis of dreams. Dreams, in his view, provided 'the royal road to a knowledge of the unconscious'. Freud's *The Interpretation of Dreams* – a work widely regarded as among his most enduring – was published in 1900 and it was this book which first drew Carl Jung into Freud's circle. It also made a strong impression on Alfred Adler, Otto Rank and Ernest Jones, all of whom were early members of Freud's psychoanalytic movement.

Freud originally believed that dreams were a garbled expression of mental events but after formulating the concept of the id in 1897 he came to the view that we all dream because the id yearns for self-expression. Sleep relaxes the ego's censoring control of the unconscious, allowing fantasies and wish-fulfillments to rise up. For Freud, all dreams – even nightmares or anxiety dreams – represented attempts to fulfill various wishes, and these wish-fulfillments could stem as much from early childhood as from current daily events.

Freud also noted that in neurotic behavior sexuality was invariably associated with repressed or suppressed wishes and these patterns could be uncovered through dream analysis, or, as Freud termed it, 'dream-work'. During sleep the dreamer's mind would find expression in dreams. Freud therefore developed the technique of talking his patients through their dreams, heeding their own 'free association' of ideas and memories, and then scrutinizing the dream reports in detail. Basically, Freud believed that dreams help the psyche to protect and satisfy itself, channeling previously unfulfilled desires through to awareness without arousing the resting physical body. Dreams could therefore be seen as a way of playing out fantasies which could not be fulfilled during the day. It was intriguing how often dreams allowed a person to overstep boundaries of conventional morality, but this in turn was a key to understanding their role: dreams were able to help release tension because the id made no distinction between the resolution of needs in the physical world or the dream-world.

Although dreams often appeared jumbled and distorted, Freud showed that they could be unraveled and decoded. However, he was somewhat inclined to look for recurring motifs in dreams, with fixed or specific connotations. Symbols usually represented the human body in some way – long stiff objects equating with the penis, hair-cutting with castration, boxes and chests with the womb, walking up and down steps with coitus, and so on – and the dreams were symbolic expressions of sex-wishes.[18] It was here, in particular, that he would later part company with Carl Jung, whose analysis of dreams, as we shall see shortly, had quite a different emphasis.

Nevertheless, Freud was the first person to undertake the enormous task of unraveling the contents of the unconscious mind and it is this, more than anything, which aligns him in spirit with the intent of the New Age. And it is clear that his contribution to our understanding of the inner world of the psyche derived substantially from his evaluation of dreams. As Freud wrote in 1900:

Dreams are not to be likened to the unregulated sounds that rise from a musical instrument struck by the blow of some external force instead of a player's hand; they are not meaningless; they are not absurd; they do not imply that one portion of our store of ideas is asleep while another portion is beginning to wake. On the contrary, they are psychical phenomena of complete validity – fulfilment of wishes; they can be inserted into the chain of intelligible waking mental acts; they are constructed by a highly complicated activity of the mind.[19]

Carl Jung (1875–1961)

Freud's *Interpretation of Dreams* stimulated Jung's own forays into dream analysis, and for a time Freud considered Jung to be his chosen successor and protégé in the psychoanalytic movement. However, unlike Freud, Jung was deeply interested in psychical research and the paranormal, and this would eventually emerge as a major sticking point between the two men. In his memoir, *Memories, Dreams, Reflections*, Jung provides a fascinating account of his discussions with Freud:

It interested me to hear Freud's views on precognition and on parapsychology in general. When I visited him in Vienna in 1909 I asked him what he thought of these matters. Because of his materialistic prejudice, he rejected this entire complex of questions as nonsensical, and did so in terms of so shallow a positivism that I had difficulty in checking the sharp retort on the tip of my tongue. It was some years before he recognized the seriousness of parapsychology and acknowledged the factuality of 'occult' phenomena.[20]

Jung soon discovered the depth of Freud's commitment to the sexual paradigm and his antipathy to metaphysical interpretations of the unconscious mind:

> I can still recall vividly how Freud said to me, 'My dear Jung, promise me never to abandon the sexual theory. That is the most essential thing of all. You see, we must make a dogma of it, an unshakable bulwark.' ... In some astonishment I asked him, 'A bulwark – against what?' To which he replied, 'Against the black tide of mud' – and here he hesitated for a moment, then added – 'of occultism' ... It was the words 'bulwark' and 'dogma' that alarmed me ... that no longer had anything to do with scientific judgment; only with a personal power drive.
> This was the thing that struck at the heart of our friendship. I knew that I would never be able to accept such an attitude. What Freud seemed to mean by 'occultism' was virtually everything that philosophy and religion, including the rising contemporary science of parapsychology, had learned about the psyche.[21]

While Jung had originally accepted the Freudian concept of the personal unconscious he soon began to conceive of a 'collective' unconscious which transcended the individual psyche. He also found himself increasingly dissatisfied with Freud's model of sexual repression and made the final split with him in 1912 following the publication of *Symbols of Transformation*, in which he rejected the concept of the sexual libido.

Jung would come to view the unconscious mind as a vast storehouse of imagery that was much greater than the repressions of the individual. He also began to move away from Freud's approach to dream analysis, relying less and less on his 'free association' technique. Gradually Jung came to believe that Freud's method of allowing a patient to discuss dreams at random could lead one away from the dream itself. For Jung each dream was complete within itself and was expressing 'something specific that the unconscious was trying to say'. Whereas Freud invariably tended to uncover sexual motifs in dreams, Jung regarded each individual dream as conveying its own innate message – a message based on a specific context and situation – and he was much less interested in attempting to identify fixed motifs like the penis or breast. Jung emphasized this point when he wrote:

> A man may dream of inserting a key in a lock, of wielding a heavy stick, or of breaking down a door with a battering ram. Each of these can be regarded as a sexual allegory. But the fact that his unconscious, for its own purposes, has chosen one of these specific images – it may be the key, the stick or the battering ram – is also of major significance. The real task is to understand why the key has been preferred to the stick or the stick to the ram. And sometimes this might even lead one to discover that it is not the sexual act at all that is represented but some quite different psychological point.[22]

Jung concluded that every dream had 'its own limitation' and that specific symbols could have different meanings in different dreams. At the same time it was important to recognize that dreams were not random occurrences. Each dream was 'a specific expression of the unconscious' and would arise because the unconscious was seeking to address aspects of the personality that were fundamentally unbalanced. Nevertheless Jung's clinical observations led him to believe that there were also certain dream-motifs of a religious or mythic nature that did not belong to the individual psyche. It was the study of these particular symbols that gave rise to his concept of the 'collective unconscious'. According to Jung:

There are many symbols that are not individual but collective in their nature and origin. These are chiefly religious images; their origin is so far buried in the mystery of the past that they seem to have no human source. But they are, in fact, 'collective representations' emanating from primeval dreams and creative fantasies. As such, these images are involuntary spontaneous manifestations and by no means intentional inventions.[23]

Jung noted that while these 'collective' symbols could manifest in individual dreams the symbols themselves appeared to be based on what he called 'the constantly repeated experiences of humanity' – recurrent and universal experiences that had subsequently become embedded in the psychic patterns of the whole human species. Jung called these primordial images 'archetypes' and in a publication titled *Two Essays on Analytical Psychology* he provided an example of how an archetype is formed:

One of the commonest and at the same time most impressive experiences is the apparent movement of the sun every day. We certainly cannot discover anything of the kind in the unconscious, so far as the known physical process is concerned. What we do find, on the other hand, is the myth of the sun hero in all its countless modifications. It is this myth and *not* the *physical* process that forms the sun archetype.[24]

Jung was intrigued by the relationship between the archetypes of the collective unconscious and the myths and religious beliefs embraced by different cultures. He also emphasized that archetypes had their own life and ongoing presence in the psyche. 'The archetypes,' he said, 'are always there and they produce certain processes in the unconscious one could best compare with myths. That's the origin of mythology. Mythology is a dramatization of a series of images that formulate the life of the archetypes.'[25] For

Jung, myths were also an expression of the divine life of humanity. 'It is not we who invent myth,' wrote Jung, 'rather, it speaks to us as a Word of God.'[26]

The archetypes clearly had their own numinous power, a power that could manifest in religious visions and other transcendent experiences. Indeed, archetypes were so powerful that they could seize hold of the psyche 'with a kind of primeval force.'[27] They also appeared to have their own independent existence in the psyche so that individuals who had personal encounters with the archetypes would readily come to believe that the voice of the Divine had communicated with them directly:

The 'primordial images', or archetypes, lead their own independent life ... as can easily be seen in those philosophical or gnostic systems which rely on awareness of the unconscious as the source of knowledge. The idea of angels, archangels, 'principalities and powers' in St Paul, the archons of the Gnostics, the heavenly hierarchy of Dionysius the Areopagite, all come from the perception of the relative autonomy of the archetypes.[28]

With the development of Jung's concept of archetypes, it was clear that his thinking had begun to diverge markedly from Freud's. Jung now considered the deepest regions of the psyche to be profoundly spiritual, whereas Freud's concept of the id suggested formlessness or chaos. Increasingly Jung began to explore what he believed to be the major structures of the personality. These included the persona – the face we use to present ourselves to the world – and the ego, which includes all the conscious contents of personal experience. However, Jung also believed that men and women should accommodate opposite gender polarities within their consciousness – and he termed these the 'anima' for men and the 'animus' for women.

He also referred to the 'shadow', an embodiment of memories and experiences repressed from consciousness that would often appear in dreams and nightmares as a dark and repellent figure. Jung argued, however, that if material from the shadow was acknowledged and brought into consciousness, much of its dark and frightening nature would disappear. Dealing with the dark and repressed aspects of the psyche remains an important aspect of all Jungian forms of psychotherapy.

Jung regarded all of these specific aspects of the personality – the ego, the persona, the shadow, the animus (in women), the anima (in men), and the shadow – as archetypes in their own right. But there was another archetype that was even more central – this was the archetype of the 'self'. Whereas the ego could be considered the center of consciousness, Jung's concept of the 'self' included both the conscious and unconscious realms of the psyche and therefore represented the totality of the personality. Appropriately, the symbol he used for the self was the circle or mandala, because it represented wholeness. According to Jung, the 'conscious and unconscious [were] not necessarily in opposition to one another, but [complemented] one another to form a totality, which is the *self*.[29] The thrust of all individual self-development was therefore towards wholeness of being. Self-realization, which Jung referred to as 'individuation', simply meant 'becoming oneself' in a true and total sense. Jung described this process of personal growth in his essay 'The Relations Between the Ego and the Unconscious' (1928):

The more we become conscious of ourselves through self-knowledge, and act accordingly, the more the layer of the personal unconscious that is superimposed on the collective unconscious will be diminished. In this way there arises a consciousness which is no longer imprisoned in the petty, oversensitive, personal world of objective interests. This widened consciousness is no longer that touchy, egotistical bundle of personal wishes, fears, hopes and ambitions which always has to be compensated or corrected by unconscious countertendencies; instead, it is a function of relationship to the world of objects, bringing the individual into absolute, binding and indissoluble communion with the world at large.[30]

Jung's impact on New Age thinking has been enormous, greater, perhaps, than many people realize. Jung emphasized dreams as living realities – direct communications from the psyche – and we find the idea of heeding the inner voice not only in New Age dream workshops, but as a broad-based principle underlying the widespread resurgence of inner-directed growth and visualization techniques in general. Jung also believed that spontaneous manifestations of the psyche were very important, and this is reflected in the free-form sketch-drawings of psychic and spiritual states which feature so prominently in many New Age workshops. And while some Jungian scholars, like Dr David Tacey, have portrayed contemporary New Age devotees as narcissistic hedonists unwilling to encounter the 'shadow',[31] Jung's insights on this important point have percolated through to the New Age movement via works by bestselling authors like Robert A. Johnson and Susan Jeffers.[32]

Meanwhile, Jung's idea of the collective unconscious has encouraged many to look at myths, fables and legends for insights into the human condition, and also to relate the cycles of symbolic rebirth, found in many of the world's major religions, to the process of personal individuation. Jung's focus is undoubtedly on *individual* transformation, although one would expect the individuation process to enrich one's relationships with other people. Nevertheless, Jung's orientation reinforces a commonly held New Age perception that one must work on oneself first before expanding the process of self-development to include others – otherwise it is simply a matter of the blind leading the blind. In the final analysis Jung is saying that we hold our spiritual destinies in our own hands and this has endeared him to many in the New Age.

Jung clearly believed that as human beings we are all connected to the universal realm of sacred archetypes and this in turn has led many to ask whether Jung was himself a mystic or a prophet of Gnosis. Jung had his own response to this question. Although he found himself addressing matters of the spirit throughout his professional life, Jung continued to regard himself as an empirical scientist rather than a metaphysician: 'I am a researcher and not a prophet,' he wrote to one of his many correspondents. 'What matters to me is what can be verified by experience. But I am not interested at all in what can be specu-lated about experience without any proof.'[33] Elsewhere, in an essay titled 'Spirit and Life', Jung says of himself: 'Not being a philosopher, but an empiricist, I am inclined in all difficult questions to let experience decide.'[34]

Nevertheless, Jung sometimes acted like a spiritual prophet, whether he intended to or not. During a celebrated session with the BBC in 1959 Jung was asked by interviewer John Freeman whether he believed in God. Jung replied that he didn't believe, *he knew* – a response clearly based on spiritual experience rather than on faith. Jung later elaborated on this point in a letter to Valentine Brooke:

> When I say that I don't need to believe in God because I 'know', I mean I know of the existence of God-images in general and in particular. I know it is a matter of universal experience and, in so far as I am no exception, I know that I have such experience also, which I call God.[35]

If Jung says he *knows* God, does this make him a Gnostic? After all, the word *gnosis* itself refers to a personal knowledge of the sacred and transcendent. Jung's approach to personal spiritual experience has led Jungian scholar Robert A. Segal to the conclusion that even if Jung is not a Gnostic in the classical and historical sense – he would never have rejected the physical world as the evil creation of a misguided demiurge as the early Gnostics were inclined to do – Jung nevertheless emerges as a type of 'contemporary' Gnostic:

Like ancient Gnostics, Jung seeks reconnection with the lost essence of human nature and treats reconnection as tantamount to salvation. For Jung, as for ancient Gnostics, reconnection is a lifelong process and typically requires the guidance of one who has already undertaken it – the therapist functioning as the Gnostic revealer. Knowledge for both Jung and ancient Gnostics is the key to the effort, and knowledge for both means self-knowledge. In these respects Jung can legitimately be typed a Gnostic. He is, however, a contemporary Gnostic because the rediscovered essence is entirely human, not divine, and lies entirely within oneself, not within divinity as well.[36]

Reverend Don Cupitt, theologian and Chaplain of Emmanuel College, Cambridge, has a more direct way of explaining Jung's relationship with the realm of the Spirit. In the Jungian approach, says Cupitt, 'the real encounter with God is the encounter with your own unconscious. Religious experience is the psyche's own struggle towards integration.'[37]

Alfred Adler (1870–1937)

Alfred Adler was born in Vienna in 1870 and studied medicine at the University of Vienna, graduating in 1895. One of the first four members of Freud's circle, he was recommended by Freud as the first president of the Viennese Psychoanalytic Society. However, by the following year he had developed perspectives that Freud found unacceptable and he resigned his position. Adler then founded the Association for Individual Psychology, which achieved widespread recognition in Europe, but in due course he was forced to flee the rise of Nazism. He emigrated to the United States in 1932.

Adler's formulation of Individual Psychology, like Jung's concept of individuation, has had a major impact on humanistic psychology, and this impact in turn has flowed on to the New Age movement. Adler's thinking, reinforced by various childhood tragedies and struggles in his own life, focused heavily on the notion of self-improvement. For Adler, the task of all healthy, motivated individuals was to develop their own capacities and potential. As Adler wrote, 'The striving for perfection is innate, in the sense that it is part of life …'[38]

Adler accepted Darwin's idea of living forms adapting to the environment and he conceived of what he termed 'life-goals' as a focus for individual achievement in their efforts to overcome life's obstacles. Life-goals, he believed, generally served as a defense against feelings of impotence, as a bridge from the unsatisfying present to a bright, powerful and fulfilling future.[39]

Adler emphasized individualism even more than Jung, ascribing to individual human beings such qualities as uniqueness, genuine awareness and an ability to take control of one's own life – aspects he felt Freud had downplayed. Adler was convinced, in fact, that we can mold our own personalities and to this extent he championed a belief which has continued, in force, in the New Age. 'Every individual,' said Adler, 'represents both a unity of personality and the individual fashioning of that unity. The individual is thus both the picture and the artist. He is the artist of his own personality.'[40]

Nevertheless, while one can find considerable support in his writings for the idea of developing human potential, Adler was more inclined than Jung to express this endeavor in a social context. For Adler, all human behavior was ultimately *social* – one had to develop a sense of fellowship within the community, a feeling of kinship which ultimately would embrace all humanity. Adler thus moved the emphasis from individual self-growth towards contributing to the community at large:

Psychological growth is primarily a matter of moving from a self-centered attitude and the goal of personal superiority to an attitude of constructive mastery of the environment and socially useful development. Constructive striving for superiority plus strong social interest and co-operation are the basic traits of the healthy individual.[41]

It is worth noting that Adler was also influenced by two other philosophers who in turn held views compatible with New Age thought. The first of these was Hans Vaihinger, the other Jan Smuts. Vaihinger subscribed to the interesting view that people are more affected by their future expectations in life than they are by past experiences – a completely different emphasis from Freud's. According to Vaihinger, human behavior is a type of fiction based on personal conceptualizations of the world. Vaihinger's idea influenced Adler's concept of life-goals and is also reflected in the New Age dictum that the way we see ourselves influences what we finally become: *ultimately our thoughts create our reality.*

The other influence on Adler was Jan Smuts, the distinguished statesman and field-marshal who became Premier of the Union of South Africa for two periods, between 1919 and 1948. Aside from his military and political career, Smuts was deeply interested in science and philosophy and he produced a book titled *Holism and Evolution.* Here he took the unorthodox scientific view that there is a tendency in Nature to produce wholes which are not explicable in terms of the sum of their parts. According to Smuts there was an impulse always towards greater organization in Nature and within all individuals an innate movement towards wholeness.

Adler and Smuts corresponded with each other and Adler made holism an integral part of his Individual Psychology, defining the self as the personality viewed as an integrated whole. Adler believed that we should regard each individual as a unified being. He wrote: 'The foremost task of Individual Psychology is to prove this unity in each individual – in his thinking, feeling, acting; in his so-called conscious and unconscious – in every expression of his personality.'[42]

Wilhelm Reich (1897–1957)

Among the other pioneers of psychology who have influenced the New Age we must also acknowledge Wilhelm Reich. Reich's concepts of sexual energy and body armoring continue to have a major impact on contemporary holistic bodywork practices and Reich himself represents a tangible link between the early days of Freudian psychoanalysis and the body/mind frameworks adopted by the New Age.

Reich studied at the University of Vienna, qualified as an MD in 1922, and then went to work with Sigmund Freud. However, as with Jung and Adler before him, Reich soon began to differ from Freud and a rift developed between them. Freud refused to give Reich personal analysis and did not share the latter's strong Marxist leanings. Nevertheless, a strongly Freudian flavor characterizes much of Reich's thinking on sexual energy, although Reich developed his theories especially in relation to the body, rather than to the mind.

Reich believed in the concept of 'bioenergy flow' through the body and considered that repression of the emotions and sexual instincts could lead to 'blockages' resulting in rigid patterns of behavior (character armor) and the tightening of specific muscle groups (body armor). As such blockages increased, the energy flow in the organism was impeded and in chronic instances would lead to a marked deterioration of health.

For Reich, as for Freud, sexual energy was the very essence of human existence. The climax of orgasm was a completely satisfying release from tension that allowed sexual energy to be discharged in an act of physical embrace and love. Reich later postulated his formula of 'biological tension and charge' which involved four stages: mechanical tension, bioenergetic charge, bioenergetic discharge and relaxation. He noted, too, that the full orgasm had an almost transcendent quality, involving loss of ego and a profound sense of peace. By contrast, people who felt guilty in sexual expression worked against the current of bioenergy or 'orgone energy' as he called it, and produced frustrations and emotions that were subsequently repressed. This brought with it the neurotic, negative behavior that Reich termed 'character armoring'. Sexual energy produced an effect on the autonomic nervous system which, in turn, via sympathetic and parasympathetic actions, caused a tangible influence on specific organs in the body. While a healthy organism would normally exhibit patterns of contraction and expansion – a type of rhythm of life – in the case of an 'armored' organism there was a permanent state of contraction. Reich was appalled by the fact that mass neurosis appeared to be the norm in Western society and believed that such character patterns derived primarily from defenses against the free flow of sexual energy.

In essence Reich's therapy is a dismantling of layers of pent-up emotion. Reich divided the body into seven zones at right-angles to the spine and centered in the eyes, mouth, neck, chest, diaphragm, abdomen and pelvis (including the legs). Reich believed that orgone energy was bound up in chronic muscular spasms and that it was necessary to free this energy progressively. Reichian 'bodywork' therapy entails dissolving the armor, beginning with the eyes and working down the body. Several approaches are used:

- *Deep breathing* Breathing conforms to patterns proposed by the therapist. The patient may feel the stream of bioenergy in the form of prickling or tingling sensations.

- *Deep massage* Pressure is applied to muscle spasms. Sometimes such areas of tension are pinched to loosen them up.
- *Facial expressions* The patient 'makes faces' expressing certain emotions while retaining eye-contact with the therapist and maintaining certain patterns of breathing.
- *Chest-work* The therapist pushes down on the chest while the patient exhales or screams. Such bodywork is designed to remove blockages to breathing.
- *Convulsive reflex-work* Convulsions break down armoring. The therapist may work with the disruptive effects of coughing and yawning.
- *Stress positions* Stress positions may be maintained to produce an effect of bodily irritation. This may lead in turn to tremors or 'clonisms' which similarly break down the body armor.
- *Active movements* The therapist may encourage the patient to kick and stamp and move parts of the body vigorously as a 'loosening up' exercise.

In general, Reichian therapy penetrates from the outer, accessible layers of armoring through to the deeper levels. Reichian therapists believe it is important that such probing occur at a pace that the patient can handle. Different effects are noted in each of the body segments:

- *The eyes* The eyes may appear dull and lifeless. The patient is encouraged to roll them from side to side and perhaps open them wide, as if in a state of sudden amazement.
- *The mouth* This area includes the muscles of the chin, throat and back of the head. The patient may be asked to cry, shout or suck, or move the lips in various ways, in order to loosen up the muscles concerned.

- *The neck* Screaming and yelling may be used intentionally to free up tensions.
- *The chest* Any armoring in this region will show up when the patient breathes or laughs. Inhibition of breathing is a means of suppressing the emotions and may require the use of special gestures involving the arms and hands.
- *The diaphragm* Armoring tends to reveal itself via body posture in this segment. The spine may curve forward, constricting outward breath. Such armoring is loosened with breathing exercises and the so-called 'gag reflex'.
- *The abdomen* This segment includes the back and abdominal muscles which are often tense if a person is defensive. Armoring is loosened up in these muscle regions.
- *The pelvis and lower limbs* With strong armoring the pelvis is pulled back and may stick out, revealing signs of deep-seated repressed anxiety. There is also a tightening of the pelvis, inhibiting sexual expression and pleasure. The patient may be asked to strike the couch with the pelvis region or kick the feet until a sense of freedom in this region develops.

Reichian therapy provides a systematic loosening of body tensions aimed at releasing the natural flow of energy through the body and seeks to do for the body what Freudian psychoanalysis seeks to do for the mind. Reich's approach has been a major influence on New Age bodywork therapies like Bioenergetics, Rolfing and the Feldenkrais method of Awareness Through Movement – all modalities which have played a distinctive role in the personal growth movement pioneered by Esalen Institute and other experiential holistic health centers. Reichian therapy provides further evidence of the way in which the work first undertaken by Freud and his former associates continues to flow through to the New Age movement today.

Chapter 3

Towards the Transpersonal

While Wilhelm Reich's contribution to bodywork provides a specific link between the early schools of psychology and the rise of the personal growth movement, another development in psychology also had a major role to play. This was the emergence of the 'humanistic' school and its important offshoot, transpersonal psychology.

Transpersonal psychology is sometimes referred to as the 'fourth force' following Freudian psychoanalysis, behaviorism and humanistic psychology. As its name suggests, transpersonal psychology refers to states of being beyond the ego. The transpersonal perspective seeks to broaden the traditional scope of psychological enquiry, taking in such studies as the nature of holistic well-being, peak religious and mystical experiences, the experiential psychotherapies and the wisdom traditions of East and West. Humanistic and transpersonal psychology both emerged as a response to the reductionist and mechanistic approach of behaviorism.

If we consider the literal derivation of the term, psychology ought to refer to the study of the *psyche* – that is to say, the study of mind, consciousness or 'soul'. However in the early years of the 20th century American and European psychologists wrestled with the need to become truly scientific and became increasingly concerned with a desire to measure, validate and objectify. As a consequence the discipline of psychology began to turn away from the intangibles of human experience like emotions, feelings, intuition and aesthetic values – intangibles that William James had been willing to explore – and more emphasis was placed instead on the more specific, and measurable, aspects of human behavior.

Leading the early charge towards objectivity was the American psychologist Dr John B. Watson, who is widely regarded as the first behaviorist – his approach would subsequently be consolidated by the highly influential psychologist B.F. Skinner. Watson denied the existence of consciousness, arguing that all learning was a response to the environment, that despite genetic variables human actions could be readily conditioned and modified. Watson defined psychology as follows:

Psychology as the behaviorist views it is a purely objective branch of natural science. Its theoretical goal is the prediction and control of behaviour. Introspection forms no essential part of its methods. ... The behaviourist, in his efforts to get a unitary scheme of animal response, recognizes no dividing line between man and brute.[1]

The behaviorist approach was consolidated by Ivan Pavlov's work on controlling behavior and by B.F. Skinner's concepts relating to conditioning and reinforcement as part of learning theory. Skinner rejected the concept of the 'personality', arguing that the latter was simply a collection of behavior patterns, as were the emotions and intellect. Likewise, for Skinner the notion of the 'self' was not essential in analyzing behavior and any idea of self-knowledge was a convenient fiction. 'There is no place in the scientific position,' Skinner wrote in 1974, 'for a self as a true originator or initiator of action.'[2]

However, with the development of phenomenology, transpersonal research and the experiential psychotherapies in the 1970s, Skinner's approach began to look less and less complete. The Californian-inspired personal growth movement – sometimes referred to in the late 1960s and early 1970s as the Human Potential Movement – can be seen in part as a response against the limitations of behaviorism. The movement consisted substantially of people intent on uncovering the motivating forces that reflected and influenced human behavior: habitual patterns, fears, intuitions, repressions – and how these interactions worked. Personal growth seemed then, as it does now, to be very much about understanding inner states of being as well as modifying outer forms of behavior.

Maslow and Sutich

Humanistic and transpersonal psychology both owe their development to two key figures: Abraham Maslow (1908–1970) and Anthony J. Sutich (1907–1976). Their personal interest in creative and spiritual values as part of the ultimate definition of a human being led historically to a psychological approach which has continued to thrive on a more popular level in the New Age movement.

Abraham Maslow was born in New York in 1908, the son of Jewish immigrant parents who had come to the United States from the Ukrainian city of Kiev. He grew up in New York and then went to the University of Wisconsin for his undergraduate and graduate studies, finally gaining his PhD in 1934. After receiving his doctorate he returned to New York, undertook further studies at Columbia University, and then joined the psychology faculty at Brooklyn College.

Maslow had studied with several distinguished psychotherapists including Erich Fromm, Alfred Adler and Karen Horney – who was a key mentor during the 1930s and 1940s. He was also strongly influenced by Max Wertheimer, one of the founders of Gestalt psychology, and in later years he would also have contact with Viktor Frankl and Rollo May. In 1952 Maslow moved to Brandeis University, which had just been established. He became chairman of the first psychology department and stayed at Brandeis until 1968. Maslow spent the last two years of his life in the Bay Area of California as a Fellow of the W.P. Laughlin Foundation.

By the time he joined the faculty at Brandeis University Maslow had become strongly opposed to the behavioristic frameworks which dominated most American psychology departments in the 1950s. In 1954 Maslow began to develop a mailing list of other psychologists around the country who shared his own personal interests – these were people concerned with such issues as creativity, love, self-actualization and personal growth in human beings. Three years later the list still comprised fewer than 125 people!

Maslow's personal orientation drew on cultural anthropology and neuropsychiatry, but he was also influenced by Gestalt psychology and was strongly holistic in his approach. Like Jung and Adler before him, he emphasized that the human organism should be viewed in terms of its total potential. As a result, Maslow developed his well-known 'hierarchy of needs', which included physiological considerations like hunger and sleep; safety (stability and order); belonging and love (family and friendship); and esteem (self-respect and recognition). Maslow's hierarchy culminated in the need for self-actualization, or, as he defined it, 'the full use and exploitation of talents, capacities [and] potentialities'.[3] He was also very interested in the sorts of people capable of self-actualization. Maslow found that such people tended to be spontaneous and independent in their natures, given to deep interpersonal relations, democratic in their character, creative in their approach to life, and able to rise above cultural limitations. He also found that self-actualizers often had the ability to have mystical or peak experiences.

Maslow's particular research focus was to evaluate people who seemed healthy and creative, rather than those who were unhealthy or neurotic. Maslow felt that unhealthy, psychologically unbalanced or maladjusted people did not provide adequate research data relating to the true nature of human potential in terms of personal growth. On the other hand, self-actualization had everything to do with personal growth.

According to Maslow it was vital that we transcend the distorting images we have of ourselves and overcome the defense mechanisms we develop which hide the real person inside. As Maslow noted: 'One cannot choose wisely for a life unless he dares to listen to himself, his own self, at each moment in life ...'[4]

The other key figure in the emergence of humanistic and transpersonal psychology, as mentioned earlier, was Anthony Sutich. Sutich was not an academic in the strict sense of the word and he would come to think of himself in due course as a 'maverick psychotherapist'. However, he brought to the new orientation a profound interest in spiritual and mystical concerns.

Sutich had developed progressive rheumatoid arthritis following an accident in a baseball game when he was 12 years old. By the time he was 18, he was totally physically disabled and his formal education had to finish in grade nine. The remainder of his life would be spent for the most part on a gurney – a four-wheeled stretcher fitted with a telephone, reading stand and other devices. Nevertheless, despite his physical disability, Sutich continued to function very effectively. He would often talk with nursing staff about their personal problems and soon acquired a reputation as a trusted friend and counselor. For many years people would come to him in hospital seeking advice, and in 1938 he was asked to become a group counselor for the Palo Alto Society for the Blind. In 1941 he began a full-time private practice in both individual and group counseling.

In due course Sutich became involved in political and social issues related to the labor movement and also worked as a Serbo-Croatian translator for the State Department during World War II. However, he also had a longstanding interest in both Western and Eastern religion – especially the latter. He read widely in the fields of Yoga, Vedanta, Theosophy and Christian Science. He had a personal interest, too, in psychedelic and mystical states of consciousness, and, as he wrote in a dissertation presented shortly before his death, 'I myself had had a mystical experience, or something like one, several times, with and without psychedelic substances, as early as 1935.'[5]

Sutich was especially impressed by Swami Ashokananda of the San Francisco Vedanta Society, who emphasized in his lectures 'the strong case for the value and validity of scientific investigation directed toward the inner realm of human potentialities, especially the spiritual potential'.[6] Sutich was already familiar with the spiritual philosophies of Swami Ramakrishna and Swami Vivekananda, and after having adjustments made to his car to accommodate his physical disability was able to travel to psychology and mysticism seminars in person. In the summer of 1948 he attended a series of lectures by Krishnamurti at Ojai, California. However, he found Krishnamurti's 'vague generalities about "Reality"' disappointing. 'He struck me as a cold, detached, rather negative person,' wrote Sutich later. 'It was his lack of warmth and humorless manner that made me feel that something was lacking in Eastern mysticism.'[7]

Sutich's interest in mysticism was rekindled, however, by reading Swami Akhilananda's *Hindu Psychology*, while at the same time he began to feel increasingly alienated by the rising wave of behaviorist psychology at nearby Stanford University. Sutich would often test the attitudes and expressions of his clients and he began to think very much in terms of their 'psychological growth'. However, few of his colleagues used terms like this in their practices.

Sutich was particularly keen on group therapy which emphasized spiritual as well as emotional development and he was delighted when he heard about Maslow's work. Sutich decided to write to him in November 1948 in an effort to make contact:

I understand that you have recently been working on something that has been vaguely described to me as the 'extremely well-adjusted personality'; alternatively, the 'super-normal personality'. The reference to your work came up as a result of my exploratory and experimental counseling work on what I call the 'growth-centered attitude' ('growth-conscious' or 'growth-minded') as the 'core' of a 'full-valued personality'.[8]

Maslow did not reply directly but in March 1949 he visited Berkeley and one of Sutich's clients arranged for the two to meet. It was a friendly meeting and on Maslow's recommendation Sutich submitted an article to the *Journal of Psychology* titled 'The growth-experience and growth-centered attitude', which was accepted for publication. Between 1949 and 1957 Sutich had little contact with Maslow but he did attend a lecture at Stanford University where he noted that there was strong opposition from Ernest Hilgard's behaviorist Department of Psychology to Maslow's concept of self-actualization. However, in 1952 Sutich met the expatriate British author Alan Watts and this lifted his spirits considerably, once again renewing his interest in mysticism and psychotherapy. Sutich notes:

The more I talked with him, the more I read about mysticism. In addition to Watts' books I read everything in mysticism I could get hold of. This carried me into the works of Sri Aurobindo (1948), Besant (1897), Blavatsky (1927), the *Bhagavad Gita* (Isherwood, 1947), Muller (1899), the *Upanishads* (Radhakrishnan, 1953) and a variety of books dealing with yoga.[9]

Sutich subsequently began to help Watts with various counseling techniques and was intrigued when Watts said he intended combining these methods with Zen Buddhism. Watts felt he could apply 'non-directive counseling', the main idea being 'to help those who run into certain kinds of paradoxes or contradictions'. Sutich and Watts also discussed the idea of *satori* – the Zen experience of sudden enlightenment – in some detail.

As mentioned earlier, Abraham Maslow kept a mailing list of like-minded psychologists who shared his interest in peak experiences and self-actualization. Sutich took a personal interest in this list and would later reflect upon it as the very basis of the new humanistic psychology. 'The mailing list,' he commented, 'was like the Committee on Correspondence that played such an important part in the history of the American Revolution.'[10]

However, Sutich noticed that even though the mailing list was growing, no substantial inroads were being made against the behaviorists, who still dominated the academic journals with their publications. Maslow, who had recently had an article on peak experiences turned down by the *Psychology Review*, urged Sutich to start a new journal. It could focus on all the aspects of human potential which were being ignored by mainstream psychology. It was proposed that the new publication be called the *Journal of Ortho-Psychology* (from the Greek *ortho*, 'to grow straight'), and Maslow proposed the following statement of purpose:

The *Journal of Ortho-Psychology* is being founded by a group of psychologists who are interested in those human capacities and potentialities that have no systematic place either in positivistic or behavioristic theory or in classical psychoanalytic theory, e.g. creativeness, love, self-actualization, 'higher' values, ego-transcendence, objectivity, autonomy, responsibility, psychological health etc. This approach to psychology can also be characterized by the writings of Goldstein, Fromm, Horney, Rogers, Maslow, Allport, Angyal, Buhler, Moustakas etc. As well as by certain aspects of the writings of Jung, Adler and the psychoanalytic ego-psychologists. While the point of view of this 'Third Force' in psychology has not yet been synthesized, unified or systematized, nor is it yet as comprehensive as the Freudian or Behavioristic systems, it is our feeling that this can come to pass, and probably soon will ...[11]

At this time Maslow numbered among his sympathizers not only the distinguished figures mentioned above but also Rollo May and Gardner Murphy, both noted psychologists. Articles for the new journal began to arrive from March 1958 onwards, and then Lewis Mumford, David Riesman and Erich Fromm joined the Board of Editors. There were difficulties with the title, however, because it clashed with *The American Journal of Orthopsychiatry*. In December 1959 Sutich received a letter from Maslow's son-in-law, Stephen Cohen, proposing that the journal be renamed *The Journal of Humanistic Psychology*, and he was pleased with this new title. Soon afterwards, the American Association of Humanistic Psychology and the journal were established under the auspices of Brandeis University.

Around a year later, in 1962, Maslow wrote to Sutich about an exciting new contact he had made. Michael Murphy and his friend Richard Price had established a center called the Esalen Institute in Big Sur, California, south of Monterey. 'They are planning a conference center there devoted, among other topics, to just the things you are interested in,' wrote Maslow. He added: 'By the way, I suggested you as a teacher to them.'[12]

Murphy later contacted Sutich, inviting him down as a guest once things were established. 'We are planning seminars and conferences for next fall and beyond and so are gathering ideas,' wrote Murphy. 'I have written to several people already, asking them to suggest ideas and people who would be good leaders. One interest we hope to develop is the inter-disciplinary approach to human nature – getting people together who usually don't get together.'[13]

The Beginnings of the Transpersonal Movement

In one of his information newsletters circulated at Esalen Institute in May 1965 Michael Murphy posed a question which would become central to the transpersonal perspective as a whole: 'What is the fundamental growth process' he asked, 'which takes the human organism beyond its present situation into the yet unrealized potential of its particular future?'[14]

Ensuing programs at Esalen would hope to tackle this important question. In January 1966 a seminar on humanistic theology was held at Esalen and attended by a number of Jesuit theologians as well as leading humanists like James Fadiman, Willis Harman, Miles Vich and, of course, Anthony Sutich. One of the lecturers at the seminar asked the Jesuits present whether they had ever had a mystical experience and whether it was Church policy to encourage attainment of that experience. To both questions they replied 'No', and Sutich recalled that he was very surprised by these answers.[15]

Shortly after this seminar, Sutich attended two further meetings at Big Sur which focused on the limitations of humanistic psychology. He began to feel that the original idea of self-actualization was no longer comprehensive enough and he expressed these views in a letter to Maslow in August 1966, noting that a humanistic therapist could hardly avoid the issue of 'ultimate goals' and mystical experiences. Accordingly, the therapist should also be able to assist his client in developing skills and pertinent techniques for awakening these faculties. 'Esalen and other places and processes,' he added hopefully, 'may become at least the American equivalent of Zen monasteries. The residential program that has just begun at Esalen may be a more concrete example of what may develop eventually throughout the country.'[16]

Increasingly, Sutich felt inclined to blend mysticism and humanistic psychology. He even proposed a new term – 'humanisticism' – but Maslow pointed out that the noted British biologist Julian Huxley was already using a comparable expression, 'trans-humanistic', with the same idea in mind. Ever keen on new publications, Sutich suggested to Maslow in February 1967 that a new journal be founded: a *Journal of Transhumanism* or *Transhumanistic Psychology*. Sutich also wrote to Huxley requesting a detailed definition of the new term.

Meanwhile on 14 September 1967, in an address to the San Francisco Unitarian Church titled 'The Farther Reaches of Human Nature', Maslow made the first reference to what he called the new 'Fourth Force', a school of psychology dedicated to the transformation of human life. Fond of delineating specific objectives, Sutich proposed to Maslow a more complete definition of the new school:

Transhumanistic (or Fourth Force) Psychology is the title given to an emerging force in the psychology field by a group of psychologists and professional men and women from other fields who are interested in those ultimate human capacities and potentialities and their actualization that have no systematic place in either the First Force (classical psychoanalytical theory), Second Force (positivistic or behavioristic theory), or Third Force (humanistic psychology which deals with such concepts as creativity, love, growth, basic need-gratification, psychological health, self-actualization etc.). The emerging 'Fourth Force' is specifically concerned with the study, understanding, and responsible implementation of such states as being, becoming, self-actualization, expression and actualization of meta-needs (individual and 'species-wide'), ultimate values, self-transcendence, unitive consciousness, peak experiences, ecstasy, mystical experience, awe, wonder, ultimate meaning, transformation of the self, spirit, species-wide transformation, oneness, cosmic awareness, maximal sensory responsiveness, cosmic play, individual and species-wide synergy, optimal or maximal relevant interpersonal encounter, realization, and expression of transpersonal and transcendental potentialities, and related concepts, experiences and activities.[17]

It was certainly a complex and rather long-winded definition. However Sutich was not without a sense of humor and, as a playful aside to his far-reaching statement – which surely must rank as one of the earliest descriptions of what would later become the New Age – he added, 'How's that for a nice ride on "Astro-Bike" or perhaps better still, "Inner Space Bike"!'

Meanwhile, the correspondence between Sutich and Maslow continued. In November 1967 Maslow wrote suggesting that the word 'transpersonal' might be the best expression of all. 'The more I think of it,' he noted, 'the more this word says what we are all trying to say, that is, beyond individuality, beyond the development of the individual person into something which is more inclusive than the individual person, or which is bigger than he is.'[18]

The term 'transpersonal' had already been used by Czechoslovakian psychiatrist Dr Stanislav Grof – later to become scholar-in-residence at Esalen Institute – during a lecture in Berkeley some two months earlier, and the expression finally carried the day. It was generally agreed that it was the most appropriate term for describing a psychology dedicated primarily to 'the advancement of mankind'.

There was now a sense that something really exciting was about to unfold – a new exploratory approach dedicated to studying the depths of human nature, the possibility of a new scientific synthesis of knowledge relating to interpersonal relationships, self-realization and transcendental potentialities. As Maslow's biographer, Edward Hoffman, has observed: 'Soon terms like *peak-experience* and *self-actualization* began to penetrate the popular vocabulary and help shape the zeitgeist of 1960s America.'[19] And the following decade would indeed see the full flowering of what would become known as the Human Potential Movement – a significant precursor of the New Age – coinciding especially with the increasing influence of the Esalen Institute in Big Sur and the rapid development of personal growth centers around the United States. There could be no doubt about it; a new era was dawning.

Chapter 4

Esalen, Gestalt and Encounter

North of San Simeon, the Californian coastline becomes increasingly craggy and precipitous. Highway 1 soon transforms into a narrow, winding courseway with spectacular cliff-edges falling away to the left and the sudden and dramatic Santa Lucia mountains rising up on the right. Wildflowers and lichen provide flashes of color here and there, but much of the terrain is rugged and severe. However, there are pockets of beautiful greenery as well – regal cypresses which grow in precarious positions, on impossible ledges, above sharp rock spurs which jut out from the crashing sea below.

Big Sur is only superficially tamed by human presence. Highway 1 was only completed in 1937 and even now is often blocked by falls of stone or pockets of fog which roll in from the ocean. It is a route which dictates its own pace, for drivers who venture here do not speed along but wind carefully and humbly round the seemingly endless successions of hairpin bends, ever aware of the precarious balance between human life, cliff edge and ocean.

The Spanish called this region after the river El Rio Grande de Sur, and the jagged, weaving coastline extends for some 50 miles, almost as far north as Carmel and Monterey. The town of Big Sur itself is still only a small settlement, famous mostly for its Nepenthe Inn, a vegetarian restaurant with impressive wooden sculptures and a wonderful view to the south. The controversial novelist Henry Miller also spent many years living in this region as a recluse.

Esalen Institute is located between Big Sur township and the charming hamlet of Lucia. One comes upon it suddenly, and it too rests literally on the cliff-edge. A place of considerable natural beauty, it is now part of local folklore and has had much to do with the rise of the new consciousness.

Esalen Institute used to be known simply as Slate's Hot Springs. The land was acquired in 1910 by Henry Murphy, a doctor from Salinas, and he built the dwelling now known as the Big House as a holiday home. By the late 1950s, however, the land had fallen into disrepair and Slate's Hot Springs was being visited mostly by Henry Miller and his circle of bohemian friends. Old Dr Murphy had long since died and the Big House was being maintained by a young macho writer named Hunter S. Thompson. Nothing much was happening except occasional brawls among the locals.

In 1962, however, things changed substantially after Dr Murphy's son Michael and Zen Buddhist enthusiast Richard Price drove down to the property to have a new look at it. They came up with an idea that was to have far-reaching consequences – Big Sur Hot Springs, as it was now called, could be a meeting place for different spiritual traditions and for the exploration of consciousness. Philosophers, writers and mystics could come here to impart their knowledge and share their experiences. It could become a very special place indeed.

With this vision, the spirit of Esalen was born, although the Springs would still be known by their old name for three more years. The Lodge, a meeting room on the property up the hill from the Big House, became the center for seminars, and early visitors associated with the Institute included Alan Watts, Aldous Huxley, Gerald Heard, Ken Kesey, Joan Baez, J.B. Rhine, Carlos Castaneda, Linus Pauling, Paul Tillich and, as we have already mentioned, Abraham Maslow.

By the latter half of the 1960s Esalen had extended its range of famous visitors to include Indian musician Ali Akbar Khan, environmentalist Buckminster Fuller and bodywork pioneer Ida Rolf. Esalen soon acquired a reputation as an idyllic therapeutic hideaway – a place to enjoy weekend seminars and workshops, and discover your inner being. It was a place to get in touch with your feelings, awaken your senses, reach out to your partner and enjoy the communal experience of bathing and massage on the cliff-edge above the Pacific Ocean.

Not everyone at Esalen was mystical, however, a notable exception being Fritz Perls, the distinguished founder of Gestalt therapy. Arguably the most important single influence in the early years of Esalen, Perls took up residence in a two-bedroom stone house built especially for him on the property. As Edward Hoffman notes, Perls was something of a controversial figure at Esalen:

Unquestionably a brilliant and masterful therapist, Perls was nevertheless well known among the Esalen community as an aged womanizer with a vulgar tongue and enormous ego. With his large, unkempt beard and predilection for jumpsuits, Perls strolled around Esalen as if he owned it.[1]

Perls despised what he called the 'woolly-headed' spiritual aspect of the personal growth movement and endeavored to bring his own, much more confronting and sometimes brutal style of therapy to the fore.

While Gestalt therapy was particular to Fritz Perls, Gestalt psychology itself was much older – the movement dating back to a paper published by Max Wertheimer in 1912. The German word *gestalt* refers to a pattern of parts making up a whole, and the underlying principle of Gestalt psychology is that an analysis of parts does not lead to an understanding of the whole because parts by themselves have no meaning. Building on the pioneering work of Wertheimer and also Wolfgang Kohler and Kurt Koffka, Perls maintained that Gestalt theory could be applied to the personality and to basic human needs:

Every organ, the senses, movements, thoughts, subordinate to [an] emerging need and are quick to change loyalty and function as soon as that need is satisfied and then retreat into the background. ... All the parts of the organism identify themselves temporarily with the emergent gestalt.[2]

Born in Berlin in 1893, Perls had struggled through his youth and school years but went on to gain his MD in psychiatry. He then moved to Vienna where he met Wilhelm Reich. Perls returned to Germany in 1936 to deliver a paper at a psychoanalytic congress attended by the founding father himself, Sigmund Freud.

Despite Freud's influence on his conceptual frameworks, Perls came to the view quite early in his professional career that Freud's focus on sex and destructiveness as the twin motivating forces of human existence was incomplete. He rejected the idea of rigidly classifying instincts and analyzing a patient's past, and chose to focus instead on the here and now. For people to be whole, or balanced, they needed to recognize bodily yearnings and impulses instead of disguising them. In fact, life was a series of gestalts that emerged one after the other – a variety of needs requiring satisfaction. Perls developed Gestalt therapy to allow people to recognize their projections and disguises as real feelings and subsequently to be able to fulfill themselves.

After breaking with the psychoanalytic movement, Fritz Perls emigrated to the United States in 1946 and established the New York Institute for Gestalt Therapy in 1952. He moved to California in 1959. His friend, fellow psychologist Wilson Van Dusen, explains how, at the time, Perls' views were revolutionary:

We were all basically retrospective, strongly retrospective, in both our analysis and therapies. We wouldn't conceive of understanding a patient without an extensive history. And for a man just to walk into a room and describe people's behavior so accurately added a whole new dimension. This is where I considered Fritz very great. His incomparable capacity to observe ...[3]

Fritz Perls had been strongly influenced by Reich's idea that the body reflected internal psychological processes. The person here and now showed everything through his or her being and behavior – there was no need to delve into analysis. 'Nothing is ever really repressed,' he once commented. 'All relevant *gestalten* are emerging, they are on the surface, they are obvious like the emperor's nakedness ...'[4]

As a therapist, Perls was often extremely curt and blunt, cutting through the niceties of social interaction to the person behind the image. At Esalen he would give demonstrations of Gestalt therapy before over a hundred people. Sitting on a dais, he would invite members of the audience to participate with him in role play. He had two chairs beside him. One was the so-called 'hot seat' which the participant sat in, engaging in dialogue with Perls. The other chair was there to help the person switch roles and enact different parts, engaging in the self-questioning process. Frequently volunteers revealed their weaknesses and limitations during these sessions but there was, after all, a lesson to be learnt.

Perls was very wary of the 'fun generation' who came to Esalen just for entertainment, and his dialogues with these people were always brutally honest. For some these were moments of revelation and awe, for others quite shattering experiences. Fritz Perls' publisher, Arthur Ceppos, recalls:

I think that Fritz's greatest contribution was his horror at how ridiculous man permits himself to become; and by becoming aware of how ridiculous he is, he can emerge into an identity that is no longer ridiculous, but is relatively free. This is the whole secret behind Fritz's hot seat. He would show people how they made fools of themselves.[5]

Essentially Perls believed, like the Existentialists, that each person lived in his or her own universe and had to take the responsibility for their own behavior and growth. The well-known Gestalt therapy prayer, which was often displayed as a poster at this time, reads as follows:

I do my thing, and you do your thing,
I am not in this world to live up to your expectations
And you are not in this world to live up to mine.
You are you and I am I,
And if by chance we find each other, it's beautiful.
If not, it can't be helped.[6]

Self-awareness and honesty were crucial to Perls' concept of Gestalt therapy: the essential point was to be aware of what you are experiencing, how you experience your existence *now*. Perls would urge people to pay particular attention to the ways in which they sabotaged their own attempts at sustained awareness, for these were ways in which they habitually prevented themselves from fully contacting the world and their own experiences.

Extending his scope from here-and-now interactions through dialogue and self-recognition, Perls also placed considerable emphasis on dreams. Dreams presented messages that could help people understand the unfinished situations they were still carrying around. In *Gestalt Therapy Verbatim* he wrote:

In Gestalt therapy we don't interpret dreams. We do something more interesting with them. Instead of analyzing and further cutting up the dream, we want to bring it back to life. And the way to bring it back to life is to re-live the dream as if it were happening now. Instead of telling the dream as if it were a story in the past, act it out in the present, so that it becomes a part of yourself, so that you are really involved.[7]

Perls suggested dreams be written down with their various details as completely as possible. Then a dialogue or encounter between the different component parts or figures could be held. As the encounter process continued, a new integration could be arrived at. Perls described the dream, in fact, as 'an excellent opportunity to find the holes in the personality ... if you understand the meaning of each time you identify with some bit of a dream, each time you translate an *it* into an *I*, you increase in vitality and in your potential'.

At Esalen, Perls worked alongside notable figures like Bernard Gunther, who taught massage and sensory awakening, Gia-fu Feng who instructed in Tai Chi, and George Leonard, who held seminars on interracial issues, but Perls remained the 'star attraction' for several years. However, in the late 1960s a major rival emerged who would increasingly take much of the limelight – Will Schutz.

Schutz was a social psychologist who had graduated with a PhD from UCLA in 1951, worked at the University of Chicago, and later taught at Harvard and Berkeley. Like Perls, he too advocated a way of liberating people from their social conditioning and false self-images. However, whereas Perls relied mainly on acute personal observation and direct verbal interchange with his clients, Schutz used a method called 'open encounter' and was building on an approach already developed by Carl Rogers and other American social scientists.

The concept of modern encounter therapy derives substantially from a training program developed for community leaders in Connecticut in 1946. A feature of this program was regular feedback between trainers and participants, the idea being that such feedback would enhance the experience of all involved. Trainers from the Connecticut groups helped establish National Training Laboratories in 1947 to assist government and industry in assessing the efficiency of personnel. NTL established a system of providing direct personal feedback through what became known as training groups, or T-groups. Schutz was thoroughly conversant with group therapy and the T-group approach when he arrived at Esalen in 1967.

In the classic encounter groups there were usually between ten and fifteen people who sat in a circle on the floor. Often there was no specified leader. An encounter session could last for a few hours or extend into days and even weeks on end. People taking part in an encounter group would try to 'reach' and perceive each other in real ways and experience genuine inner feelings. Such therapy depended, of course, on developing honest relationships with the others involved and expressing such feelings verbally or physically.

In the approach adopted by Carl Rogers, members of the encounter group would initially interact loosely, waiting for information on what to expect and how to act. A sense of frustration would often develop as the group came to realize that it had to determine its own direction. Often members would resist expressing themselves personally, but then ease out of this by beginning to discuss events and situations that occurred in the past.

Rogers discovered that it was quite common for the first encounter exchanges to be negative ('You don't appeal to me'; 'Your manner of talking irritates me'; 'You are very superficial') but this was because deep positive feelings were harder to express than negative sentiments. Usually, however, providing the group passed through this phase without fragmenting, personally meaningful material would begin to come through and a sense of trust would emerge. As sensitive and important recollections rose to the surface, the members of the group would begin to respond by seeking to help other members of the group who had deep inner problems.

It was this type of orientation that Schutz brought to Esalen. An admirer of Rogers, his particular emphasis in group therapy was to help people feel good about themselves. In fact, Schutz published a bestselling book titled *Joy: Expanding Human Awareness*, soon after his arrival at Esalen. In it, he explained that the attainment of joy was at the very core of his approach:

> Joy is the feeling that comes from the fulfilment of one's potential. Fulfilment brings to an individual the feeling that he can cope with his environment; the sense of confidence in himself as a significant, competent, lovable person who is capable of handling situations as they arise, able to use fully his own capacities, and free to express his feelings.[8]

Initially Perls welcomed Schutz's presence at Esalen. He seemed to have solid academic credentials and was not a dreamy mystic like so many other visitors to the Institute. Perls may also have thought of Schutz as a potential convert to Gestalt therapy. But it soon became clear that Schutz was intent on being his own person and developing his own reputation. His book brought considerable publicity to Esalen and when *Time* magazine published a largely favorable article on Esalen in 1967, ironically there was no mention of either Perls or Gestalt therapy. Not surprisingly, Perls felt slighted and the somewhat embittered Gestalt therapist now began describing Schutz's open encounter sessions as insubstantial distractions – good fun perhaps, but not to be taken seriously. A sense of resentment was beginning to take hold.

Schutz continued to hold successful seminars at Esalen, although in due course he also began to attract critics in addition to Fritz Perls. Several mainstream psychotherapists working in other regions of the United States voiced the opinion that it was unwise to encourage the sort of encounter sessions Schutz was holding, because there was no scope for further follow-up: the therapist in charge could hardly assume responsibility for what might happen to participants later on. Schutz responded to this by emphasizing that anyone could do whatever they were willing to take responsibility for, and that included any clients wishing to involve themselves in encounter therapy. Obviously, open encounter was potentially a risk-taking exercise, since there was always the possibility that hurtful or damaging material could come to the surface during an encounter session. However, Schutz also pointed out that Esalen was essentially for people who were healthy, its main aim being to help already compara-tively well-balanced individuals with their self-actualization process, rather than providing care for people who were mentally ill. In the final analysis, said Schutz, everyone coming to Esalen had to take the responsibility for what they experienced there. It was up to them to respond to the personal challenge of self-trans-formation.

During the late 1960s the range of seminars offered at Esalen expanded rapidly – from some 20 program options in 1965 to around 120 in 1968. However, the exciting expansion of activities at Esalen was not without its human casualties and part of the problem was related to casual experimentation with mind-altering drugs.

The attitude to psychedelics at Esalen in the early years had always been comparatively relaxed – Alan Watts had described his aesthetic and mystical experiences with psilocybin and LSD in his 1962 publication *The Joyous Cosmology* and Aldous Huxley, who, like Watts, was an early visitor to Big Sur, had related his wondrous encounter with mescaline in *The Doors of Perception*. Michael Murphy had himself experimented with peyote in the Big House at Esalen in the early 1960s and Carlos Castaneda explained the shamanic use of psychedelics during a celebrated visit to Esalen around the same time. However, the psychedelic experience *per se* was not promoted at Esalen. Seminars on the relationship between drugs and mystical and religious experi-ences were held there from time to time but they were intended as theoretical seminars, not experiential workshops. It soon became necessary to include a note in Esalen brochures to the effect that no drugs would be used in such sessions.

Nevertheless, the first death associated with Esalen was drug-
-related. Lois Delattre was a member of the first residential
program at Esalen and later went to work in Esalen's San
Francisco office. Like many others in the personal growth
movement at that time, she had experimented with LSD, but she
also wanted to explore the effects of the so-called 'love drug',
MDA, an amphetamine derivative of isosaffrole which
heightened sensory awareness and was said to produce states of
emotional openness.[9] Delattre succeeded in locating some MDA
and took it with three other friends. However, she soon became
very introspective and withdrew to lie down on a bed. For a
while she seemed to be breathing deeply, as if in a trance, but
when her companions later returned they found her dead.
Delattre's death caused a distinct sense of panic at Esalen. Even
though it was not directly attributable to an Institute program, it
did highlight what no one had yet seriously considered – that the
quest for heightened realms of consciousness could result in a
fatality.

The next deaths at Esalen were not drug-related but they too
had a strong impact on the Esalen community. Marcia Price had
attended Fritz Perls' Gestalt therapy workshops and was
employed in the Esalen office. She was also involved sexually
with Perls, who had acquired a well-earned reputation as a
womanizer. The news that Marcia Price had committed suicide
by shooting herself devastated members of the residential
program at Esalen and had a profoundly sobering effect on
everyone who knew her. It was later revealed that Fritz Perls had
mocked her suicide threats during a Gestalt therapy session.
Then, to exacerbate matters still further, a young woman named
Judith Gold drowned herself in the Esalen baths, early in 1969.
Gold, too, had experienced a traumatic encounter with Perls; she
had similarly threatened suicide while sitting in his 'hot seat' and
had been savagely jeered by Perls in response.

Perls himself was not especially compassionate or conciliatory after these deaths, maintaining that people who were potential suicide cases should be treated just like anyone else. If you were threatening to kill yourself, Perls would tell you to go right ahead and do it. However, the mood at Esalen changed dramatically after these unfortunate incidents, and Perls' relationship with Michael Murphy began to sour. Perls in turn became increasingly disturbed by the escalating street violence in California and also felt that the political ascendancy of Ronald Reagan as Governor of California and the resurgence of George Wallace and Richard Nixon heralded a new right-wing direction in the United States which reminded him of events in Nazi Germany. With these factors dwelling heavily in his mind, and colleagues on all sides accusing him of paranoia, Perls decided to leave Esalen in 1969. Perls went to Canada, where he had a number of students, and purchased a motel alongside Lake Cowichan on Vancouver Island. He named his new establishment the Gestalt Institute of British Columbia, but did not live to see its development. He died six months after founding it, in March 1970.

The dramatic years of Fritz Perls at Esalen were undoubtedly a potent lesson for the personal growth movement and provided ample demonstration that the brutal stripping away of personal defense mechanisms could, in some instances, have tragic consequences. At the end of it all, Will Schutz's more optimistic mode of encounter therapy seemed more compatible with the Esalen style, and Schutz outlasted Fritz Perls by several years, continuing with his open encounter sessions at Esalen Institute until 1973, before deciding to leave and head north to San Francisco.

Today the range of experiential workshops offered at Esalen is enormous. Visitors come to learn techniques of Tai Chi, massage, Zen, hypnosis, dance, shamanism, Taoism, 'creative sexuality' and Feldenkrais body awareness, or to attend lectures on quantum physics, Gnosticism, Tibetan Buddhism, deep ecology or feminist spirituality. The range is diverse and ever-changing, but Esalen is also much less controversial than it used to be. The general public now has a much greater familiarity with mysticism, the vast range of mind and body therapies, and the philosophy of 'health for the whole person'.

However, it took some time for these holistic frameworks to emerge. In the late 1960s the full impact of the psychedelic era was still to be felt, and there would be important lessons to be learned as the youth culture began to pursue its often reckless exploration of drug-induced altered states of consciousness.

Chapter 5

The Psychedelic Years

For many people the psychedelic era is epitomized by the so-called 'Summer of Love' in 1966–67, which shrouded San Francisco's Haight-Ashbury district in a haze of drug-induced joy-consciousness. It was at this time that the media first began to draw attention to the emergent counterculture – that rapidly increasing group of mostly well-educated, young middle-class Americans who were rebelling against the materialism of the 'American Dream', against the hostilities perpetrated upon the gentle people of South Vietnam, and against the rising levels of violence in cities at home.

Interestingly, the controversy surrounding psychedelic mind-altering drugs and the quest for spiritual transcendence had already surfaced several years prior to the Summer of Love. The issue of psychedelics and mystical enlightenment was already a hot topic amongst those who attended workshops at Esalen, and it had also been raised by influential writers like Aldous Huxley and Alan Watts. The key issues in the debate were whether psychedelics could produce authentic mystical states of awareness and whether such states were simply 'artificial' forms of 'chemical ecstasy'.

Huxley, Watts and Psychedelics
The debate over 'drugs and mysticism' had been triggered initially by the publication in 1954 of Aldous Huxley's *The Doors of Perception*. Huxley had taken his title from William Blake's pronouncement that 'if the doors of perception were cleansed, everything would appear to man as it is, infinite'. Huxley's book would later inspire the well-known rock singer Jim Morrison to

name his band The Doors, by way of tribute.

Huxley related how in May 1953 he had swallowed four-tenths of a gram of mescaline dissolved in a glass of water and sat down to wait for results. For Huxley, mescaline brought revelation: his 'I' became 'Not-Self' and the everyday objects around him – flowers, books and furniture – seemed to radiate jewel-like colors and profound significance. Here, he felt, was 'contemplation at its height'. Huxley later conceded that mescaline could plunge some people into hell rather than lifting them into heaven, but on balance he decided that it could certainly serve as a catalyst to mystical awareness – especially for rational or 'verbal' intellectuals like himself who felt 'compelled to take an occasional trip through some chemical Door in the Wall into the world of transcendental experience'. Later, in 1958, in the *Saturday Evening Post*, Huxley emphasized the mystical relevance of both mescaline and the more recently discovered psychedelic, LSD. Referring specifically to LSD, Huxley noted that 'It lowers the barrier between conscious and subconscious and permits the patient to look more deeply and understandingly into the recesses of his own mind. The deepening of self-knowledge takes place against a background of visionary and even mystical experience.'[1]

Huxley's views on LSD were subsequently endorsed by British philosopher Alan Watts in his book *The Joyous Cosmology*, published in 1962. Referring both to LSD in particular and to psychedelics in general, Watts wrote that 'these drugs ... provide the raw materials of wisdom, and are useful to the extent that the individual can integrate what they reveal into the whole pattern of his behavior and the whole system of his knowledge ... the hours of heightened perception are wasted unless occupied with sustained reflection or meditation upon whatever themes may be suggested.'[2]

Watts had emigrated to the United States in 1936 – a year before Huxley – and was best known for his writings on Zen

Buddhism. After switching his allegiance to Christianity, Watts was ordained as an Anglican priest in 1944 and then served as the Episcopal chaplain at Northwestern University for six years. However, he then renounced Christianity as his spiritual path, left Northwestern University, and accepted an offer to teach at the School of Asian Studies in San Francisco. Retaining his ongoing interest in Zen Buddhism and Taoism, Watts now sought to reconcile these Eastern philosophies with contemporary West Coast values. He also began experimenting with LSD. From this time onward he would embrace an alternative lifestyle which blended free love, mysticism and psychedelics.

Watts had come to the view that Christianity did not trust humanity's natural urges – that it was always downplaying the flesh in favor of the spirit – and that it had inherited this dualism from the ancient Greeks. 'It has often been said,' wrote Watts, 'that the human being is a combination of angel and animal, a spirit imprisoned in flesh, a descent of divinity into materiality, charged with the duty of transforming the gross elements of the lower world into the image of God. ... Not to cherish both the angel and the animal, both the spirit and the flesh, is to renounce the whole interest and greatness of being human.'[3]

Watts had been fascinated for many years by the way in which Zen Buddhism could help alienated and lonely people find spiritual 'release'. Watts was a friend of the Beat poet Gary Snyder, who had spent over a decade in Zen temples in Kyoto, and knew a number of the other Beats – including Jack Kerouac, Lawrence Ferlinghetti and Allen Ginsberg – all of whom were already familiar with Zen Buddhism and the concept of *satori*, or direct enlightenment. Together, Watts, Snyder and Kerouac denounced bourgeois suburban values, and Watts took up residence on an old ferry boat called the *Vallejo*, moored in Sausalito – across the bay from San Francisco.

A skilled teacher and radio broadcaster, Watts soon became a frequent visitor on college campuses across the country. In 1961 he addressed students and academics at Columbia, Cornell, Chicago, Harvard and Yale Medical School, while at other times he held seminars on the *Vallejo*. During these meetings Watts would address all the current issues of the day – sexuality, sensuality, mind-expanding drugs, food and popular lifestyles – everything which at the time was considered risqué in conventional middle-class society. Watts had taken LSD on several occasions and believed, like Aldous Huxley, that psychedelics could be used meaningfully as spiritual sacraments rather than for recreational 'kicks'. In like fashion, Snyder believed that Zen meditators who had previously experienced LSD would find it easier to practice *zazen* in their quest for *dhyana*, or ultimate enlightenment. However there were other prominent voices in the debate over drugs and mysticism. They included a small group of radical psychologists working at Harvard University, who had already attracted national attention for their views on psychedelic and personal transformation.

The Harvard Triumvirate: Metzner, Alpert and Leary

Ralph Metzner, Richard Alpert and Timothy Leary all had distinguished academic backgrounds. German-born Metzner had graduated from Oxford University in 1958 and received a doctorate in clinical psychology from Harvard University in 1962. The following year he became a post-doctoral fellow at Harvard Medical School, specializing in psychopharmacology. Richard Alpert – who would later be known to the world as Baba Ram Dass – had taken his doctorate at Stanford University. In 1953 he became an assistant professor at Harvard University and in 1956 he was appointed co-director of the Harvard Psychedelic Drug Research Project. And Timothy Leary, who would later become famous for his psychedelic dictum 'Turn On, Tune In and Drop Out', had a similarly impeccable academic background. After gaining a Masters degree at Washington State University in 1946 he earned his PhD from the University of

California in 1950 for his thesis 'The Social Dimensions of Personality'. He published a conventional textbook, *The Interpersonal Diagnosis of Personality*, in 1957 and was appointed to the Harvard Center for Personality Research in 1960. As it transpired, this triumvirate of PhDs – Metzner, Alpert and Leary – were poised to become pioneers of the psychedelic revolution.

During his summer vacation in 1960, in the first year of his new position at Harvard, Leary took his two children down to Cuernavaca in Mexico. As Leary would later relate in his autobiography, *Flashbacks*, 'In the days of Montezuma this town, called "horn-of-the-cow", was the home of soothsayers, wise men and magicians. Cuernavaca lies south of a line of volcanic peaks, Popo, Ixtacihuatl, and Toluca. On the slopes of the volcanoes grow the sacred mushrooms of Mexico, divinatory fungi, *teonanacatl*, flesh of the gods.'[4] In Cuernavaca Leary would experience the flesh of the gods for the first time and it would change his life forever.

Several guests called on the Learys at their holiday villa, among them Gerhart Braun, an anthropologist from the University of Mexico. Braun had studied Aztec culture, had translated various Nahuatl texts, and was intrigued by the references he had found in their literature to sacred mushrooms, known locally as *hongos*. Leary asked if he could perhaps locate some. A week later Braun phoned to say that he had obtained several such mushrooms from a *curandera*, or folk healer, in the village of San Pedro near Toluca, and perhaps they should try them. Braun came round with some friends, spread the mushrooms out in two bowls, and said to Leary that everyone should take six. It was generally agreed that they tasted a lot worse than they looked, but expectations were high.

The *hongos* made Leary slightly nauseous at first, and his face began to tingle. Soon his vision was awash with wafty hallucinatory impressions and, like Aldous Huxley who had charted this strange terrain many years earlier, he began to discover a profound richness in the kaleidoscopic imagery unfolding before his eyes:

> Mosaics flaming color Muzo emerald, Burma Rubies Ceylon Sapphire,
> Mosaics lighted from within, glowing, moving, changing,
> Hundred reptiles, jewel encrusted ...[5]

Leary now began to ponder the nature of his own life-force, his bloodstream, his pulsing arteries. The organic basis of all creativity overwhelmed him. His body contained a myriad universes; his cell tissue seemed to hold the secret of life and energy. Leary was perceiving the motions of the universe at the atomic and subatomic levels. Finite imagery had been left far behind. He was witnessing the tides and motions of energy and form in their most profoundly elementary and essential phases of manifestation. And surprising though it must have seemed, the experience was quintessentially *religious*: 'I came back a changed man,' Leary later recalled. 'You are never the same after you have had that one flash glimpse down the cellular time tunnel. You are never the same after you have had the veil drawn.'[6]

It was this initiatory experience which led Leary and his friends towards a systematic exploration of inner space. It seemed to him at that time that a new chapter in the development of human thought was beginning: the quest for the very source of mystical awareness. There had been visionaries before, but they had all been isolated individuals. Now a *movement* could get underway. The earlier mystics and seers were forerunners and could act as guides:

> We did sense that we were not alone. The quest for internal freedom, for the elixir of life, for the draught of immortal revelation was not new. We were part of an ancient and

honorable fellowship which had pursued this journey since the dawn of recorded history. We began to read the accounts of early trippers – Dante, Hesse, Rene Daumal, Tolkien, Homer, Blake, George Fox, Swedenborg, Bosch, and the explorers from the Orient – Tantrics, Sufis, Bauls, Gnostics, Hermetics, Sivits, Saddhus ... no, we were not alone.[7]

During the autumn and winter of 1960, Leary spent most of his spare time studying the hallucinogenic qualities of psychotropic mushrooms. By day he continued to deliver lectures on clinical psychology at the Harvard Graduate School. One of his students – a man who seemed to Leary at the time to be rather academic and somewhat 'ivory towerish' in his attitudes but who was nevertheless brilliant at his work – was Ralph Metzner. Metzner said he wanted to experiment with psilocybin – a psychedelic synthesized from the mushroom *Psilocybe mexicana* – and was keen to evaluate its impact on prison inmates. He thought that it could provide them with an experience which would change the pattern of their lives. Of course there was no way in which they could predict the outcome, or the reaction of either inmates or wardens, but perhaps it could lead to new methods of integration and rehabilitation.

And so began a series of psychedelic prison sessions. At first they weren't entirely successful. Leary on one occasion found himself viewing one of the inmates, a Polish embezzler, with acute distrust. Someone put on a jazz record, alleviating the tension, and everyone relaxed. However, the mood ebbed and flowed. As Leary later wrote: 'There were high points and low points, ecstasies and terror.'

There were more sessions. Some of the convicts were able to leave on parole. Mild-mannered and changed men, they were sometimes – on Leary's admission – unable to cope with society's pressures. However, the prison and its psychiatric unit had become, in certain measure, a 'spiritual center'. It felt like a step towards a new understanding.

The prison sessions inspired Leary towards a sense of brotherhood. He had been able to communicate with men of a quite different ilk. The psilocybin had unshackled the psychiatric doctor-inmate-warden roles and they were 'all men at one ... all two-billion year-old seed centers pulsing together'. But the effect was not enduring. 'As time slowly froze,' noted Leary, 'we were reborn in the old costumes and picked up the tired games. We weren't yet ready to act on our revelation.'

It took an eccentric Englishman, Michael Hollingshead, to point out the next stage along the way. Hollingshead was a yoga practitioner and fiction writer whose novels were semi-autobiographical. He also had a strong interest in psychedelics. Furthermore, he had taken LSD – the most potent of all hallucinogens in terms of dose and quantity – and he urged Leary to do so. At first Leary refrained. After all, LSD was a chemical that had been synthesized in a laboratory, whereas the mushrooms had a natural and cultural origin. They grew in the ground; the Aztecs regarded them as holy.

Hollingshead insisted that LSD was of overwhelming 'religious' significance, paling the mushrooms into insignificance, and Leary was eventually won over. Together with a group of friends, he and Hollingshead consumed a dose in November 1961. Once again Leary found himself caught up in an eddy of transforming shapes and forms. As he reflected on these visionary sequences he thought of his role as father of his children. Had he been living a sham existence based merely on a routine form of parental devotion? Suddenly he seemed to be surrounded with death and falsity. Amidst all this confusion, what could be said to be real? Leary considered the structures and patterns of society: the cultivation of crops, the growth of cities, the nature of invasions, migrations, moral codes and laws – but eventually these too seemed illusory and insubstantial as a basis for *being*. They were merely constructs and episodes of man; they did not identify his origins.

Leary now found himself falling inwards, beyond structure, into a swirling vortex of energy: 'nothing existed except whirring vibrations, and each illusory form was simply a different frequency.' His perception had been reduced to a primal level, but then, as the effects of the psychedelic began to wear off, he experienced a terrible sense of loss. He had entered the heart of an energy vortex. 'Why had we lost it?' he asked himself. 'Why were we being reborn? ... in these silly leather bodies with these trivial little cheese-board minds?'

Leary had reached a level of consciousness which for the first time had seemed to define a sense of reality and being-ness. He had never reached this level before. He had never been to the core. Why couldn't it be more accessible?

Meanwhile he continued to explore other hallucinogens as a means of entry to these states of self-realization. He took DMT with his colleague Richard Alpert, and discussed these experiences with Alan Watts. He also had lengthy discussions with William Burroughs who had chronicled his personal experiences in the South American jungle with the shamanic potion known as *yage*, or *ahayuasca*. Burroughs had begun to ponder whether the visions of the mystics and seers of the past had a biochemical origin. Had he entered the same 'psychic spaces' as Jacob Boehme, William Blake and St John of the Cross had before him? Leary, meanwhile, received some insights into these matters from an unexpected source.

The Good Friday Experiment

As with the prison experiments suggested by Ralph Metzner, the new development similarly owed its impetus to the enthusiasm of a Harvard student. This time it was Walter Pahnke, young and eager, with a medical degree and a divinity qualification already under his belt. Pahnke was undertaking PhD studies in the philosophy of religion and wanted to pin down the visionary experience within experimental parameters. Twenty theological students could be assembled in a church setting. Some would be given psilocybin while others would remain as the 'control group'. There would be organ music, prayers and a sermon – all the normal things in a Protestant service – and it would be interesting to see whether anyone found themselves expanding their consciousness in a transcendental, mystical direction.

Leary thought Pahnke's suggestion was outrageous, but Pahnke insisted. He had a medical degree, after all, and would undertake psychiatric interviews to screen out 'pre-psychotics' beforehand. The volunteers would be carefully chosen and the experiment would proceed in the respectable presence of Dean Howard Thurman of the Boston University Chapel and Dr Walter Huston Clark, a visiting theological scholar.

Pahnke suggested using as his framework a list of common mystical attributes that had been drawn up by W.T. Stace, a leading scholar in the field of comparative religion.[8] These attributes, or qualities, fell under nine headings which represented the most commonly reported aspects of mystical experience. Stace's defining attributes were as follows:

- *Unity* The mystic experiences a profound sense of 'oneness' both within his or her own being, and also in the external world.
- *Transcendence of time and space* The mystical experience is not contained within three-dimensional space. It is often described as 'eternal' and 'infinite'.
- *Deeply felt positive mood* Feelings of joy, blessedness and peace impart to the person the sense that the mystical experience has been of incalculable value.
- *The sense of sacredness* There is a profound sense of awe. Something is experienced which is able to be 'profaned'.
- *Objectivity and reality* Knowledge and illumination come together: the experience seems to be overwhelmingly

authoritative. No 'proof' is necessary – 'ultimate reality carries its own sense of certainty.'

- *Paradoxicality* Following the illumination, rational interpretations seem to be logically contradictory. There is a feeling of an all-encompassing Unity devoid of specific attributes.
- *Alleged ineffability* Words fail to adequately express the mystical experience.
- *Transiency* Mystical consciousness is not sustained indefinitely; it is more of a 'peak experience'.
- *Persisting positive changes in attitude and behavior* Lasting psychological changes are experienced which affect the quality of one's interaction with others, and with life itself. The mystical experience itself is held in awe, and one is more at peace with oneself than before.

Walter Pahnke's proposed session took place, as planned, on Good Friday 1962 in the chapel at Boston University, and would become known as the 'Good Friday Experiment'. Ten theological students were given psilocybin while the others were given nicotinic acid, a vitamin which causes transient feelings of warmth and tingling in the skin. The participants engaged in a two-and-a-half-hour religious service consisting of organ music, four solos, readings, prayers and personal meditation. During the weeks before the experiment, special care had been taken to reduce fear and maximize expectancy, and during the experimental session itself participants did not know whether they had taken the psilocybin or the placebo.

Walter Pahnke collected data for up to six months afterwards, and each student had, by this time, prepared an account of his own personal experiences. Pahnke's statistics, condensed into percentages, are admittedly clinical but they do, however, make interesting reading.

Of those who had taken psilocybin, 70 percent experienced *inner* unity, and 38 percent *external* unity. 84 percent felt they had transcended time and space, 57 percent experienced a deeply felt positive mood, 53 percent a feeling of sacredness, 63 percent the sense of objectivity and reality, 61 percent the element of paradoxicality, 66 percent ineffability, 79 percent transiency, and an average of 50 percent were substantially changed in psychological attitudes, along the lines of Stace's mystical framework.

The control group, that is to say, those who had taken nicotinic acid, for the most part had much less intense religious experiences. The most pronounced sentiment was the feeling of love (positive mood) which was felt by 33 percent. Otherwise the figures were: unity (7 percent); time and space (6 percent); positive mood (23 percent); sacredness (28 percent); objectivity and reality (18 percent); paradoxicality (13 percent); ineffability (18 percent); transiency (8 percent); and psychological changes (8 percent).

Pahnke's experiment did not in itself offer proof that a person partaking of psychedelic substances would necessarily have a mystical experience, and it is clear that this is not the case. However, the session did seem to show the value of hallucinogens in intensifying what would normally be a mild and rare religious experience. Within a religious setting it was therefore not surprising that any expansion of consciousness would tend in a mystical direction.

The Good Friday Experiment helped consolidate Leary's belief that 'set' (mental attitude) and 'setting' (the chosen supportive environment) were important factors in the outcome of a psychedelic session: 'Our studies, naturalistic and experimental ... demonstrate that if the expectation, preparation and setting are spiritual, an intense mystical or revelatory experience can be expected in from 40 to 90 percent of subjects.'[9]

As Leary noted, when a human being ascends to the lofty heights of enhanced spiritual consciousness during a mystical illumination, the personality undergoes a dramatic process of transformation. The capacity for visionary insight reveals the limitations of all ego-based human frameworks – jealousies, fears, guilt, insecurities and so on – as if from a new and more far-reaching vantage point. On returning to everyday awareness the person who has had this peak illumination may find they are able to bring some of this unifying spiritual knowledge back into normal consciousness, assimilating it and hopefully re-molding the earlier and more limited personality that existed prior to the mystical experience. It was meaningful, therefore, to regard mystical illumination as a type of rebirth. Not only did one change, but the more negative, or non-integrated, aspects of one's being were subsumed in favor of a more positive and integrated perspective.

This, at least, was the apparent promise of psychedelically assisted mystical illumination. However, on a more mundane level, Leary's excursions from normality into altered states of consciousness were heading for a political showdown at Harvard University. Media reports of the controversial drug experiments conducted at the Center for Personality Research had enraged Professor Herbert Kelman, a fellow psychologist on the faculty. They had also infuriated Professor Brendan Maher, who dismissed Leary's findings and believed psilocybin and LSD were dangerous drugs that should only be administered by physicians in a medical setting.

The campus debate was highlighted in the media and in turn came to the notice of the Massachusetts State Narcotics Bureau. After several police investigations and a considerable amount of departmental wrangling, Timothy Leary and Richard Alpert were dismissed from Harvard University in May 1963. It was the first time in 300 years that faculty members had been asked to leave because of controversy surrounding current research.

The Summer of Love

Just three years later, recreational drug use in the counterculture in both Britain and the USA was already widespread. In San

Francisco – the center of the Summer of Love in 1966–67 – LSD was readily available to 'acid trippers' in such forms as White Lightning or Orange Sunshine, marijuana was commonplace and smoked openly in the streets, and 'hash cookies' were favorite fare at parties.

In political terms the 1960s were tumultuous years, dominated by the war in Vietnam. Between 1961 and 1963 President Kennedy committed 16,000 military personnel to the campaign. At the end of 1965, after President Johnson had ordered the bombing of North Vietnam, this number had escalated to 200,000, and in early 1968 exceeded 500,000. The anti-war movement had been steadily building in the United States since October 1964, when vigils began on a weekly basis in Times Square. Soon opposition to the war began to spill over on university campuses. In May 1965 the Interreligious Committee on Vietnam, which included Martin Luther King and Daniel Corrigan, the Episcopal bishop of New York, sponsored a vigil at the Pentagon to protest against the human tragedy of Vietnam, and on 2 November 1965 American Quaker Norman Morrison doused himself with kerosene and burnt to death in front of the Pentagon, emulating the suffering of napalm victims in North Vietnam. In the same year an apocalyptic message entered popular music for the first time with the release of Barry McGuire's chart-topping protest song 'Eve of Destruction', suggesting that the Vietnam conflict was bringing the world to the brink of catastrophe.

The anti-war movement also mobilized a powerful response in Europe. In March 1968 hundreds of anti-Vietnam-war demonstrators attempted to storm the American Embassy in London's Grosvenor Square, and in the following October a massive anti-war march was staged in central London on such a scale that shops and banks were boarded up and newspaper offices placed under extra guard.

Psychedelics, and marijuana in particular, had already

become part of the international anti-war protest. In Berlin in 1968 a popular slogan appeared everywhere: 'A gun in your right hand – a joint in your left.' And as Felix Scorpio reported in the British radical newspaper *IT* (formerly *International Times*) in April 1969: 'Of course, the real change in the scene here has been the dope revolution. ... Berlin is alive with heads dropping acid and STP in cinemas, parks, buses, and this too is a kind of revolution, and an interesting antithesis to America, where pot came first and politics followed.'

Meanwhile, on the American West Coast and elsewhere, the response of the hippies to the conflict engulfing mainstream Western society was essentially a message of peace. Hippies wore flowers in their hair, and although some projected an idyllic sense of innocence regained, many were also determined to overthrow cultural and social norms through displays of bizarre behavior. This was a time of hand-painted, multicolored Volkswagen vans, exotic and unconventional clothes, patchouli incense, politically driven itinerant folksingers, and innovative rock groups. In the USA Fritz Perls was proclaiming a message of personal liberation at Esalen, and so were street banners in San Francisco: 'The time has come to be free. BE FREE. Do your thing. Be what you are. Do it NOW.'[10]

The Psychedelic Shop, run by Jay and Ron Thelin, opened at 1535 Haight Street, San Francisco, on New Year's Day 1966. It sold all manner of books, records and psychedelic posters while also reserving a third of its floor space for a 'calm center', where hippies could come to meditate or sleep. Meanwhile The Print Mint sold old movie posters, doubled as a community center where people could leave messages for each other, and was invariably populated by wandering musicians and appreciative hippies. Nearby were eateries like Tracy's and the psychedelically decorated Drog Store Café. Gonzo journalist Hunter S. Thompson provides us with a tantalizing description of everyday life at the Drog Store:

The best show on Haight Street is usually on the sidewalk in front of the Drog Store, a new coffee bar at the corner of Masonic Street. The Drog Store features an all-hippie revue that runs day and night. The acts change sporadically, but nobody cares. There will always be at least one man with long hair and sunglasses playing a wooden pipe of some kind. He will be wearing a Dracula cape, a long Buddhist robe, or a Sioux Indian costume. There will also be a hairy blond fellow wearing a Black Bart cowboy hat and spangled jacket that originally belonged to a drum major in the 1949 Rose Bowl parade. He will be playing the bongo drums. Next to the drummer will be a dazed-looking girl wearing a blouse (but no bra) and a plastic mini-skirt, slapping her thighs to the rhythm of it all.[11]

The Haight-Ashbury district was served by a newspaper called *The Oracle*, which was hawked in the streets and distributed through various 'alternative' outlets around the Haight. Printed in different-colored inks that fused together in rainbow patterns, *The Oracle* kept residents up to date with what was happening in the local community, as well as publishing controversial articles on such diverse topics as the horrors of prisoner-of-war camps and the joys of masturbation.

Joyce Ann Francisco, who sold advertising for *The Oracle*, told *Time* reporter Judson Gooding that she loved being a hippie. 'Human beings need total freedom,' she said enthusiastically. 'That's where God is at. We need to shed hypocrisy, dishonesty, phoniness, and go back to the purity of our childhood values.' She also endorsed the casual, hedonistic approach to drugs in the Haight-Ashbury subculture. 'Whatever turns me on is a sacrament – LSD, sex, my bells, my colors. This is the holy communion. … When I find myself becoming confused, I drop out and take a dose of acid. It's a short-cut to reality – throws you right into it.'[12]

The Haight-Ashbury soon came to be known as the Hashbury and it had its own pantheon of heroes. One of these was novelist Richard Brautigan, who would later become fashionable as the avant-garde author of *Trout Fishing in America* and *In Watermelon Sugar*. Brautigan liked to parade in the streets carrying a large mirror and he would then call out 'Know thyself!' as the surprised visitors and tourists saw their own reflections in his mirror. Other notables on the local scene included psychedelic artist Michael Bowen, who would later help create the Love Pageant Rally; The Diggers, who fed hundreds of hungry passers-by free of charge at The Panhandle; poets Allen Ginsberg and Michael McClure; Jerry Garcia , the much-loved lead singer with The Grateful Dead; and poster artists Stanley Mouse, Alton Kelley and Wilfried Satty. Local entrepreneur Bill Graham staged many of the early acid-rock concerts at San Francisco's Fillmore Auditorium – including performances by Janis Joplin and Grace Slick – so that made him a special figure in the counterculture, and there were dramatic impromptu street theater performances by the Mime Troupe who were dedicated to 'undermining society'. Meanwhile, hippie poetess Lenore Kandel gained notoriety overnight for her collection of rapturous, sexually explicit poems, *The Love Book*, and LSD biochemist August Owsley Stanley III was already famous for producing the best 'acid' in the country.

One of the best-loved psychedelic heroes in the Bay Area was Ken Kesey, author of the acclaimed novels *One Flew Over the Cuckoo's Nest* and *Sometimes a Great Notion*. Kesey had studied at the University of Oregon and later went on to Stanford in 1958 after winning a literary competition. It was while studying at Stanford that he completed *One Flew Over the Cuckoo's Nest*, a work which provides profound insights into the oppression and loss of freedom experienced by mental patients. Meanwhile, one of Kesey's fellow graduate students at Stanford, Vik Lovell, suggested that Kesey might like to participate in a CIA-funded research study involving mind-altering drugs. Kesey and Lovell were actually paid $75 a night by the CIA to take psilocybin and LSD under clinical conditions and this, predictably, earned them hero status in the Hashbury counterculture. Kesey dedicated *One Flew Over the Cuckoo's Nest* to his friend. The dedication read: 'To Vik Lovell – who told me there were no dragons, then led me to their lairs.'[13]

Kesey also gathered around him a group of musicians, jugglers, magicians and clowns known as the Merry Pranksters. The idea was to mount spontaneous recreational 'acid-happenings', anyplace, anytime. The Pranksters had their own transportation – a 1939 International Harvester bus that had been hand-painted in bright psychedelic colors. Its name, *Further*, was proudly displayed above the windscreen, and the word 'magic' was daubed in large capital letters on the front bumper bar. Wherever the Pranksters traveled and performed, their presence was guaranteed to make an impact.[14]

It was a crazy, wild and happy time and for a while it must have seemed it could go on forever. Kesey himself said the main idea was 'to be peaceful without being stupid, to be interested without being compulsive, to be happy without being hysterical'.[15] But then on 6 October 1966 came the announcement that the State of California would ban the use of LSD, a date many in the Hashbury would come to associate with the symbolism of 666 – the mark of the Beast.

However, if the people's sacrament was about to be taken away, a strong response would soon be forthcoming. Accordingly, Michael Bowen and the Psychedelic Rangers declared that on the very day proposed for the banning of LSD there would also be a Love Pageant Rally at Panhandle Park between Masonic Avenue and Ashbury Street. The 'protest' invitation sent by the Rangers to Mayor John F. Shelley provides a clear indication of the schism that was now rapidly developing between the psychedelic generation and mainstream 'straight' society:

Sir,

Opposition to an unjust law creates futility for citizens who are its victims and increases the hostility between the governed and the governors. In the case of the LSD prohibition, the State has entered directly into the sacrosanct, personal psyches of its citizens. Our Love Pageant Rally is intended to overcome the paranoia and separation with which the State wishes to divide and silence the increasing revolutionary sense of Californians. Similar rallies will be held in communities such as ours all over the country and in Europe. You are invited to attend and address our rally. Thankyou.

Sincerely yours,

Citizens for the Love Pageant Rally

October 6, 1966[16]

The rally began, as promised, on the morning of 6 October, as employees of *The Oracle* and the Psychedelic Shop intent on 'turning on' Mayor Shelley led a delegation to City Hall, laden with flowers and morning glory seeds. Later, as crowds steadily gathered, an impromptu stage was created on the back of a truck for The Grateful Dead, Janis Joplin, and Big Brother and the Holding Company, and the rally burst into full flight. It was a joyous time, 'a hell of a gathering', with 3,000 people really enjoying themselves. One observer was moved to say: 'It's just being. Humans *being*. Being together …' 'Yes', agreed Michael Bowen, 'it's a Human *Be-In*.'

The term 'Be-In' soon became popular with the street culture of the time. But Bowen didn't want things to stop there, and after meeting with Allen Cohen, editor of *The Oracle*, it was agreed that there should be a much bigger love rally in San Francisco – a rally which would be remembered for years to come.

The date planned was 14 January 1967, in the afternoon. There would be a 'Gathering of the Tribes for a Human Be-In at the Polo Fields in Golden Gate Park'. In a press release issued two days prior to the event it was announced that:

> Berkeley political activists and the love generation of the
> Haight-Ashbury will join together with members of the new
> nation who will be coming from every state in the nation,
> every tribe of the young (the emerging soul of the nation) to
> powwow, celebrate and prophesy the epoch of liberation,
> love, peace, compassion and unity of mankind. The night of
> bruted fear of the American eagle-breast-body is over. Hang
> your fear at the door and join the future. If you do not believe,
> please wipe your eyes and see.[17]

Another press release provided more specific details of what one
could expect:

> Twenty to fifty thousand people are expected to gather for a
> joyful powwow and Peace Dance to be celebrated with
> leaders, guides and heroes of our generation. Timothy Leary
> will make his first Bay Area public appearance; Allen
> Ginsberg will chant and read with Gary Snyder. Michael
> McClure and Lenore Kandel; Dick Alpert, Jerry Rubin, Dick
> Gregory and Jack Weinberg will speak. Music will be played
> by all the Bay Area rock bands, including The Grateful Dead,
> Big Brother and the Holding Company, Quicksilver
> Messenger Service, and many others. Everyone is invited to
> bring costumes, blankets, bells, flags, symbols, cymbals,
> drums, beads, feathers, flowers.[18]

This time a crowd of around 10,000 people would come together
in a rapturous union of love and activism. It was clearly an
auspicious day, for as astrologer Ambrose Hollingsworth had
calculated, it marked a time when the present population of the
Earth would be equal in number to the total number of dead in
the whole of human history. Obviously, an effusive and positive

demonstration of human exuberance was called for on this special occasion.

Luckily 14 January was a crisp winter day, the sun beaming down as thousands of hippies mingled together, waving their colorful banners, burning incense, smoking marijuana, sharing food, and carrying flowers. There were giggling children, frolicking animals, Hare Krishnas beating on drums, and a procession of guest speakers and musicians. Jefferson Airplane and Quicksilver Messenger Service played their rock songs before an enthusiastic audience.

Near the grandstands a group of white and African-American musicians played guitars and flutes together. A few members of the famous Hell's Angels motorcycle gang also came to watch, clad in black-leather sleeveless jackets, and they too mingled amidst the incense and the flowers. Amazingly, there were no fights and the crowd was extraordinarily well behaved all afternoon. Psychedelic guru Dr Timothy Leary, who had flown in from the East Coast, declared 'Whatever you do is beautiful' and poet Allen Ginsberg chanted 'We are one! We are all one!' As the sun set across the park there was a profound feeling of deep and pervasive peace.

The gathering was acclaimed by all who had participated as a great success and afterwards Michael Bowen and Allen Ginsberg were ecstatic – they felt it was the birth of a new era, a newfound harmony of consciousness. For others it even seemed like Eden regained, lost innocence rediscovered. But the question on everyone's lips was: Would it last? Would the Summer of Love simply prove ephemeral? Would the joy-consciousness endure? Would psychedelics transform the nation? As it turned out, the hippie phenomenon of Haight-Ashbury would not last very long at all. Within a year the Psychedelic Shop had closed down, Michael Bowen had moved to Mexico to paint, *The Oracle*'s editor, Allen Cohen, had moved to Northern California to write, and there was a general dispersal of local energy.

However, it would be a mistake to identify the impact of 'hippie consciousness' simply with what happened in San Francisco during the Summer of Love. In many ways this particular manifestation of psychedelic culture was just the most visible expression of a much wider phenomenon that had now begun to filter across the whole country. There were hippies all over the United States – in Boston, Seattle, Detroit, New Orleans, Austin, and New York. In June 1967 a gathering of hippies met in Greenwich Village's Washington Square Park to assist the cause of dog owners protesting against the leash laws. Here, reveling in playful paradox, they chanted 'What is dog spelled backwards?' And in Stone Place Mall in Dallas, around a hundred 'flower children' assembled to protest against a proposed ban against large public gatherings. There were also small hippie communities springing up all around the country, like the group who lived in a cluster of geodesic domes constructed from old automobile tops at 'Drop City' near Trinidad, Colorado, and the hippies at Morning Star Ranch near Sebastopol, north of San Francisco.

In one of the most symbolic occurrences of the psychedelic period, in October 1967, Abbie Hoffman, Jerry Rubin and a large group of counterculture devotees organized the National Mobilization demonstration at the Pentagon in Washington DC. An underground publication, *The East Village Other,* called for the presence at this event of 'mystics, saints, artists, holymen, astrologers, witches, sorcerers, warlocks, druids, hippies, priests, shamen, ministers, rabbis, troubadours, prophets, minstrels, bards [and] roadmen' in a magical ceremony which would attempt to levitate the Pentagon. This was a period of quasi-surreal political activity in which a group of hippies formed the Youth International Party and the so-called 'yippies' were formed, as a 'cross-fertilization of the hippie and New Left philosophies'.[19] And even though the magical levitation did not of course occur, this very public magical ceremony would nevertheless come to symbolize, in the popular mythology of the day, the encounter between the cosmological forces of love and magic on the one hand, and the symbolic military might of the Pentagon on the other – a clear distinction between the country's rulers, with their symbols of external political strength, and the youth culture with its internal vitality and magic.

Chapter 6

Maps for Inner Space

Timothy Leary, Ralph Metzner and Richard Alpert had become intrigued by the transformative potential of psychedelics long before their dismissal from Harvard University and they had already discussed the idea of developing some sort of guiding framework for their mystical ventures. It somehow seemed appropriate that they should now venture towards the East – the direction of the rising Sun – for their inspiration.

Looking for insights into the nature of mystical and visionary experiences, Leary and his colleagues decided to explore Tibetan Buddhism. They chose as a key work the *Bardo Thodol* or *Tibetan Book of the Dead*, which had been translated into English by the American Buddhist scholar W.Y. Evans-Wentz. Aldous Huxley, who was also a practicing Buddhist, prized this Mahayana text and had alluded to it in *The Doors of Perception*.[1]

Although *The Tibetan Book of the Dead* seemed oriented towards the needs of the dying – traditionally Tibetan priests read passages from it to those approaching death – Leary believed it was also extremely relevant to the living. After all, sooner or later everyone would have to face the inevitability of death. *The Tibetan Book of the Dead* described a series of post-mortem events – the so-called *Bardo* visions experienced between incarnations – and Leary believed these descriptions could also be used as a guide to mind-expansion. The Bardo levels of consciousness were psychic realms one could explore while one was well and truly alive, long before the final post-mortem separation of mind and body.

The *Bardo Thodol* begins with the loftiest mystical experience of all: the Clear Light of Illumination experienced as the beholder loses his own ego in surrendering to the Void. This is a state of supreme transcendence, of Unity with All. It is a state of sublime Liberation from the constrictions of the sensory world.

According to the *Bardo Thodol*, if this state of consciousness cannot be sustained a realm of awareness known as the Secondary Clear Light then arises in its place. At this level the beholder is swept up in a state of ecstasy which Leary calls *wave energy flow*: 'The individual becomes aware that he is part of and surrounded by a charged field of energy, which seems almost electrical.' If he rides with the flow he may find he can sustain this sublime level of consciousness. However, should he attempt to control it, this in itself represents an act of ego, which in turn reflects *duality* – a state of consciousness where one is aware of oneself as separate and distinct from the immediate surroundings. In such a dualistic state the flow of energy associated with the experience of Unity begins to ebb away and the individual falls into lower levels of the mind referred to in the *Bardo Thodol* as the *Chonyid Bardo*, or karmic hallucinatory stages.

In the second Bardo, writes Leary,

> ... strange sounds, weird sights and disturbed visions may occur. These can awe, frighten and terrify unless one is prepared ... any and every shape – human, divine, diabolic, heroic, evil, animal, thing – which the human brain conjured up or the past life recalls, can present itself to consciousness; shapes and forms and sounds whirling by endlessly. The underlying solution – repeated again and again – is to recognize that your brain is producing the visions. They do not exist. Nothing exists except as your consciousness gives it life.[2]

It is in this phase that Tibetan Buddhists believe they encounter the Seven Peaceful Deities and the Seven Visions of the Wrathful Deities – their own counterpart of the Western Heaven and Hell.

These deities incorporate 58 embodiments of the human personality couched within traditional, culturally delineated forms. Evans-Wentz describes these deities as follows:

> The chief deities themselves are the embodiments of universal divine forces, with which the deceased is inseparably related, for through him, as being the microcosm of the macrocosm, penetrate all impulses and forces, good and bad alike. Samanta-Bhadra, the All-Good, thus personifies Reality, the Primordial Clear Light of the Unborn, Unshaped *Dharma-Kaya*. Vairochana is the Originator of all phenomena, the Cause of all Causes. As the Universal Father, Vairochana manifests or spreads forth as seed, or semen, all things; his *shakti*, the Mother of Great Space, is the Universal Womb into which the seed falls and evolves as the world systems. Vajra-Sattva symbolises Immutability. Ratna-Sambhava is the Beautifier, the Source of all Beauty in the Universe. Amitabha is Infinite Compassion and Love Divine, the *Christos*. Amogha-Siddhi is the personification of Almighty Power or Omnipotence. And the minor deities, heroes, *dakinis* (or 'fairies'), goddesses, lords of death, *rakshasas*, demons, spirits and all others, correspond to definite human thoughts, passions and impulses, high and low, human and sub-human and super-human, in karmic form, as they take shape from the seeds of thought forming in the percipient's consciousness content.[3]

The third phase, or *Sidpa Bardo*, is the period of 're-entry' – the descent from the transcendental heights of spiritual awareness through to the more familiar context of one's everyday environment. According to Mahayana Buddhist tradition, a person who brings full knowledge of spiritual Unity through into incarnation can rightly be considered an avatar, or saint. However, such people are rare indeed, and most human beings function on a far less exalted level. Below the saintly level of spiritual enlightenment exists a vast spectrum of dualistic states of awareness ranging from greater-than-normal human perception through to the lowest forms of animal consciousness re-awakened in man.

According to the *Tibetan Book of the Dead* one should try to avoid being trapped or seduced by the apparent reality of the visionary images encountered in the Bardo states. For this reason it is important during the 're-entry' phase to focus the will as much as possible on spiritual values rather than on symbols of the ego. If this does not happen the individual may find himself enmeshed in 'Judgment' visions resulting from karma associated with his personality, debased sexual fantasies, or other projections of the psyche.

To summarize the essential teaching of the *Bardo Thodol*: The Great Liberation is achieved by ego-loss, or 'the death of the ego'; this state of spiritual self-realization may be achieved in the first Bardo of the Clear Light or by transcending the images of deities which arise in the second Bardo. Below these levels the ego gains more and more strength, and seeks 'rebirth' in the world of the senses where it is able to assert itself once more as dominant. Most of us, says Leary, are doomed to return to normality after our encounter with the realms of Spirit. However, training for these levels of consciousness provides greater familiarity with the most sacred dimensions of the psyche. It is inevitable that each of us will one day have to make the choice for spiritual Liberation.

The *Bardo Thodol* was the ideal map for inner space that Leary, Metzner and Alpert had been looking for. It clearly provided one of the best available frameworks for exploring the heights of mystical perception as well as the 'rebirth', or return-phase of coming back to waking reality. Leary and his co-authors decided, therefore, to base *The Psychedelic Experience* almost entirely on the Bardo sequences in the *Tibetan Book of the Dead*. Published in New

York in 1963, *The Psychedelic Experience* became a classic in the literature of altered states of consciousness and remained a key reference guide for the wisdom-seeking hippie counterculture through the rest of the decade.

As one might expect, however, the trauma of Alpert and Leary's dismissal from Harvard led to a temporary parting of the ways. The third member of the triumvirate, Ralph Metzner, later collaborated with Leary in creating the International Foundation for Internal Freedom and the Castalia Foundation. Metzner also edited *The Psychedelic Review* for several years and went on to produce a number of notable books, including *The Ecstatic Adventure, Maps of Consciousness* and *The Unfolding Self*. He is currently Professor of Psychology at the California Institute of Integral Studies in San Francisco.

Richard Alpert, meanwhile, went off to India in 1967, initially to discover what the holy men of the East could make of LSD. A Californian named Bhagwan Dass took Alpert into the foothills of the Himalayas and subsequently Alpert showed his sacrament to Dass's guru, Neem Karoli Baba – known to his followers as Maharaj-ji. The holy man consumed Alpert's entire stock – 900 micrograms – and was apparently totally unaffected by his psychedelic intake! Someone explained to Alpert that the sage operated in a mental space called *sahaj samadhi* which was not dependent on sources of stimulation from the biophysical level, and Alpert realized he had found a higher source of spiritual authority than he had anticipated. The Maharaj-ji allowed Alpert to stay and provided him with a teacher, and the former Harvard professor became Baba Ram Dass.

Ram Dass now says that 'the only thing you have to offer to another human being, ever, is your own state of being'. He remains a Westerner, if only by heritage, and has spent much of his time communicating the spiritual truths of Eastern mysticism to Western audiences. A serious stroke, however, has confined him to a wheelchair and is likely to curtail his public appearances in the future. Ram Dass's most famous book is *Be Here Now*, which has sold over two million copies. His other books include *Doing Your Own Being, Journey of Awakening* and *Grist for the Mill* (co-authored with Stephen Levine) and an insightful book on ageing, changing and dying titled *Still Here*.

Leary, meanwhile, became a scapegoat for the widespread political distrust of psychedelics. For many years after his dismissal from Harvard he lived the unfortunate life of a jail escapee-cum-hunted man on the basis of an initial charge of possessing less than one ounce of marijuana. However in his later years Leary's life returned to a state of comparative normality. Following the successful publication of his autobiography, *Flashbacks*, in 1983, Leary spent much of his time working as a talk-show host and as a lecturer on the American campus circuit. He also became passionately interested in cyberspace technology, and towards the end of his life advocated what he called 'designer death' – the act of consciously planning one's personal transition through death. Leary died in 1996.

However, Metzner, Alpert and Leary were not alone among the early psychedelic pioneers of inner space. During the 1970s two other figures, Dr John C. Lilly and Dr Stanislav Grof, would also gain increasing recognition for their innovative exploration of psychedelic states of consciousness. Both believed the psychedelic experience had important therapeutic and transformative potential, and both would also have a significant impact on the personal growth movement in the years ahead – Lilly as the inventor of the float-tank used for sensory isolation and meditation, and Grof as a pioneer of holotropic breath therapy, a variant on the holistic modality known as rebirthing.

John Lilly and Sensory Isolation

Born in 1915, Lilly graduated from the California Institute of Technology and went on to receive his doctorate in medicine from the University of Pennsylvania in 1942. He then worked extensively in various research fields of science including biophysics, neurophysiology, electronics and neuro-anatomy and became well known for his research on dolphin-human relationships. This led to the publication of two books, *Man and Dolphin* and *The Mind of the Dolphin*, before his acute awareness of the sensitivity and intelligence of dolphins caused him to have ethical objections to further clinical research on these creatures. He then adopted the position that it is preferable for a scientist to be his own guinea pig before inflicting himself on his subjects.

Lilly therefore began to switch his emphasis to the study of human consciousness, using his own experiences as a focal point. A few years after gaining his doctorate from the University of Pennsylvania he decided to test the idea that a person remains awake because he is bombarded with sensory stimuli. It was while working for the National Institute of Mental Health in Bethesda, Maryland, that he developed the first prototype of the float-tank. His idea was to produce an environment of solitude, isolation and confinement where sensory input was minimized as far as was humanly possible. Wearing a special latex rubber mask fitted with a breathing apparatus, Lilly floated naked in quiet solitude and darkness, in sea-water heated to a constant 93°F, the temperature at which one is neither hot nor cold. In the darkness Lilly felt as if he were floating in a gravity-free dimension. He discovered that the brain compensates for the reduction of sensory stimulation by producing a marked degree of heightened inner awareness. 'I went through dream-like states, trance-like states, mystical states,' he wrote later. 'In all of those states I was totally intact.' At all times he remained simultaneously aware of his floating body and the nature of the experiment.[4]

This inquiry into sensory deprivation was Lilly's first scientific contact with mystical reality. It seemed to him that under these conditions the brain, or 'bio-computer', released a particular 'program' of sensory experiences. This program would be directly related to one's concepts and beliefs, that is to say, one would only perceive things within the grasp of the imagination. A person with narrow conceptual confines would find himself in a barren, constricting 'space' when his mind contents were revealed. Lilly found that, potentially, sensory deprivation states offered tremendous freedom. External reality had been shut out. He could program a mental journey to any place which his imagination could conceive – his choice of program could take him to various specific 'spaces', or to states of consciousness representing various levels of transcendence.

During the early 1960s Lilly also took LSD for the first time, and he found that he was capable of entering mystical dimensions by this means. He had been raised as a devout Roman Catholic in his youth and he knew full well that, at death, the pure soul winged its way to God. Now, years later, while listening to Beethoven's Ninth Symphony under hallucinatory influence, Lilly found himself experiencing a similar 'flight of the soul'. He saw angelic beings and an aged patriarchal God seated on a throne. The programmed learning from his youth had been re-activated by the LSD! 'Later,' wrote Lilly, 'I was to realize that the limits of one's belief set the limits of the experience.'

Sometimes on his inner journeys Lilly contacted entities he called his 'two guides'. However, he resists describing these beings beyond indicating that they represented a particular type of direction and knowledge applicable only to his own wanderings on the inner planes. On occasions they appeared to epitomize his higher self talking down to the more constricted everyday personality, showing the way towards more integrated being. At other times they took the form of 'karmic' conscience, reminding Lilly that he had commitments to his friends and family, and could not become an 'inner-plane drop-out' without dire consequences.

As he continued to explore the various states of inner space, Lilly also began to seek what he called a 'safe place', a point of reference. Lilly's was the dark and silent void of the water tank – 'absolute zero point' – a place 'out of the body, out of the universe as we know it'. Before him lay endless planes of possibilities barred only by the limits of the imagination.

On one occasion Lilly found himself in a space which he called the 'cosmic computer.' It seemed to him that he was a very small and insignificant part of someone else's macro-computer, in rather the same way that the famous Argentinian short-story writer Jorge Luis Borges had described individuals being 'dreamed' into reality by the power of another person's imagination. Lilly sensed tremendous waves of energy, of the same intensity as those described in the Tibetan Bardo of the Secondary Clear Light. However, there was no sense of well-being in this experience. Instead he found himself overwhelmed with feelings of total terror, swept up in a whirlpool of swirling, meaningless energy – a loveless cosmic dance with 'no human value.'

Afterwards Lilly thought over his conceptions of the origin of the physical universe, which had been formulated during his scientific training. There had been no room here for mystical trance elements, or doctrines of 'love' and 'meaning.' His negative Bardo visions showed that a new program was necessary. He had failed to acknowledge the energies of the Godhead working through him.

Later Lilly had discussions with Alan Watts about Eastern mysticism. At Esalen he talked over the merits of Gestalt therapy with Fritz Perls and Ida Rolf, and here too he met Ram Dass – the former Richard Alpert – who had recently returned from India.

Ram Dass introduced him to the *sutras* of Patanjali, a classic text on yoga, and Lilly came to realize that if he wished to find Union with the Infinity of the Void he would have to stand back from both the programmer and the program. He would have to see his results and frameworks in a new light, for the twofold division of seer and seen could no longer apply in a state of

Unity Consciousness. He would later write, 'Beyond transcendence is an infinite variety of unknowns. ... Beyond these unknowns, now unknown, is *full complete Truth*.'

For Lilly, this meant that even when we hold to a set of beliefs, they must always remain open-ended, for they cannot hope to encompass the Transcendent Unknown and contain it within finite expressions and concepts. Lilly subsequently had a close involvement with Oscar Ichazo, a Bolivian spiritual teacher who headed a mystery school in Arica, a town on the Pacific coast of Chile. With Ichazo he discussed the concept of 'negative spaces' and the 'burning of karma'. A high degree of concentration was called for: in this approach negative qualitites would be mentally 'seized' and ruthlessly exhumed in transcendentally negative spaces where they would fail to exert any further influence on one's state of being. Never again would they register on one's personal map of inner consciousness.

Oscar Ichazo's system was based partly on the teachings of George Gurdjieff, whose approach, as we saw in Chapter 1, was to push his followers physically to the edge of their endurance. Only through this type of effort, Gurdjieff argued, could one overcome the slavery of robot-like existence that most people confuse with real life.

Like Gurdjieff, Ichazo similarly emphasized the need for authentic spiritual awakening and he claimed in an interview in *Psychology Today* that one of his major aims was to destroy ego-dominated thoughts.[5] According to Ichazo, when the ego, or a society of egos, reaps the full hell they have sown in their quest for false security and status, they come to a point of collapse and rebirth. The collapse comes at the moment when the ego games are completely exposed and understood: illusion is shattered, subjectivity is destroyed, karma is burned. For Ichazo, the decline of society also brings with it the first moment of enlightenment – its roles and 'programs' are suspended. The only thing left is the *first Satori* – the *first enlightenment*.

Lilly had come to Ichazo for an alternative to current scientific conceptual frameworks, and it was Ichazo who provided Lilly with a structure of the positive and negative states of consciousness from *Satori* through to *anti-Satori*. Following Gurdjieff's system, Ichazo had identified nine states of consciousness, beginning with the highest state – which was assigned a 'vibrational' number of 3, through to successive states, which were identified symbolically by doubling the number of the previous state:

3   6   12   24   48   96   192   384   768

The last of these states in the Gurdjieff/Ichazo model was considered to be a type of hell state.

Lilly now redesigned the scale, assigning positive and negative values to states on either side of what he called 'the middle of the range', or 'normal reality' (state 48). This made the nine-level spectrum of consciousness look quite different:

+3   +6   +12   +24   +48   and   -48   -24   -12   -6   -3

Lilly's sequence identified the highest state of awareness as +3 and the lowest as -3. In the composite framework presented in Lilly's book *The Center of the Cyclone*, he identifies these states as follows (I have presented them in a simplified form here, for greater accessibility):

State of Consciousness	Description
+3 *Dharma-Megha/Samadhi* **Classical *Satori***	Death of the ego. Fusion with the Universal Mind. Union with the Godhead.

+6 *Sasmita-nir bija*
Buddha Consciousness

A point source of consciousness, energy, light and love. Communication at the level of essence.

+12 *Sananda*
Christ Consciousness
of bodily awareness.

A state of cosmic love and divine grace. Highest state

+24 *Vicara*
Basic *Satori*

Control of the human biocomputer. Ability to act knowledgeably and freely.

+48 *Vitarka*

Normal human consciousness.

-48

Openness to new ideas.

-24

Pain, guilt and fear.

-12

Extremely negative bodily state. Consciousness dominated by pain.

-6

A purgatory-like situation. A sense of meaninglessness is prominent.

-3

The 'quintessence of evil, the deepest hell of which one can conceive.'[6]

In a memoir published in 1990 titled *John Lilly, So Far...* Lilly mentions that while his initial relationship with Ichazo was one of 'immediate rapport', they soon came to a major hurdle over the issue of ego. Ichazo's philosophy focused on reducing ego, while, as Lilly himself puts it, his role 'wasn't to get rid of ego but rather to spend as much time as possible near the top end of the scale'.[7] Lilly meanwhile became gradually disenchanted by what he perceived as Ichazo's unwillingness to entertain any belief systems other than those which he had developed through the Gurdjieff work. Lilly acknowledged that his six-month stay in Arica had helped him find his own center – 'the eye of his storm of Being' – but by the end of 1970 their paths were diverging. Intent on pursuing complete freedom of spiritual belief, Lilly realized he could not confine himself to the restrictions of spiritual organizations – even those based on the work of Gurdjieff and the Arica mystery school teachings. In the later years of his life he opted instead to go his own way, maintaining that there were few answers he took for granted. Instead he had begun looking for 'a few good questions' – new scientific ideas to stretch his mind.[8] Lilly died in 2001.

Stanislav Grof

As with Dr John Lilly, Dr Stanislav Grof similarly became involved in the personal growth movement following years of research into psychedelics and altered states of consciousness. Born in Prague in 1931, Grof studied medicine at the Czechoslovakian Academy of Science. In 1954 he began research into the psychotherapeutic uses of LSD, a controversial line of enquiry which he continued after migrating to the United States in 1967. Grof worked in Baltimore at the Maryland Psychiatric Research Center and became an assistant professor at Johns Hopkins University. One of his particular fields of interest was research into the use of psychedelics for easing the pain of terminal cancer patients. He also conducted studies with depressed and alcoholic patients, schizophrenics, narcotic drug addicts and people suffering from psychosomatic illnesses. However, Grof soon discovered that his research was leading him into deeper levels of consciousness than he expected. Reflecting on this during an interview in 1984, he explained how he was increasingly drawn towards a transpersonal view of the human psyche:

I was brought up and educated as a Freudian analyst and so when we started doing the LSD work I expected that we would mostly be working with biographical material. I was looking for a tool that would somehow bring out the unconscious material much faster, so that it would deepen and intensify psychoanalysis. To my surprise people would not stay in the biographical domain which, according to Western psychology, is considered to be the only domain available – memories from childhood and the individual unconscious. Without any programming, and actually against my will, my subjects started moving into realms that hadn't been charted in psychoanalysis at all. The first encounter was powerful – death and birth. People started having sequences of dying and feeling reborn, frequently with details from their biological birth. But this experience of death then reversed and became like a gateway into the transcendental, the archetypal – the transpersonal as we call it now. All this material emerged as a great surprise for me.[9]

As a result of his LSD research, Grof began to develop a model of the human mind which could accommodate these new elements. According to Grof's model there are basically four levels in the psychedelic encounter with the mind. The first of these, experienced at the most superficial level, involves sensory and aesthetic phenomena – for example, visionary episodes characterized by vibrant colors, geometric patterns, and experiences of beautiful natural vistas and exquisite architectural forms. At this level there is also an increased awareness of sounds – humming, chimes and so on.

The next level Grof refers to as the 'biographical' level and its content includes important memories, emotional problems, repressed material and unresolved conflicts from one's present life. Basically this is the realm of the individual unconscious, associated with areas of the personality accessible in usual states of awareness – the unconscious mind as conceived by Freud. Grof coined the term 'COEX System' to describe a 'specific constellation of memories consisting of condensed experiences (and related fantasies) from different life periods of the individual' and he recognized early on that these COEX patterns in individual patients could be triggered into conscious awareness using LSD in a therapeutically controlled environment.[10] However, Grof felt obliged, on the basis of the data he was uncovering, to move beyond Freud's model of the mind, because he came to believe that restricting his framework of the unconscious to one based only on 'biographical' or ego-based elements was no longer tenable.

Grof's third level of consciousness encompasses levels 'characterized by a degree of experiential intensity that transcends anything that is usually conceived to be the limit for the individual human being'. This might involve a 'deep, overwhelming confrontation with the existential realities of death and dying, pain and suffering, birth and agony' but could also open the individual to profound religious and spiritual experiences.[11]

Grof calls these third-level realms of perception – which relate closely to the process of birth and the intra-uterine experience – 'Basic Perinatal Matrices', and he identifies four of them (BPM 1 to 4). Grof believes that each of these four matrices in turn can be linked to different types of religious or spiritual experience.

BPM 1 is associated with the intra-uterine bond of the fetus to the mother, a type of 'symbiotic unity' reflected in the mystical experience as feelings of cosmic unity, tranquility, bliss and transcendence of time and space – they are often what Grof calls 'good womb' experiences. Grof correlates BPM 1 with Maslow's 'peak experiences' and has described them as 'an important gateway to a variety of transpersonal experiences'.[12]

BPM 2 is related to the first clinical stage of biological delivery, a process characterized by muscular uterine contractions while the cervix is closed. This is experienced as a feeling of 'no exit', of cosmic engulfment, or being trapped in a torturous domain. Understandably, it is often a terrifying time for the subject, who feels overwhelmed by increasing levels of anxiety, unseen sources of danger and sometimes a strong sense of lurking evil. Grof correlates this level with Hell states and the 'expulsion from Paradise'.[13] Examples of this type of experience include Prometheus chained to a rock and tortured by an eagle who feeds on his liver, Christ's visions in the Garden of Gethsemane, and the Dark Night of the Soul as described by St John of the Cross.

BPM 3 is associated in the birth process with the second stage of delivery, when the cervix is dilated. Here, although the uterine contractions are still continuing, the open cervix offers the prospects of survival, albeit through a process of struggling along the birth canal. Grof associates this, in the LSD experience, with death-rebirth struggles, and says that at this time the individual can still have frightening encounters with repulsive materials – the experience of eating feces, drinking blood and urine, and so on. However, there is also the sense of impending release – the distinct impression that transcendence is possible. Grof believes that this level sometimes produces visions associated with bloody sacrifice – mythic images of Moloch, Astarte, Kali, or Aztec/Mayan ceremonies – but he also associates BPM 3 with 'the transcending aspects of the crucifixion and of Christ's suffering, as well as the positive aspects of the Last Judgment'.[14]

The final matrix, *BPM 4,* is associated with the spiritual experience of death and rebirth and, according to Grof, is linked in the birth process with the actual birth of the individual. LSD subjects entering this phase report visions of vivid white or golden light, the universe is perceived as indescribably beautiful and radiant, and those experiencing it feel cleansed and purged, as if they have entered a state of spiritual redemption or salvation. Grof associates this state mythically with the rebirth of Osiris – the ancient Egyptian god who was brought back to life by Isis after being murdered and dismembered by Set – and also with the resurrected Christ, who is crucified on the cross but triumphs over death.[15]

However, Grof does not believe that the correlations between the birth process and the levels of consciousness accessed through LSD are coincidental. Sometimes individuals appear to relive their actual birth experiences and even seem to tap into the thought processes experienced by their mothers at the time. He also maintains that his LSD research confirms the presence of Jungian archetypes in the collective unconscious – that it is no longer appropriate to consider such a concept as simply theoretical:

LSD subjects frequently report that in their transpersonal sessions they have had a vivid and authentic sense of confrontation or identification with archetypes representing generalized biological, psychological or social types and roles; these can reflect various levels of abstraction and different degrees of generalization. The Old Wise Man, Good Samaritan, Conqueror, Martyr, Fugitive, Outcast, Tyrant, Fool or Hermit are examples of the more specialized archetypal images. The most general archetypes always have strong elements of numinosity, as exemplified by the Great Mother, Terrible Mother, Father, Child-King, Great Hermaphrodite, Animus and Anima, or Cosmic Man. Frequently transper-

sonal experiences of this kind have concrete cultural characteristics and take the forms of specific deities, demons, demi-
gods and heroes ... Quite common also are experiences with
spirits of deceased human beings and suprahuman spiritual
entities.[16]

Significant and powerful though they are, Grof does not,
however, regard perinatal and archetypal experiences as the most
profound or transcendent levels of human awareness. In his view,
it is possible to extend still further on the spectrum of
consciousness – from the four perinatal levels to an experience of
the complete transcendence of human individuality. Here, he
writes, 'we begin to free ourselves from the preconception that
consciousness is something created within the human brain.
Transpersonal consciousness is infinite, rather than finite,
stretching beyond the limits of time and space.'[17]

For Grof, consciousness would seem to be an innate characteristic of the natural universe:

Mind and consciousness might not be exclusive privileges of
the human species but [may] permeate all of Nature, existing
in the most elemental to the most complex forms. Struggle as
we might, we seem unable to free ourselves from preconcep-
tions imposed on us by our culture and by what we believe to
be common sense. However if we are to maintain these
illusions it becomes necessary to ignore a vast body of observations and information coming from modern consciousness
research and from a variety of other scientific disciplines.
From all these sources comes evidence strongly suggesting
that the universe and the human psyche have no boundaries
or limits. Each of us is connected with, and is an expression of,
all of existence.[18]

When research into the medical and therapeutic potentials of

LSD became politically untenable in the mid-1970s, Grof was forced by circumstance to explore other techniques of achieving transpersonal states. Gradually he began shifting his emphasis towards what he now calls 'holotropic breath therapy', an approach which resembles the more widely known technique of 'rebirthing'. The latter modality was developed by Leonard Orr in California during the early 1970s, and both rebirthing and holotropic breath therapy derive substantially from *Pranayama* – the Indian Yoga of breath – which employs a connected breathing rhythm to produce an altered state of consciousness. In both therapies the subject lies horizontally in a comfortable position with a facilitator, or helper, sitting nearby to assist in any experiential crisis. The session begins as the subject engages in rhythmic in-and-out breathing, with no pauses in between. As Orr has written: 'You merge with your breath, flowing, glowing, soaring, relaxing profoundly, your mind melting into your spirit, surging, awakening your inner being and the quiet sounds of your soul ...'

In holotropic breath therapy, however, the technique is somewhat more intense and the results more sudden and dramatic. The breathing is accompanied by recorded music which is chosen to reflect different phases of the cathartic process. As Grof explains: 'The music is the vehicle itself, so at the beginning we start with some very activating, powerful music. Then, maybe an hour into the session, we move into a kind of culminating, "breakthrough" type of music – for example using the sounds of bells or similar, very powerful, transcendental sounds.'[19] His musical selections are very varied, including African tribal rhythms, Sufi chants, Indian ragas, Japanese flutes and various forms of ambient music.

Paradoxically, the type of hyperventilation breathing employed in the holotropic approach actually reduces the amount of oxygen transmitted to the cortex of the brain, producing a natural 'high'. The technique simulates the experience of mystics who live in high altitudes where the air is more rarefied, and is therefore ideal, as Grof himself says casually, for those who can't make the trip to the Himalayas! However, more importantly, Grof has found that holotropic breathing, like LSD psychotherapy, can resolve profound emotional problems associated with the birth process, and can also take subjects into the furthest transpersonal realms. A significant finding of Grof's more recent work is that his original model of consciousness remains basically unchanged: the same transpersonal levels of awareness can be accessed either through psychedelics like LSD or through non-drug, altered-state modalities like holotropic breathwork. The human mind and the universe are as they are. Different techniques and modalities may be used to explore what remains, essentially, the same terrain.

Chapter 7

The Holistic Perspective

The 1960s psychedelic consciousness brought in its wake an important aftermath – a widespread awareness that inner states of being were vitally important in any definition of essential human-ness.[1] This, of course, was a central component of both humanistic and transpersonal psychology, but it now began to influence concepts of health and medical care as well. A characteristic definition, epitomizing the new orientation, appeared in a work titled *Dimensions of Humanistic Medicine*, published in San Francisco in 1975. Here the authors described human health care in a way which acknowledged the *total* human being both in physical and spiritual terms:

> A person is more than his body. Every human being is a holistic, interdependent relationship of body, emotions, mind and spirit. The clinical process which causes the patient to consult the medical profession is best understood as this whole and dynamic relationship. The maintenance of continued health depends on harmony of this whole.[2]

The idea of tapping one's own innate healing potential, of regarding the process of overcoming disease as a learning experience, and of becoming more self-reliant, were all perceptions that had spilled over from the earlier years of Maslow, Sutich and Esalen. Whereas, in more traditional styles of Western medical practice, patients were generally regarded as dependent on the doctor and illness was considered a complaint to be eliminated, the new focus was now on helping the patient to become more knowledgeable about his condition and to participate in the healing process. The complaint could then provide the patient with insights and opportunities for self-discovery. The old concept was that health could be defined as the absence of disease and that in states of illness one should pay attention primarily to the specific symptoms, or body parts, which had 'gone wrong'. Now, however, the emphasis was being placed on health as a positive and natural state of human well-being – the whole person, and not just the symptom or organ, was now the subject of the medical enquiry.

There was also an increasing recognition that the frame of reference should not be physical alone but should also encompass mental and emotional aspects of health and could even include such areas as spiritual values, the search for personal meaning, and the integrative elements of religious beliefs. At the same time in the holistic paradigm there was a shift away from curative medicine towards the prevention of illness. This brought with it the long overdue recognition that self-help factors like sensible nutrition, regular exercise and personal preventive health-care measures were all vital considerations in avoiding illness. As Schutz and Perls had stressed at Esalen, it was a matter of taking substantial responsibility for your own health care. And where treatments *were* required from a doctor, they would preferably be intended not just to repress isolated symptoms but to help restore balance to the organism as a whole.

Most importantly, there was a dramatic switch away from synthetic medicines towards natural remedies, whenever they were available. The emphasis in the new holistic health paradigm was now on the remarkable capacity of the human organism to rectify imbalance and initiate processes of self-healing. Meditation and yoga could be used to help reduce stress, and 'natural' modalities like naturopathy, acupuncture, shiatsu and homeopathy, all of which stimulated healing processes from within the organism itself, were to be preferred to conventional medical treatments whenever possible. This brought with it the accompanying belief that healing should be as non-intrusive as possible and that synthetic chemicals and other 'unnatural' agents were to be totally avoided, or used only as a last resort.[3]

However, perhaps the most far-reaching implication of the holistic health perspective was that mind, body and spirit were now regarded as interrelated and health care was being called upon to address all of these aspects collectively. It was an orientation that tended towards mysticism and which still attracts widespread resistance among many conventional Western doctors. Indeed, the whole issue of the interrelatedness of mind and body – quite apart from spirit – has only recently begun to gain momentum in orthodox medical circles. From a medical perspective it has been clinically difficult to identify specific links between mind (psyche) and body (soma) in causing disease, even though many individual doctors have believed for some time that such connections do indeed exist.

Psychosomatic Aspects of Disease
Professor Hans Selye – Emeritus Professor at the University of Montreal, President of the International Institute of Stress and a pioneering figure in the holistic health movement – had long regarded stress as an extremely important factor in causing illness. However, he emphasized that stress could not be equated simply with intensity of lifestyle. Stress, he believed, was best thought of as deriving from the perception of events in our lives and was therefore a reflection of our ability to deal with the demands of those events. Stress could be measured by such factors as general irritability, depression, high blood pressure, impulsive and aggressive behavior, inability to concentrate, emotional tension, sexual problems, insomnia, migraine headaches and a variety of other symptoms. Selye also noted that people react differently to the demands made upon them. We all learn to adapt to pressures, but stress arises when the process of coping begins to fail. We then have to develop daily priorities for

regaining equilibrium – by slowing down or altering our pace of life, and so on. Otherwise we risk a breakdown of health – beginning, perhaps, with relatively minor conditions like skin complaints and intestinal upsets but leading perhaps to more serious illnesses.[4]

Many studies have since been made to determine whether stress is related to the incidence of cancer and heart attacks, and researchers have also wondered whether certain personality types are more susceptible than others to outbreaks of ill-health. In 1974 the Californian cardiologists Dr Ray Rosenman and Dr Meyer Friedman published a highly influential book which described how a behavioral pattern known as 'Type A' correlated with the likelihood of heart disease.[5] The Type A person was typically extremely competitive and aggressive, was inclined to schedule more and more activities into less and less time, was usually in too much of a hurry to derive any sense of beauty from the environment, did not delegate tasks easily, exhibited explosive speech patterns, had trouble sitting and doing nothing, and was given to lip clicking, head nodding, fist clenching and other related traits. In a business setting, the typical Type A person could appear to be productive and full of confidence, but underneath felt inferior and was prone to failure. By contrast, the Type B person was much calmer, had more inner composure, and was less demonstrative in his actions. He could be equally as self-motivated as Type A, but his behavior was not as competitive or aggressive.

A similar relationship also seemed to exist between psychological factors, stress, and the outbreak of cancer. Dr Lawrence Le Shan, a research psychotherapist currently based in New York, was a leading advocate of meditation and holistic health during the 1970s. After studying 250 cancer patients and administering personality tests, Le Shan compared them with 150 non-cancer subjects. The following factors emerged:

- 77 percent of cancer subjects but only 14 percent of healthy subjects showed extreme tension over the loss of a close relative or friend.
- 64 percent of cancer subjects as opposed to 32 percent of non-cancer subjects showed signs of not being able to adequately express anger, resentment and aggression towards other people, but bottled up their feelings instead.
- 69 percent of cancer patients had low personal esteem and culpability while only 34 percent of the control group showed this characteristic.

Le Shan also found that, typically, cancer patients had experienced a major emotional trauma six to eighteen months prior to the development of the disease.[6]

Meanwhile Dr Carl Simonton, a physician from the University of Oregon who specialized in the holistic treatment of cancer, extended the hypothesis of Dr Friedman and Dr Rosenman and put forward the idea that there was also a 'cancer' personality. The most pronounced characteristics of this personality type were as follows:

- A tendency to hold resentment and a marked inability to forgive.
- An inclination towards self-pity.
- A poor ability to develop and maintain meaningful, long-term relationships.
- A very poor self-image.[7]

Dr Simonton placed great emphasis on Professor Selye's discovery that chronic stress suppressed the immune system, and drew attention to the fact that it was the immune system that provided the mechanism for destroying or keeping at bay the cancerous cells present in the body. Dr Simonton summarized his conclusions during the May Lectures held in London in 1974:

All human beings have cancer cells within them. The problem is not the cancer cells but the breakdown of the body's ability to deal with them and rid itself of disease. I see cancer, therefore, as having much in common with diseases like tuberculosis, the common cold and so forth. We are continually exposed to many dangerous agents both from within and without, but it is only when we become susceptible to them that the disease actually develops.[8]

One of Simonton's most distinctive techniques, introduced as an adjunct to orthodox radiation therapy, was the use of visualization and relaxation to help his patients focus on their cancerous growths – and it was Simonton's focus on visualization for health that would be taken up in earnest by the New Age movement. Simonton asked his patients, three times a day, every day, to visualize their medical treatment and the body's own immune mechanisms (white blood cells) acting positively and victoriously over the disease. Dr Simonton discovered that patients with a positive attitude towards their disease had a much more favorable clinical response to treatment than those with a poor attitude.

While many orthodox doctors continue to be wary of psychosomatic treatments and are wary of acknowledging that meditation and visualization can really produce clinical effects, important insights have been provided by a relatively new science, psycho-neuroimmunology (PNI), which has gone a long way towards endorsing the holistic health perspective. Since the 1980s PNI researchers have been involved in the ongoing task of investigating how the brain interacts with the body's immune cells – how the brain sends signals via the nerves to enable the body to fight disease. Because these neural pathways can be triggered by thoughts and emotions, such research has been useful for discovering how seemingly subjective or intangible holistic therapies like visualization and meditation are in fact working with something physiologically real. It would seem that the brain and immune system constitute a closed circuit and that there is a two-way interaction between the immune system and the brain which monitors the presence of intrusive bacteria, tumors and viruses in the body.

Neuropharmacologist Dr Candace Pert, a former research professor in the Department of Physiology and Biophysics at the Georgetown University Medical Center in Washington DC and who has written the bestselling book *Molecules of Emotion* – a popular work among many New Age readers – believes the mind is not confined to the brain. In fact, she says, we can regard the mind as being present in every cell of the body.[9] According to Dr Pert every cell in the human organism has intelligence and every cell has receptors that can send and receive information. Considered in this light, we can think of human beings as a flow of information and memory.

Pert's scientific focus has been on neuropeptides, small protein-like chemicals made in the brain that operate rather like 'biochemical units of emotion'. These neuropeptides, which include the well-known category of endorphins, are morphine-like chemicals generated in the brain, which produce marked changes in mood. However, it also appears that neuropeptides can connect with macrophages (cells which help destroy infection and disease), influencing the speed and direction of their movement. The interaction of these two classes of chemicals in the body appears to offer a scientific explanation for a phenomenon most of us acknowledge intuitively – that our moods and state of mind can affect our state of health. For example, it may be the sheer emotional power of optimism and positive thinking which helps some people recover from seemingly 'terminal' types of illness. The reason for this is that the positive attitude itself helps to keep the immune system fighting. As PNI researcher Professor Ed Blalock of the University of Texas has observed:

Your classical sensory systems recognize things you can see, taste, touch, smell and hear. Bacteria and viruses have none of these qualities, so how are you going to know they are there unless the immune system lets your brain in on the secret? The immune system may be the sixth sense we've been seeking all these years ...[10]

The Prophets of Self-help

An awareness of psychosomatic factors in health is one thing, the exploration of 'personal growth' and 'human potential' quite another. As the widespread interest in holistic health gathered momentum during the 1970s, the body-mind-spirit paradigm soon began to acquire a particular focus that would lead the youthful wisdom seekers of the Leary generation in an entirely new direction. The new focus was based on *personal motivation* – on the idea, central to the American dream, that we all have the potential to achieve wealth, success and happiness if we have the drive and vision to bring it about.

The United States had long had its share of popular 'you too can be a success' writers, most of whom were self-taught and essentially self-educated. Introducing the elements of 'self-help' and 'success' to the holistic concept of inner balance and well-being proved to be decisive in the birthing of what has now become known as the New Age movement.

One of these early motivational writers was William H. Danforth, founder of the Ralston Purina Company, whose book *I Dare You!* ran through numerous editions in the 1950s. One of the chapters in this book was titled 'You can be bigger than you are', and it epitomized his approach. Danforth's book contained the potent message that everyone could help to transform themselves into happier, more prosperous individuals.

Another work in this genre was Napoleon Hill's *Think and Grow Rich*, which announced to the reader that it would 'help you to negotiate your way through life with harmony and understanding [since] you are the master of your fate and the captain of your soul'. Hill was well aware that one's destiny depended on positive motivation and in turn on positive thoughts, and he believed that to implant the concept of achievement in the mind was a necessary precondition for success. To this end, argued Hill, one should 'feed his subconscious mind on thoughts of a creative nature' and visualize oneself 'on the road to success'. He advocated a type of self-hypnosis, which he called 'auto-suggestion', as a way of doing this.

Hill's approach is mirrored in the New Age notion of 'prosperity and abundance consciousness', where devotees 'visualize' their future wealth and happiness, bolstering it all the time with 'affirmations' intended to guarantee a successful outcome. Interestingly Hill also anticipated the New Age in other ways. He maintained that to contact the Infinite Intelligence in the universe, one's mind would have to operate with the highest 'vibrations', transcending the barriers of ordinary perception to look beyond to richer horizons.

Also in this style, but somewhat more sophisticated, was the bestselling book *Psycho-Cybernetics* by Maxwell Maltz. A plastic surgeon by profession, Maltz had noticed that modifying his patients' facial features often led to positive changes in personality, so he postulated the idea that one could similarly visualize a more positive internal self-image to effect constructive change in one's life.

The term 'cybernetics' itself had been coined in 1947 by mathematician Norbert Wiener and the physicist Arturo Rosenblueth and was defined as the 'science of control and communication in the animal and the machine'. Wiener and Rosenblueth were aware that biological organisms seemed to have sensors that measured deviations from set goals, which in turn provided 'feedback' that would allow such behavior to be corrected. Basically, Maltz believed that the internal self-image one visualized could similarly help to provide a base for the personality and behavior, and that, as long as the self-image was positively reinforced, there were potentially no limits to individual accomplishment. In this way, as one hears so often in the New Age today, people could readily learn to 'create their own reality' through a process of transforming the self.

Maltz's book was undoubtedly an advance on the simpler motivational emphasis on the power of positive thinking advocated by Napoleon Hill. According to Maltz, however, 'positive thinking' by itself wasn't enough – the self-image had to be positive as well. A person endeavoring to think positively with a negative self-image could hardly hope to be successful because the two dimensions of the personality would simply fight against each other. Maltz also noted that traits like resentment and guilt were associated with a negative self-image. A person harboring resentment, for example, was effectively allowing others to determine how he should feel or act by fixating on past events. This was completely inconsistent with striving for a positive future in which one could gain success and self-fulfillment. Guilt was also a matter of living in the past by trying to atone in the present for something 'wrong' which had occurred at an earlier time. Maltz argued that since one could not change the past, guilt was hardly warranted. The appropriate task, emotionally, was to respond to the present situation.

Maltz believed that the main tools for changing the self-image from negative to positive were physical relaxation, imagination and hypnosis. As Maltz noted in his book:

The proper use of the imagination can be equivalent to the beginning of a goal and a belief in this goal. And if this belief is strong enough we hypnotize ourselves with it. ... all our habits, good and bad, are daily forms of self-hypnosis. Belief is a form of creative hypnotism.[11]

The New Age counterpart of Maxwell Maltz is an energetic

woman named Shakti Gawain, bestselling author of *Creative Visualization* and *Living in the Light* – works now regarded as New Age classics. In *Creative Visualization* Gawain describes a variety of exercises, meditations and affirmations to assist readers in visualizing health, prosperity, loving relationships and 'the fulfillment of desires'. As she noted in an interview in 1988 with New Age newspaper *LA Resources*, creative visualization is a technique 'of being able to imagine having what you want in your life so that you can create the internal experience of having your life be the way you want it to be. ... Creating that internal experience seems to open us up to creating it externally as well.'[12]

With publication of her second book, *Living in the Light*, however, Gawain moved more towards recognition of an internal guiding intelligence that could be accessed by trusting and following one's deep intuitions. During her interview she mentioned that this heightened awareness provided her with a much more qualitative approach to life: 'Moving with the energy of life and with the energy of the universe in a really spontaneous way is just the most exciting and wonderful way to live.' Clearly, Gawain's approach to visualization and intuition had taken her beyond the more specifically goal-oriented concepts of Hill and Maltz. Her vision now also extended to acknowledging Carl Jung's idea of confronting the 'shadow'. Gawain even maintained that facing one's darker side was a vital ingredient in the ongoing process of planetary transformation:

To 'live in the light' you really have to be willing to go into what you feel is the darkness. You have to face your shadow self and bring that into the light. I believe that as we are doing that individually we are also doing that on a worldwide level. The world is going through a lot of darkness, upheaval and pain, but we are becoming conscious of the things which we have repressed in the past – the things we have not been willing to deal with. Just as each of us are doing that in our own lives, it's happening on a mass consciousness level too. I feel that if we keep having the courage, those of us who are willing to really face ourselves and really do delve into ourselves and really start living in accordance with our own inner truths to the best of our abilities, we will see that reflected in the world around us. We're just going to keep seeing that, more and more. We really live in a very exciting time.[13]

Mention should also be made at this point of Alexander Everett (1921–2005), creator of Mind Dynamics and an organization known as Inward Bound. Like Shakti Gawain, Everett moved gradually from an approach which initially utilized visualization and imagination towards a method based on transcending thought itself.

Everett was an important influence on such figures as Werner Erhard (founder of est and Forum); Jim Quinn (Life Stream), Peter and Ruth Honzatko (Alpha Dynamics) and a variety of other mind-control groups. And like Napoleon Hill and Maxwell Maltz before him, his initial impetus was as an exponent of 'self-improvement'.

Alexander Everett was born in Exeter, England. At the age of 24, after returning from six years in the British Army during World War II, he managed to obtain a teaching position without any formal university training. Then, when he was 32, he established the private Shiplake School for boys, in a manor house in Henley-on-Thames, near London.

However, it is not for these achievements that he is best known in the personal growth movement. In 1968, having moved from England to the United States, Everett founded a system of personal development training called Mind Dynamics. Based initially in Texas and later in the San Francisco Bay Area, Everett promoted his ideas to a large audience through seminars and training programs in which he explained how the mind affected the emotions and how emotions affected the body. However, despite their financial success, Everett did not find his Mind Dynamics seminars very fulfilling. What he discovered was that only around 10 percent of people attending benefited substantially from what he was teaching, and they were already successful in their lives. He became increasingly concerned to develop new ways of helping a much larger percentage of the population and this led him to disband Mind Dynamics in 1973. Everett then undertook a spiritual search of his own:

> I travelled to India and began to realize that there was a power beyond the mind – and that was the *self*. In the West we may be inclined to call it the 'spirit' or the 'soul' – according to the religious tradition we belong to   but I found out that the level of the self is perfect: there is no duality at that point. It seemed to me that if I got into that level, the highest power could control the lower powers. Most people try to find out who they are through the mind and you can't do it. The mind is designed to work at the outer levels. Until you get to the inner levels there is no way you can know about these higher powers. This is the big mistake the Western world makes. The mind is a lower level of consciousness. It cannot perceive that which is above.

Everett incorporated the fruits of his spiritual search into a program called Inward Bound which he organized from his center near Eugene, Oregon. Focusing on the idea that the God-principle can be found deep within every human being, Everett came to believe that there are four levels of human functioning – physical, emotional, mental and spiritual:

> I teach that we should stop thinking – that we should still the mind – and when that happens we are awakened to a Higher

Source, the Eternal, the I Am, or whatever you care to call it. I train people through a process called 'centering' to make contact, to be open, to wake up to this Higher Source. The idea of Inward Bound is to go to this inner state. When you do that you *know*. At the lower levels you only think you know. To me, God is not somebody 'out there'. God is a principle. God is within you. As you awaken to that fact, you change. In my seminars I aim for this process of centering on the God part within ...[14]

During an interview I conducted with him in November 1988, I asked Everett what he felt were the implications of his approach, both within the human potential movement and in a broader, international context. His response was both encouraging and optimistic:

Human potential in the ultimate sense is developing the highest state of consciousness. When you function at the lower level you want power; you want money, you want possessions, but you are on your own at this level. However, when you open yourself to the highest level, you get a sense of Oneness, you are one with everybody else, and then you realize you can serve other people – you're not in it just for yourself. I believe this is the big quantum leap that is coming to the planet in the next few years. Man is going to have to switch over from the lower self to the level of co-operation and service. At the moment only a minority group is doing this – but it's growing. At the moment man is Homo Sapiens – the 'wise intellectual'. Later man will be known as 'Homo Noeticus' – the knowing man, who is guided by intuition and inspiration, Selfishness is out of date: co-operation is coming. People are going to have to share and work together.[15]

Chapter 8

Mystics and Metaphysicians

On one level, as Alexander Everett has intimated, the New Age has been all about developing a capacity for greater intuition, striving for inner spiritual knowledge and the quest for communal co-operation – these are some of its most positive and worthwhile elements. However, it is also true that many New Age enthusiasts have become excessively eclectic and undiscriminating in their pursuit of mystical enlightenment. In the New Age, with equal abandon, we find a liberal sprinkling of healing with crystals, metaphysical communication with dolphins, affirmations for prosperity consciousness, and a seemingly never-ending procession of 'spiritual masters' from both East and West – some of whom hold workshops on the perennial wisdom teachings while simultaneously presiding over wealthy, well-endowed corporate organizations.

There are those who are attracted to the New Age because they hope that by attaining new levels of mystical self-realization they may come to feel that they are now a class apart – exclusive members of a group of more 'evolved' human beings, or 'spiritual illuminati'. There are men who are drawn to the New Age in order to explore their inner feminine natures, and women who seek more dynamic and assertive 'masculine' paradigms for self-renewal. There are business executives who are drawn to the New Age for its promise of material abundance and an end to 'poverty consciousness'. And there are those whose sense of self-confidence is perhaps so fragile that they grasp at all manner of oracles – from predictive astrology and fortune-telling with the *I Ching* or Tarot, through to personal communication with angels.

Voices of the New Age

The New Age is also a movement with its own superstars, among them such figures as motivational speaker and doctor Deepak Chopra, 'angel therapist' Doreen Virtue, bestselling 'channeler' Neale Donald Walsch – author of *Communications with God*, self-help seminar leaders Anthony Robbins, Louise Hay and Wayne Dyer, holistic therapists Carolyn Myss and Brandon Bays, and well-known American actress and New Age spokesperson Shirley MacLaine. They all, in their own respective fields, offer an ultimately positive outlook on life and have optimistic and often inspirational messages to convey. Sometimes, however, these messages are not received in the manner intended.

During a New Age lecture in New York in 1987, while emphasizing the divine potential latent in all human beings, Shirley MacLaine told her audience 'I am God', and when a woman rose from her seat to object MacLaine is said to have replied: 'If you don't see me as God, that's because you don't see yourself as God.'[1] While such statements seem incredibly brazen at first glance, it is likely that Shirley MacLaine was intending to convey the sense that every human being is animated by the spark of the universal Godhead – a basic principle in the wisdom traditions of both the East and West. As one writer expressed it: 'She believes that each person is the centre of creation and that power, wisdom and the strength to overcome resides in every individual.'[2]

Dr Deepak Chopra has also sent mixed messages during his extraordinary career as a leading spokesperson for the New Age. Chopra is an articulate and remarkably well-informed lecturer, and his ability to present a fusion of holistic healing principles with insights into quantum physics, 'cellular intelligence' and transpersonal states of consciousness is unquestionably impressive. It is also true that no lesser figure than the Dalai Lama has endorsed his book *How to Know God*. However, there are also times when Chopra seems to be endorsing the cause of spiritual materialism.

Born in India, and trained as a conventional doctor, Chopra eventually discarded Western medicine for Indian Ayurvedic medicine because he was less concerned with curing disease than with promoting holistic health. However, after establishing himself in America Chopra was able to transform himself into what one commentator has called 'the rock star of the new spirituality'. His numerous books – among them *The Seven Spiritual Laws of Success* – have sold millions of copies and he similarly earns millions of dollars each year from the sales of his tapes and alternative health products. He also has a close personal following among many of the Hollywood glitterati, including Elizabeth Taylor, Winona Ryder and Demi Moore, as well as television hostess Oprah Winfrey. Deepak Chopra is possibly the first New Age spiritual guru to claim wealth is God-given. 'I have no qualms about being a millionaire,' he told a journalist from *Newsweek*, 'and I want everyone else to know that they can do it too. People who have achieved an enormous amount of success are inherently very spiritual.'

Transformation – for a Fee

The blend of 'wealth and wisdom' is a successful mix in the commercial arenas of the New Age. In Western consumerist society, where anything in demand can be marketed, it is unfortunately true that assuaging spiritual thirst has itself become a commodity – and this product usually comes at a cost. And so we find ourselves in the midst of a vast array of personal and metaphysical 'transformation' seminars, many of them marketed for excessively high fees. Some of these seminars come with the promotional tag that money is simply 'a unit of power and energy' and that 'prosperity consciousness' is potentially available to all of us if we can 'take the responsibility' to recognize our own self-worth. Techniques like this have certainly worked for 'human potential communicator' Anthony Robbins, author of motivational bestsellers like *Awaken the Giant Within* and *Notes from a Friend*. Robbins reputedly earns $150,000 a day for his seminars on overcoming fear and owns an entire island in Fiji. And while he is among the most successful international self-promoters in the consciousness-raising business, there are many others who aspire to follow in his footsteps.

The group of motivational lecturers and authors focused around American self-help publisher and writer Louise Hay provide a case in point. They include Dr Doreen Virtue, Wayne Dyer, Stuart Wilde and past-lives therapist Dr Brian Weiss. As a publishing company keen to promote its products, Hay House has no peer in the holistic marketplace and is one of the most successful independent publishing companies in the United States.

American 'angel therapist' Dr Doreen Virtue is currently the bestselling author in the Hay House publishing stable. Trained originally as a psychologist and nutritionist, Dr Virtue came from a family interested in psychic and spiritual healing and this orientation gradually became more important in her work. A highly articulate and personable presenter with such titles as *Healing with the Angels, The Fairy Oracle* and *Angel Visions* to her credit, Doreen Virtue's New Age readership is predominantly female. During her lectures on the healing powers of angels, fairies and Nature spirits, she encourages her audience to call on these supernatural agencies to assist in the treatment of illness or to avoid misfortune. On two separate occasions I have myself heard her relate how an angel interceded to help her prevent the imminent theft of her car.[3]

Clearly the New Age arena is a diverse and wondrous place, and at times its scope seems almost limitless. The American New Age magazine *Interface*, which is a typical publication within its genre, lists an extraordinary number of personal transformation seminars and workshops – once again, all of them available at a price.[4] Some of the random offerings on tap: 'The Necessity of Meeting God in the Darkness'; 'Embracing the Shadow and

Reclaiming our Wholeness'; 'Freedom from Emotional Eating'; 'The Seven Stages of Money Maturity'; 'Evolving Culture through the Chakras'; 'The Tao of Now' ... and so the list continues. No doubt many of these workshops may be meaningful and worthy, but one cannot help forming an impression that in popular American culture – a culture which ultimately permeates everywhere else – spirituality and transformation can be purchased in weekend workshops like goods from a supermarket.

Where the New Age seems to have crumbled in its credibility is in its often uncritical mix of self-help, 'channeled' inspiration, confused mythologies and showbiz therapies. There is now a multi-million dollar international market in experiential workshops, lectures, crystals, relationships counseling and 'rebirthing', presented in a way which often tends to trivialize the more important findings of humanistic and transpersonal psychology. Similarly, there are numerous workshops on loving relationships, discovering the inner child, dialoguing with the inner voice, recovering the inner song, or reawakening the inner pulse – all of them variants on Carl Jung or the encounter group therapies of the 1960s.

And still the focus on self-help and personal transformation remains. It remains a truism in the New Age that one should transform oneself before seeking to transform others. While at times, and often with justification, this may appear to be an extremely self-centered attitude, the broader intent – at least, in theory – is to move beyond exploring the facets of one's own individuality to developing an integrative state of awareness in one's relationship with others and then within one's immediate environment and the planet as a whole. However, it is clear that the process of individual integration needs to occur on a number of levels – physical, mental, emotional and spiritual. A diverse range of alternative 'mind, body and spirit' modalities – some more authentic than others – has sprung up to cater for this need.

Underlying all of these modalities is the common theme of self-transformation and the credo that if we can all make the effort to transform ourselves and raise our culture to the next phase of human evolution, the world will surely be a much better place to live in.[5]

Bodywork therapies like massage, chiropractic, the Alexander Technique and yoga are now mainstream and uncontroversial, and there are many meditation, relaxation and visualization techniques that are both credible and worthwhile. However, it is in the New Age approaches to the Spirit that one finds the most controversial concepts and practices.

Channeling

One of the most popular New Age modalities is 'channeling', or psychic mediumship – an activity associated with a range of New Age personalities including Shirley MacLaine, Kevin Ryerson, John Edward, Sylvia Browne, Dolores Cannon, J.Z. Knight and the late Jane Roberts (these last two acting as channels for the discarnate beings known as Ramtha and Seth respectively). The highly regarded New Age classic *A Course in Miracles* is also a channeled work. Dictated mentally to Helen Schucman, this 1,500-page manuscript of psycho-spiritual teachings and exercises is thought by some to have emanated from Christ himself.[6]

Channeling is really a more recent name for spiritualism and as a metaphysical practice it has remained comparatively unchanged since its heyday in the late 19th century. In the act of channeling the psychic becomes a vehicle for communications from the spirit world. Channelers enter trance or meditative states and claim to make contact with spirit-helpers and guides on the inner planes. They are then able to obtain information which can in turn be offered to their clients – or workshop participants – as advice for attaining a state of well-being, dealing with bereavement, or managing one's day-to-day affairs.

One of the most successful contemporary American New Age

channelers is Neale Donald Walsch, a former public information officer and radio-show host whose first book, *Conversations with God*, spent 137 weeks on the *New York Times* bestseller list. Walsch claims to communicate not with archangels or spirits but with God himself.

According to Walsch's own account, during the early 1990s his personal life had begun falling apart and both his career and health were in a state of decline. He didn't know why his life had turned out this way and so, like Jesus, he cried out to God asking: 'My God, why have you forsaken me?' The extraordinary thing is that according to Walsch, God responded to him directly. Walsch's books – there are now three volumes in the *Conversations with God* series, a sequel titled *Communion with God*, and also an accompanying CD – present a radical and mystical vision of the universe that Walsch claims was channeled directly from God without involving the intermediary role of the Church. When radio interviewer Rachael Kohn asked him whether any of his readers were indignant that he had written in the voice of God, thereby upturning the authority of the Bible, Walsch responded positively: 'Mostly we receive letters from people who are extraordinarily grateful, who say that "My life has been touched and changed forever", who say "At last, someone who is writing what I have been thinking all of my days." Who say, as one wonderful lady from Portland, Oregon, wrote to us, "Thank you for reintroducing me to a God I can fall in love with."'[7]

As mentioned earlier, channeling has been with us in various guises for well over a century. One of the key inspirational figures in this area – a person who has influenced contemporary channelers perhaps more than anyone else – is the psychic healer and pioneering explorer of past lives, Edgar Cayce. Indeed, Edgar Cayce can almost be considered a precursor of the New Age itself, since he spans the period between the spiritualists and Theosophists of the Victorian era and the celebrity channelers of more modern times.

The 'Life Readings' of Edgar Cayce

Edgar Cayce was born on 18 March 1877 in Kentucky and came from a fundamentalist Protestant Christian background. As a young man Cayce discovered that he could give accurate healing diagnoses for other people by going into a hypnotic trance. Here he would be assisted by inner guidance towards the diagnosis of symptoms, often using medical terms which were completely unknown to him. On one occasion he gave a diagnosis in fluent Italian even though he was not familiar with this language in his everyday waking consciousness. This remarkable psychic gift led him in turn to giving 'life readings'– readings which seemed to reveal the existence of past lives and their karmic influence on present-day health problems.

It came as something of a shock to Edgar Cayce when his subconscious mind began to alert him to the possibility of past lives and reincarnation. He was already familiar with the psychic faculties of clairvoyance, telepathy, precognition and the power of prophecy, but reincarnation seemed too fantastic to be credible. In 1923 Cayce met a man named Arthur Lammers, and this meeting would change his approach to psychic diagnosis forever. Lammers was interested in occult metaphysics and it seemed to him that if Cayce could correctly diagnose health ailments by going into trance, he might also be able to uncover the metaphysical secrets of life, death and spiritual development. Lammers asked Cayce if he had ever sought to discover our true purpose on Earth, the nature of the soul, and what we were doing before each of us was born.

Cayce decided to explore these issues with Lammers himself, by giving him a trance reading. He then revealed that Lammers had been a monk in a past life and also began to use Sanskrit terms like *karma* and *akasa* which he had never referred to before. From this time onwards Cayce's trance readings would frequently refer to past lives and would often use mystical terminology to explain the secrets of the inner world. The idea of these life readings was to reveal both the positive and negative influences that past lives had brought to bear on one's present existence. The readings would also demonstrate how certain attitudes and personality characteristics were specifically connected to previous incarnations.

Cayce soon discovered that many of his present friends had been relatives or associates in a previous life. He also learned psychically that he had been an Egyptian high priest named Rata in a former incarnation, and his present wife, Gertrude, had been his wife in ancient Egypt as well. In other incarnations Edgar Cayce had been a Persian physician, an Arab tribal leader named Uhjltd, and the biblical figure Lucius – a relative of Luke and a friend of Paul. He had also incarnated in 1742 as John Bainbridge, a gambler, libertarian and soldier in the British army stationed in America prior to the War of Independence. His present lifetime as Edgar Cayce had been given to him as an opportunity to make up for the sensual excesses and materialism of his previous life as John Bainbridge.

One could easily dismiss Edgar Cayce's past life experiences simply as delusional fantasies if his legacy amounted to just a small number of isolated psychic impressions. However, it is the enormous number of life readings made for other people that have secured Edgar Cayce's enduring reputation as a psychic and healer. Here are two typical examples from the Cayce records:

David Greenwood, born on 26 August 1913, was 14 years old when Edgar Cayce gave him his life reading on 29 August 1927. Cayce told him about five previous incarnations. The first of these could be traced to a time prior to 10,000 BC when he had been heir to a throne in Atlantis. Then, around 10,000 BC, Greenwood had been an Egyptian named Isois and he had served as an intermediary between his own people and a conquering army. Later he was Abiel, a court physician in Persia, and in his fourth incarnation Colval, a tradesman who abused his position of power in a city in Thessalonika. Finally he had served Louis XIII and XIV as a loyal master of robes. Cayce warned Greenwood about his digestive problems and quick temper and told him to pursue a trade related to clothing or fabrics. Despite having no personal interest in this field, David Greenwood became a salesman in a clothing company in 1940, and proved to be very successful in his new role. He also suffered from food allergies and followed Edgar Cayce's advice by adhering to a strict diet.

Cayce also gave a reading for Patricia Farrier, aged 45, a spinster who suffered from claustrophobia and fear of crowds. Attuning himself psychically to the source of her anxieties, Cayce told her that she had died tragically in her previous life when an earth tremor had caused the floor of a building to collapse. She had been just 13 at the time, and she had been smothered to death in a farmhouse cellar as everything crumbled around her.

Edgar Cayce gave some 2,500 life readings between 1923 and 1945, and details of these readings are now housed in the library at the Association for Research and Enlightenment at Virginia Beach in the United States. Cayce's legacy remains one of a healer and psychic who was able to utilize trance states in order to tap into previous incarnations and karmic consequences – apparently at will. Cayce came to believe that groups of souls could reincarnate collectively and that people bound by ties of family friendship or common interests would very likely be related, or connected to each other in some way, in successive incarnations. Needless to say, Cayce's many publications on psychic healing, past lives and spiritual guidance continue to sell well in New Age bookstores internationally. More than 50 years after his death he remains a superstar among New Age luminaries.

Guidance from Ramtha

Sometimes channeled entities purport to provide messages of great spiritual significance. In November 1987, J.Z. Knight channeled the following thoughts from Ramtha: 'God is both male and female and yet neither. That which lives in the woman is as powerful and divine as that which lives in the man ... God is the essence, it permeates your entirety ... Within you lies the ability for profound knowingness. Like the Mother Earth, a wisdom, a courage, a dignity to evolve.'

While such pronouncements seem little more than banal platitudes – hardly life-shattering or controversial – Ramtha also spoke of a huge wave which would soon engulf Sydney. Many years later, Sydney – the city which hosted the Olympic Games in the year 2000 and a city close to where I, too, happen to live – has not yet faced this potentially devastating deluge. Nevertheless, several people in J.Z. Knight's audience were so perturbed by Ramtha's pronouncements that they decided, there and then, to move to the relative safety of the Blue Mountains, some 50 miles inland. J.Z. Knight also advised participants in her workshop to hoard their gold supplies, and she mentioned in passing that governments would soon act to reduce citizens' financial free will – 'psychic' advice that caused unwarranted alarm at the time.

From a psychological perspective, vulnerability to such messages would seem to reflect a sense of individual disempowerment and low self-esteem. And there is also the puzzling inference that advice emanating from the spirit world is implicitly superior to everyday common sense. Regrettably, there are many individuals within New Age circles who fail to heed what the New Age is actually telling them: that they can come to valid personal conclusions by drawing on their own inner resources, including the intuitive voice within.

Healing with Crystals

Another New Age practice that has attracted widespread media ridicule and which has come to personify the more credulous aspects of the New Age, is healing with crystals. In an article in an alternative New Age publication called *Southern Crossings* Lynette Mayblom described how 'crystals have wonderful uses in the area of personal healing but they can also be used on a greater scale for world healing. Crystals can be used to focus love and light on important buildings and places, to construct triangles of light in the planet's etheric body, to assist the growth of plants, and to protect and purify your home.' Mayblom went on to relate how crystals could also be used in spiritual meditation: 'Triangles of light can be set up between three people by meditating daily at the same time with crystals. These people can visualize light flowing from their third eyes to the other two, creating a triangle of light and visualizing the encompassed area filled with light. Distance is of no consequence.'[8]

Crystals are by no means a cheap commodity and it is perhaps stating the obvious that only the more affluent New Agers could hope to afford crystals of any size. New Age enthusiast Bianca Pace told journalist Mark Chipperfield that she marketed quartz crystals for between $600 and $4,000 each, and that her crystals had 'the power to cure diseases and transmit human and cosmic thoughts'. Crystals, she maintained, 'are part of the energy grid of the planet'.[9]

In fairness to the less gimmicky aspects of the personal growth movement, however, it must be emphasized that there are also other approaches, philosophies and techniques which have much greater claim to recognition within the New Age context and acceptance – especially the proven forms of experiential psychotherapy we have already referred to. One can gauge the respective merits of the various New Age modalities not in terms of the 'quick cosmic fix' they often purport to offer but through their capacity to assist the ongoing process of personal transformation.

One of the side effects of the New Age's quest for transformation and the fascination with Eastern mystical traditions has been the recent proliferation of Indian gurus visiting the West.

For many followers these gurus have become the new spiritual authority figures, replacing the more conventional leadership role of Christian prelates like priests and bishops.

The Role of the Guru

The traditional role of the guru is to lead the *chela* – the guru's pupil or follower – towards self-knowledge and mystical transcendence. In theory, the guru represents the sacred divinity within each of us, and is a catalyst for self-enlightenment. The real quest is the flowering of more complete spiritual awareness within the individual.

Some gurus give their chelas individual mantras upon which to meditate, and there is usually an unfolding program of lessons and spiritual exercises appropriate to the level of the pupil. At times the interaction between the guru and chela may become quite complex and may involve a process whereby the guru challenges the concepts and self-image of the chela in order to reduce the pupil's ego, in this way allowing a new spiritual awareness to dawn.

In some traditions the chela is required to submit totally to the spiritual leader. Many believe that without direct guidance from the guru their lives lack meaning, purpose and direction. For these followers the guru literally represents the path to Godhead and self-realization.

In 1967 and 1968 The Beatles' guru, Maharishi Mahesh Yogi, attracted enormous publicity during his visit to the West. Adorned in flowing white robes and garlands of flowers, the Maharishi promoted the practice of Transcendental Meditation and succeeded in getting his picture published in most of the leading publications of the day, including *Life, Look, Time, Esquire* and *Newsweek.* Frequently accompanied by public relations personnel and film stars like Mia Farrow, he appeared as a guest on the Johnny Carson show and even gave a presentation at Madison Square Gardens. Quite different in appeal from

Vivekananda, who had electrified American audiences 70 years earlier, the Maharishi preached a simple message: the purpose of life was to experience happiness. He also claimed that the discipline, concentration and effort associated with traditional forms of yoga and meditation were simply a waste of time. 'Transcendental Meditation,' said the Maharishi, 'is not like Zen or Jnana yoga. It does not employ concentration and contemplation, but is just the opposite of these disciplines. That's what makes it so easy. ... TM is a natural process of going to levels of your mind that are the most interesting and the most pleasurable.'[10] All that was required was to sit comfortably for a few minutes each day and silently repeat a special word or phrase called a mantra. Other than this, nothing else was needed, and one could lead whatever sort of life one wanted.

The central technique in Transcendental Meditation was to turn one's attention towards the more subtle levels of thought until the mind finally transcended thought altogether. In a brochure titled *Transcendental Meditation: An Introductory Lecture* the Maharishi explained that the quest for higher consciousness was easy and did not have to involve an intense personal struggle:

> Without our having to observe or struggle with ourselves, quite spontaneously our natural inclinations begin to come into greater harmony with the natural laws of the evolution of life. Our desires become increasingly life supporting and simultaneously increasingly fulfilled. This happens gradually. We are not angels from the first meditation, but as the sense of well-being grows, naturally the mind becomes well-intentioned, warm, loving and clear, and no longer irritable or fearful ...[11]

With his promise of instant Nirvana, the Maharishi quickly attracted a large following of Western devotees. His appeal was especially strong among the youth generation who were no doubt attracted by the idea of an effortless path to enlightenment. At times it even looked likely that he might herald a new spiritual movement – a simplified version of the Eastern wisdom tradition that could perhaps replace LSD in the post-psychedelic era.

However, it was not only the young who were captivated by the Maharishi. Jacob Needleman, Professor of Philosophy at San Francisco State College, recalls that 'tens of thousands from the solid middle-class were also paying for instruction in the magic of transcendental meditation. We saw photographs of huge auditoriums filled with well-tailored adults, their eyes closed, and their minds – the captions told us – plunged into the deeper levels of thought.'[12]

Inevitably there was a catch – all prospective converts to Transcendental Meditation, including The Beatles, would have to pay a week's salary to be given their mantra. However, in hindsight, perhaps this was not such a large fee to pay for enlightenment; it is certainly substantially less than the amounts charged at many transformational seminars today. And there was an ideological gloss to TM as well. Appealing to supporters of the anti-war movement, the Maharishi explained that if only one percent of the world's population were to practice Transcendental Meditation, this would be enough 'to neutralize the power of war for thousands of years'.

Towards the end of 1968 the Maharishi announced he was returning to India and by this time The Beatles had already moved on to other things. Interest in the Maharishi as a charismatic spiritual figure quickly began to wane and little more would be heard of him after he departed American shores. However, two years later Transcendental Meditation received support from a surprising source. The 27 March 1970 issue of the prestigious magazine *Science* – the official publication of the American Association for the Advancement of Science – included an article on the 'Physiological Effects of Transcendental Meditation' written by Robert K. Wallace from the Department of Psychology at the Center for Health Sciences in Los Angeles. The article reported that Transcendental Meditation had a specific impact on such body functions as oxygen consumption, heart rate, skin resistance and EEG measurements. During meditation oxygen consumption and heart rate decreased and this could clearly have positive benefits.[13]

The scientific endorsement of meditation as a means for attaining deep states of relaxation is perhaps the most significant legacy of the Maharishi's teachings. Few who practice yoga and meditation today would portray these disciplines as simple paths to pleasure and there can be little doubt that the Maharishi preached a basic message aimed at a generally uncritical audience. Nevertheless, it is now widely accepted that meditation reduces levels of stress, tension and anxiety in the physical organism and that this in turn reduces levels of cortisone which inhibit the immune system – thus allowing the physical organism to return to a more balanced state of health. The Maharishi deserves acknowledgment for bringing meditation into the awareness of mainstream America and popular consciousness generally. For many, meditation has now become a central part of everyday life.

Another guru who attracted widespread recognition in the West during the post-psychedelic era was Swami Muktananda (1908–1982), a leading teacher of Kundalini yoga. Muktananda became a disciple of Bhagawan Nityananda in 1947 and claimed he gained self-realization after nine years of spiritual guidance. When Nityananda died in 1961 he passed on the power of the Siddha yoga lineage to Muktananda. In India, Siddha yoga is known as 'the yoga of perfection' and a *siddha* is one who has attained an advanced state of self-knowledge – one who can claim to be a 'perfect master'. Muktananda's message was clear and direct: God dwells within you. The key task is to raise

Kundalini because 'when the Kundalini has swept away all false impressions and misunderstandings we know our own divinity and we see God everywhere. The whole world is nothing but the play of our own self.'[14]

By definition, a siddha is a person whose Kundalini has been already awakened. The siddha is then able to awaken the Kundalini in his disciples, initiating the process of their own personal transformation. This, however, requires the all-important 'grace' of the guru, which is received through *shaktipat*. According to Swami Muktananda, *shaktipat* can be received by the chela in one of four ways: through the guru's touch, *sparsha diksha*; through his words, *mantra diksha*; through his gaze, *drik diksha*; or through his power of thought, *manasa diksha*.

Devotees of Siddha yoga believe that simply being in the presence of a master whose Kundalini has been already awakened may act as a stimulus to spiritual growth in itself. As medical practitioner and longstanding Siddha yoga devotee Dr Christopher Magarey has noted: 'A holy person, a *siddha*, awakens that awareness spontaneously and initiates the process of inner transformation quite naturally and effortlessly.'[15]

In 1974 Swami Muktananda visited several cities in Australia. In Melbourne he was asked by yoga teacher John Cooper whether it was the will of the guru that actually created the transmission of the Kundalini, or the devotion and openness of the disciple. Swami Muktananda replied: 'There are different ways in which Kundalini can be awakened. Kundalini can be awakened just by seeing a guru. It can be awakened by his touch. It can be awakened even by his thought, though you may be at any distance from him. It is also awakened by the grace of the guru, which he transmits deliberately. And the awakening can also take place itself in a natural manner as a result of the disciple's devotion to his master. But the important thing is the disciple's love and the guru's grace coming together. Then the

Kundalini is awakened.'[16]

Muktananda earned widespread respect for his yoga teaching and by the time he died in 1982 he had established 31 ashrams or meditation centers around the world. Nevertheless, towards the end of his life there were persistent reports of sexual misconduct with female Siddha yoga devotees and also claims that the Siddha Yoga Foundation had begun to transfer substantial funds to its bank accounts in Switzerland.[17] However, the controversial nature of these claims does not seem to have affected the credibility of the present head of the Siddha yoga lineage, Swami Chidvilasananda (also known as Gurumayi) – Swami Muktananda's elegant female successor.[18]

Unfortunately, a recurring theme among a number of gurus who currently grace the contemporary scene in the West is the claim that their teaching in some way precludes that of other, competing teachers. Sometimes, too, a guru may be elevated to a position of apparent godliness by virtue of his or her claimed achievements. A biography of Indian spiritual leader, artist and musician Sri Chinmoy – prepared for the news media – related how in one particular calendar year

… Sri Chinmoy painted over 120,000 works of art depicting higher realms of meditation. His poetry and music became just as voluminous. On November 1st … Sri Chinmoy demonstrated the creative dynamism of meditation by writing 843 poems in a 24 hour period. Fifteen days later he painted 16,031 works of art in another 24 hour period. Three days later Sri Chinmoy celebrated a year in which he had completed 120,000 paintings. Since arriving in America he has composed over 5,000 songs and musical compositions, earning the praise of such notable composers as Leonard Bernstein and Zubin Mehta.[19]

Presumably this extraordinary data about Sri Chinmoy, released in a press kit for the media, was intended to establish him as a role model for his prospective followers. As Sri Chinmoy himself explained, 'Our goal is always to go beyond, beyond, beyond. There are no limits to our capacity because we have the infinite divine within us. Each painting, each poem, each thing that I undertake is nothing but an expression of my inner cry for more light, more truth, more delight.'[20]

However, while one could hardly fail to admire the sheer volume of his output, the effect of such statistics upon his followers would surely have been to disempower them, rather than uplift them. After all, who else but Sri Chinmoy could maintain such an exalted pace of creative manifestation?

There was also a call for devotees to come to his musical concerts, no doubt to admire him but also to gain privileged insights from his music. As a publicity notice for one of his concerts revealed: '*Unlike other musicians*, Sri Chinmoy's music is not composed for entertainment but as a guide to higher states of awareness' (my italics). The author of this publicity notice clearly believed that Sri Chinmoy was the only musician capable of providing this special path to higher consciousness.

Prior to the demise of his ashram in Oregon, Bhagwan Shree Rajneesh (also known as Osho, 1931–1990) similarly exercised a remarkable charismatic power over his followers. Each day his *sannyasins*, or devotees, would file in procession to watch as the Bhagwan drove past in his gleaming Rolls Royce, flanked by security guards armed with Uzi semi-automatic guns. And yet, double-think was clearly in evidence at Rajneeshpuram. Bhagwan's principal assistant Ma Anand Sheela, later to be jailed for conspiracy, food poisoning and attempted murder at the ashram, described during a cable network interview what Bhagwan was doing: 'What he is teaching is to be individual, to become free, free of all limitations, free of all conditioning, and just become an integrated individual, a free being.'[21]

However, the depth of this freedom was clearly limited.

Bhagwan gave each of his followers 'spiritual names', insisted on their wearing pendants bearing his photographic image, and allowed his devotees to wear clothing only of specific colors. His organization also charged substantial fees for experiential spiritual growth workshops. Such are the paradoxes of spiritual leadership.

Admittedly the charismatic Bhagwan Shree Rajneesh and his ashram in Oregon represent an extreme case, but it is one which lingers in the memory. It is not so long since Bhagwan departed the scene, and one must ask the question, as with any other guru: Are the guru's teachings intended purely for one's spiritual growth and enlightenment? How enlightened is the teacher? Are any other agendas operating? And what is the cost?

The figure of Jiddu Krishnamurti (1895–1986), meanwhile, allows us to examine the concept of the guru in a fresh light. Krishnamurti was not only one of the most respected Indian spiritual teachers of recent times but he also became famous for being the guru who renounced the very notion of being a guru. His story raises the important question of whether we need a guru at all, and whether we all have within our own inner resources the potential capacity for authentic self-realization.

During his lifetime Krishnamurti traveled widely throughout Europe, America and Asia, speaking to millions of people and becoming hugely influential. But rather than seeking followers or disciples he spoke instead about the key issues affecting daily life. His addresses – for which he would become renowned – encompassed a wide range of topics including war, violence, love, fear, death and the nature of time and freedom.[22]

Krishnamurti grew up on the Theosophical estate at Adyar in India – his father, Naraniah, was a Theosophist and lived in a small house near the Theosophical compound. Krishnamurti and his brother used to swim in the sea on the Adyar beach and it was here, in 1909, that the leading Theosophist C.W. Leadbeater first noticed him. Krishnamurti was just 13 years old at the time.

At Adyar Leadbeater had been conducting a clairvoyant investigation into past lives and when he began to investigate the past lives of Krishnamurti he discovered to his amazement that the young boy had been a disciple of the Buddha.[23] Leadbeater's enthusiasm for Krishnamurti was soon shared by Mrs Annie Besant, who had succeeded Colonel Henry Olcott in 1907 as the second president of the Theosophical Society. Leadbeater now began to refer to Krishnamurti as 'our Krishna' and claimed to take him every night onto the astral plane where he could be instructed by Madame Blavatsky's Tibetan Masters. Before long the message passed around at Adyar that Krishnamurti had been accepted by Master Koot Hoomi, and in due course the young Krishnamurti was proclaimed to be the World Teacher, or messiah, that many Theosophists had been waiting for. Soon it was said that Krishnamurti was an incarnation of the avatar Lord Maitreya, and a society known as the Order of the Star in the East was established as a vehicle for his teachings.

In 1911 Leadbeater left Adyar for a lecture tour which included Burma, Java, New Zealand and Australia and by the following year he had decided to settle in Sydney. In 1922 Leadbeater and a group of his students moved into a large house known as the Manor, located in Clifton Gardens, a fashionable harbor-side suburb. Leadbeater had now become deeply involved in the activities of a ritualistic splinter group known as the Liberal Catholic Church, whose membership included many Theosophists, but he nevertheless continued to support the cause of Krishnamurti. In 1923–24 a huge Grecian-style amphitheater was erected by members of the Order of the Star in the East on the shores of Balmoral Beach – a short distance from Clifton Gardens – and it was announced by Leadbeater and his colleagues that Krishnamurti would enter Sydney by walking across the harbor, up the beach and into the amphitheater. Seats for this miraculous event were sold well ahead of time for up to £100 each.[24]

However, none of this impressed Krishnamurti himself. Unconvinced by the need for superficial ceremonial events, he became increasingly disillusioned with Leadbeater's evangelizing tone and on 3 August 1929 he dissolved the Order of the Star in the East. At the same time he rejected any role as a World Teacher or guru, proclaiming that 'truth is a pathless land' and that all organized systems of religious belief are an 'impediment to inner liberation'.[25]

Having severed his connection with Leadbeater, Krishnamurti now decided to move to California. Krishnamurti had first visited Ojai, near Santa Barbara, in 1922 and he returned to Ojai with Annie Besant for a period of eight months in August 1926. During their visit Annie Besant acquired six acres of land in the Ojai Valley that would later become the home of the Happy Valley Foundation. Krishnamurti very much liked this area of California. According to his friend and biographer Pupul Jayakar, Krishnamurti 'cherished his walks in the silences of the mountains surrounding the Ojai Valley. He walked "enormously" for endless miles, spending whole days in the wilderness, alone.'[26]

As late as 1927 Annie Besant was still proclaiming that Krishnamurti was the World Teacher and she also told him she would be happy to resign as president of the Theosophical Society and sit at his feet listening to him. However, Krishnamurti refused these flattering overtures and after dissolving the Order of the Star he established his own Foundation in Ojai. It was here, during the late 1930s, that Krishnamurti met Aldous Huxley and Gerald Heard, who were living in nearby Los Angeles. According to Pupul Jayakar, by the mid-1940s Krishnamurti and Huxley had become close friends and would go for long walks together.[27]

Krishnamurti's essential message was that we all have the potential to perceive spiritual truth and no intermediary guru figure or spiritual organization is required. According to

Krishnamurti spiritual liberation is essentially an act of self-discovery: only through unmediated self-observation can we achieve authentic spiritual freedom. Krishnamurti believed that in order to achieve spiritual freedom we should practice a form of unconditional self-observation that he called 'attention' – because in this way the senses could be awakened to their fullest potential. Krishnamurti defined 'attention' as a state of 'complete sensory activity' and he maintained that by entering a state of authentic self-awareness, one could then experience complete harmony and true understanding. Unconditional self-observation involved transcending all aspects of one's prior conditioning and this in turn meant moving beyond the divisive and analytical aspects of the mind. According to Krishnamurti, to achieve true self-awareness, all processes of thought had to become silent and still – for only then could one move beyond thought itself. Krishnamurti had already affirmed that 'truth is a pathless land' and now he added a further insight. 'Attention,' he said, 'is a movement to eternity.'[28]

Chapter 9

Spirit, Myth and Cosmos

'It is not we who invent myth,' Carl Jung once observed, 'rather, it speaks to us as a Word of God.' Jung believed that the origin of mythology lay in the dramatization of images by the archetypes in the unconscious mind. His theories of the collective unconscious have subsequently encouraged the examination of myths and fables in order to gain profound insights into the human condition. Jung has had an immeasurable impact on studies in mythology and one of his strongest supporters was the well-known American scholar of comparative religion, Joseph Campbell (1904–1987). Campbell visited Jung in Zurich in 1953 and was enthusiastic about Jung's interpretation of the universal themes in world mythology.

During his productive life as a teacher and writer, Campbell produced a number of authoritative but accessible studies on oriental, indigenous and Western mythology and many insightful essays on metaphor and symbol in comparative religion. This work culminated in a fine series of television interviews with Bill Moyers, *The Power of Myth*, which explored the universality of myth and brought his wisdom and articulate thought to literally millions of viewers across the world.

Campbell's career reflects a life of solid scholarship. After gaining his Masters degree in cultural history from Columbia University in 1927, Campbell went on to study at the University of Paris from 1927 to 1928 and then spent a further year at the University of Munich exploring Sanskrit and oriental religion. He later taught at Sarah Lawrence College in Bronxville, New York, for 38 years. It was while he was in Paris that he began to read Freud, Jung and the works of Thomas Mann, and he also became deeply interested in the universals of the mythic imagination. Like Jung, he came to believe that myths had originated in the collective unconscious:

Myths originally came out of the individual's own dream consciousness. Within each person there is what Jung called a collective unconscious. We are not only individuals with our unconscious intentions related to a specific social environment. We are also representatives of the species *homo sapiens*. And that universality is in us whether we know it or not. We penetrate to this level by getting in touch with dreams, fantasies, and traditional myths; by using active imagination.[1]

Campbell believed that myths were highly relevant to everyday life. Although on one level they pointed to the mysteries and paradoxes of human existence, myths also validated the social and moral order in specific cultures and marked the various pathways through the different stages of life – from childhood, through to adulthood, old age and death. 'Every culture,' said Campbell, 'has rites of passage and related myths that serve this need.'[2]

Myths were also directly relevant to the life experience of the individual, a source of inspirational guidance for everyday life. Campbell liked to refer to what he called 'the journey of the hero' – the journey that every human makes simply by being purposeful in the world. According to Campbell, each of us, at some point, has to come forth and engage in battle with various obstacles or 'powers of darkness'. During our lives we may encounter demons, angels, dragons or helping spirits but then, after conquering the various obstacles thrown up along the way, we finally emerge victorious and return from our adventures with 'the gift of fire', or knowledge.

Campbell believed that as human beings we all have the same

sacred heritage: 'We share the same gods, we are informed by the same archetypes. The natural forces that animate us are common and divine.'[3] Campbell also proposed that we should explore those myths that touched us most deeply – the archetypal stories and legends that could help enrich our life's journey. As Campbell's biographers, Stephen and Robin Larsen, have observed: 'Campbell urged us to *see through* life metaphorically, and to celebrate the myths *as if* they were alive in us – providing windows for deeper insights into ourselves.'[4] Indeed, it is for his support for the mythic life that Campbell is best remembered. 'Mythology helps you to identify the mysteries of the energies pouring through you,' he once remarked. '... Therein lies your eternity.'[5]

Joseph Campbell remained primarily a scholar and teacher during his long career and probably would not have considered himself part of the personal growth movement – even though he knew many of its key figures.[6] And yet one particular saying of Campbell's has had enormous impact and is widely quoted in New Age circles; this was his famous expression: 'Follow your bliss.' Here Campbell was endorsing the idea that we should all follow a 'path with heart', a path that defines our place in the cosmos and on this earth. Campbell was not alone in articulating this view but he helped endorse it, and since his time there has been a substantial resurgence of interest in the role mythology can play in contemporary human life. We can also credit Campbell with directly influencing the rise of sacred psychology.

Mythic Consciousness and Sacred Psychology

Several key figures in the personal growth movement – among them Jean Houston, Jean Shinoda Bolen, David Feinstein and Stanley Krippner – have played a prominent role in exploring practical and inspirational ways of introducing archetypal mythic realities into everyday consciousness. Dr Jean Houston, an enthusiastic supporter of the work of Joseph Campbell, first discovered his writings at the age of 10 when she read his famous book *The Hero with a Thousand Faces*. She is now one of the leading advocates of sacred psychology.

Houston is a former president of the Association of Humanistic Psychology and a director of the Foundation for Mind Research now based in Ashland, Oregon. However, her talents also extend into many forms of creative expression. An award-winning actress in Off-Broadway theater, she has developed numerous training programs in spiritual studies which include the enactment of themes from the ancient Mystery traditions. Her many methods include visualization, chanting, storytelling and rituals. Like Joseph Campbell, Houston believes strongly in the transformative power of myth.

In an interview published in the alternative magazine *Magical Blend* she explained her own role in this process: 'My task is to evoke people into that place of identifying the god or goddess or archetype that is personal to them and allowing that being to speak for them ...'[7] She also maintains that not only mythologically, but also quite literally, our origins are in the cosmos:

Earlier peoples saw archetypes in Nature and in the starry Heavens – in the Sun, the Moon, the Earth, the vast oceans – implicitly realizing our descent from these primal entities ... Our ancestors storied this deep knowing into tales of the community of Nature: the marriage of Heaven and Earth; the churning of the ocean to create the nectar of life; the action of the wind upon the waters to bring form out of chaos. In these mythic tellings, our forerunners located higher reality and its values in the larger community – in the things of this world, shining reflections of the community of archetypes. They clearly perceived that the pattern connecting both world and archetype was the essential weave that sustains all life.[8]

Houston is personally interested in a broad range of myths,

especially those   which describe sacred journeys of transformation, and she is fascinated by archetypal figures like Parsifal,
St Francis of Assisi, Odysseus, Christ, Isis and Osiris – figures
who show us by example how we may undertake the process of
spiritual renewal. For Houston, myths and archetypes are of
central concern in our daily lives: 'Myths serve as source patterns
originating in the ground of our being. While they appear to exist
solely in the transpersonal realm, they are the keys to our
personal and historical existence, the DNA of the human
psyche.'[9]

Houston believes, like Carl Jung, that while archetypes are
universal they nevertheless manifest in unique ways within each
individual. Archetypes, she says, 'bridge spirit with nature, mind
with body, and self with universe. They are always within us,
essential structures within the structure of our psyches.'[10]
According to Jean Houston one of the key roles of sacred
psychology is to assist the individual in transforming his or her
life from what she calls the 'personal-particular' to the 'personal-
universal', thereby bringing a new vision and perspective to
everyday experience.

It is precisely because myths and archetypes transcend
cultural barriers and help define our relationship with the
cosmos as a whole that they are of such vital importance today.
For Houston our present era, with its accompanying sense of
existential crisis, is characterized not simply by a sense of
paradigm shift but by what she calls a 'whole system transition,
a shift in reality itself'. With its profound insights into the nature
of personal transformation and renewal, sacred psychology can
play a vital role in this important transition. For Jean Houston the
characteristic hallmarks of the age are an increasing sense of
planetary ecological awareness, the rebirth of the sacred
Feminine, the emergence of new forms of science and the
emergence, overall, of a global spiritual sensibility.[11] 'In this time
of whole system transition,' she writes, 'the Soul of the World, the

anima mundi, is emerging. It seems to be with us through all the things and events of the world. Speaking through myths, it enlarges our perception of the deeper story that is unfolding in our time.'[12]

Jean Shinoda Bolen is another leading figure in the personal growth movement who shares a passionate interest in sacred psychology. Bolen's special focus has been on promoting the idea that men and woman alike can become aware of the archetypal processes operating in their everyday lives.

Dr Bolen is a professor of psychiatry at the University of California in San Francisco, a Jungian analyst, and author of such works as *Goddesses in Everywoman, Gods in Everyman* and *The Tao of Psychology.* Like Jung, Bolen believes that the gods and goddesses of mythology represent different qualities in the human psyche.

Myth is a form of metaphor. It's the metaphor that's truly empowering for people. It allows us to see our ordinary lives from a different perspective, to get an intuitive sense of who we are and what is important to us ... Myths are the bridge to the collective unconscious. They tap images, symbols, feelings, possibilities and patterns – inherent, inherited human potential that we all hold in common.[13]

Like other practitioners of sacred psychology, Bolen also believes that mythic or archetypal awareness brings a true sense of meaning to everyday life: 'If you live from your own depths – that is, if there is an archetypal basis for what you're doing – then there's a meaningful level to it that otherwise might be missing ... When people "follow their bliss" as Joseph Campbell says, their heart is absorbed in what they're doing.'[14] In her book *Gods in Everyman* Bolen describes how this personal experience of 'bliss' enables the individual to tap into a universal sense of the sacred:

Bliss and joy come in moments of living our highest truth –

moments when what we do is consistent with our archetypal depths. It's when we are most authentic and trusting, and feel that whatever we are doing, which can be quite ordinary, is nonetheless sacred. This is when we sense that we are part of something divine that is in us and is everywhere.[15]

Like Jean Houston, Bolen believes that this feeling of mythic and archetypal attunement opens out finally into a greater, planetary awareness:

The current need is a return to earth as the source of sacred energy. I have a concept that I share with others that we're evolving into looking out for the earth and our connection with everybody on it. Women seem more attuned to it, but increasingly more men are too. I believe that the human psyche changes collectively, when enough individuals change. Basically, the point of life is to survive and evolve. To do both requires that we recognize our planetary community and be aware that we cannot do anything negative to our enemies without harming ourselves.[16]

Developing a Personal Mythology

Bringing mythic realities into the everyday lives of individuals has also been an important part of the work of Dr David Feinstein and Dr Stanley Krippner, authors of the influential book *Personal Mythology: The Psychology of Your Evolving Self.* Feinstein and Krippner's book had its origins in a research project at the Johns Hopkins University School of Medicine which began by comparing several emerging 'personal growth' therapies with a number of traditional therapies. Feinstein came to believe that each therapy, in its own way, helped people construct an understanding of themselves and where they stood in relation to the world as a whole. He then adopted the term 'personal mythology' to describe what he calls the 'evolving construction of inner reality'. According to Feinstein, all human constructions of reality are, in a sense, mythologies.

Dr Krippner, meanwhile, brought to the project an extensive knowledge of dreams, spiritual healing and altered states of consciousness. Together, and over a period of several years, Feinstein and Krippner held workshops to help people become aware of the mythologies that had guided them in the past. The task soon became one of helping group participants develop rituals and spiritual practices which would guide them in their ongoing daily lives.

Feinstein and Krippner divided their work with personal mythology into five stages. In the first stage individual participants were asked to recognize and define their own personal myth and to question whether this myth remained an 'ally' or not. Stage Two involved identifying an 'opposing' personal myth – one which had the potential to create conflict within the psyche. The conflicting myths were then examined to see how they were connected to personal experiences from the past. Stage Three subsequently provided a sense of synthesis and unified vision. Here the original myth and the conflicting myth were brought into confrontation and then towards a point of resolution, and any obstacles to unity were envisioned as opportunities for personal growth and self-realization. In Stage Four, the therapeutic focus came to an end and participants were asked to make a commitment to the new emergent vision. Finally, in Stage Five, they were encouraged to weave their personal mythologies into their daily lives.

For Feinstein and Krippner – as for Jean Houston and Jean Shinoda Bolen – the approach has been one of applying the principles of mythological thought to individual experience, of grounding an authentic mythic awareness in the here and now. As Feinstein and Krippner confirm:

Each of us is challenged to direct our strength and wisdom

toward creating mythological harmonies within ourselves. Within our families. Within our organizations. Within our nation. Within the world. And as we reconcile our logic with our intuition, our egos with our shadows, our old myths with our new ones, and our personal needs with those of our community, we also pave the way for a world steeped in contradictions to move forward in greater peace and creative harmony.[17]

Joseph Campbell, had, perhaps, already anticipated these sentiments in his book *Myths to Live By*:

If you really want to help this world, what you will have to teach is how to live in it. And that no-one can do who has not himself learned how to live in it in the joyful sorrow and the sorrowful joy of the knowledge of life as it is. That is the meaning of the monstrous Kirttimukha, 'Face of Glory', over the entrances to the sanctuaries of the god of yoga, whose bride is the goddess of life. No-one can know this god and goddess who will not bow to that mask in reverence and pass humbly through.[18]

Feminism and the Goddess

It is hardly surprising that the revitalizing themes of sacred psychology have resonated within the New Age movement – the ground had already been laid within the American counter-culture of the early 1970s. With the ensuing quest for new maps of spiritual awareness that followed in the aftermath of the psychedelic revolution, many had already begun to explore the pathways of magic, witchcraft, shamanism and the mythology of the Goddess. And in a clear and emphatic response to patriarchal forms of religion, the rise of feminism brought with it a resurgence of interest in ancient mythologies that supported an awareness of feminine spirituality.[19] In her book *Changing of the*

Gods: Feminism and the End of Traditional Religions, released in 1979, Naomi Goldenberg spoke of creating a 'powerful new religion' focused on the worship of the goddess,[20] while around the same time influential thinker Mary Daly was talking of a new feminist witchcraft in which woman's nature could be considered as innately divine. For neopagan women it would not be a matter of *reflecting* the goddess so much as *becoming* the goddess, or *being* the goddess[21] and this was a sacred potential in which all women could share. As Mary Farrell Bednarowski and Barbara Starret have observed:

> Feminist witchcraft elevates woman's nature above man's nature in its life-giving abilities. Feminist witches describe themselves as committing a 'political act' when they replace the Father with the Mother: The image of the Mother does not lose its old connotations of earth, intuition, nature, the body, the emotions, the unconscious etc. But it also lays claim to many of the connotations previously attributed to the father symbol: beauty, light, goodness, authority, activity etc. The feminist witch claims both sun and moon, both heaven and earth, and she invokes the goddess in herself and in other women in her efforts to make it possible.[22]

This was very much a feminist concept of self-empowerment and for some it meant taking the goddess tradition beyond the male domain altogether. Judy Davis and Juanita Weaver expressed this type of sentiment during the mid-1970s:

> Feminist spirituality has taken form in Sisterhood – in our solidarity based on a vision of personal freedom, self-definition, and in our struggle together for social and political change. The contemporary women's movement has created space for women to begin to perceive reality with a clarity that seeks to encompass many complexities. This perception

has been trivialized by male dominated cultures that present the world in primarily rational terms ... [Feminist spirituality involves] the rejoining of woman to woman.[23]

One of the leading advocates for the new Goddess-based spirituality in the late 1970s was a psychotherapist and teacher named Miriam Simos, otherwise known as Starhawk. Starhawk burst onto the American neopagan scene with the publication in 1979 of her bestselling book, *The Spiral Dance*, a handbook of ritual, mythology, spells and inspirational reflections.[24] At the time it was by no means clear whether Starhawk was simply another witch in the same tradition as contemporary neopagan practitioners like Doreen Valiente and Janet Farrar or whether this new expression of feminist spirituality involved something potentially much broader and more comprehensive. When Starhawk was asked several years later what sort of witch she was, this was her reply: 'A witch is somebody who has made a commitment to the spiritual tradition of the Goddess, the old pre-Christian religions of Western Europe. So I am a witch in the sense that that is my religion, my spiritual tradition. I am an initiated priestess of the Goddess.'[25]

Starhawk later became a founding member of an organization called Reclaiming: A Center for Feminist Spirituality and Counseling, in San Francisco, and also joined the teaching faculty at Holy Names College in Oakland, where she explored the common ground between her own form of Goddess-based neopaganism and Matthew Fox's renegade Roman Catholic-based Creation-centered spirituality. Like Jean Houston and Jean Shinoda Bolen, Starhawk maintained that the underlying impetus behind the new Goddess movement was a powerful and transformative sense of the sacred. In an interview with Alexander Blair-Ewart in Toronto she explained her perspective:

What's important about witchcraft and about the pagan

movement is, essentially, that it's not so much a way of seeing reality, as it's a different way of valuing the reality around us. We say that what is sacred, in the sense of what we are most committed to, what determines all our other values, is this living Earth, this world, the life systems of the earth, the cycles of birth and growth and death and regeneration; the air, the fire, the water, the land ...[26]

In her own writings Starhawk has referred specifically to the nurturing and revitalizing power of the Goddess-energy:

The symbolism of the Goddess has taken on an electrifying power for modern women. The rediscovery of the ancient matrifocal civilizations has given us a deep sense of pride in woman's ability to create and sustain culture. It has exposed the falsehoods of patriarchal history, and given us models of female strength and authority. The Goddess – ancient and primeval; the first of deities; patroness of the Stone Age hunt and of the first sowers of seeds; under whose guidance the herds were tamed, the healing herbs first discovered; in whose image the first works of art were created; for whom the standing stones were raised; who was the inspiration of song and poetry – is recognized once again in today's world. She is the bridge, on which we can cross the chasms within ourselves, which were created by our social conditioning, and reconnect with our lost potentials. She is the ship, on which we sail the waters of the deep self, exploring the uncharted seas within. She is the door, through which we pass to the future. She is the cauldron, in which we who have been wrenched apart simmer until we again become whole. She is the vaginal passage, through which we are reborn ...[27]

Shamanism and the New Spirituality

As interest in mythology, magic and sacred psychology became more widespread in the counterculture during the late 1960s and early 1970s it was perhaps inevitable that many Western spiritual seekers would also become increasingly attracted to indigenous and archaic cultures – cultures for which the world of myth was still a living reality. And it was equally likely that sooner or later they would also discover the most ancient spiritual tradition of all – shamanism.

At a time when there was renewed interest in Native American spirituality in particular, the works of South American author Carlos Castaneda (1925–1998) were an immediate success, eventually selling millions of copies worldwide. Castaneda's first book, *The Teachings of Don Juan*, was published by the University of California Press in 1968 and for many devotees of the new spiritual perspectives surfacing at that time in the popular culture, Castaneda and his 'teacher'– Yaqui sorcerer don Juan Matus – represented the first point of contact with the figure of the shaman. Even after his death in 1998, Castaneda's influence and fame continued to spread, and while his works are now correctly categorized as 'fiction', his early writings were unquestionably grounded in solid shamanic research – much of which had been undertaken, as we now know, in the UCLA Library.[28]

Throughout his life Castaneda remained a highly private person and only sketchy details of his personal history were ever released to the public. He gave few interviews and always refused to have any portrait photographs taken, although he did participate in a weekend seminar at the Esalen Institute in 1970 and consented to a fascinating interview with Sam Keen that was published in *Psychology Today* in December 1972.[29] Between 1959 and 1973 he undertook a series of degree courses in anthropology at the University of California, Los Angeles and was granted a PhD for his third book, *Journey to Ixtlan* (1972), for what really amounted to an imaginary ethnography.[30]

It has now been established that Castaneda's real name was Carlos Arana, and he was born in Cajamarca, Peru in 1925.[31] He adopted the name Carlos Castaneda when he acquired United States citizenship in 1959 and the following year, having commenced his studies at UCLA, he claimed that he traveled to the American southwest to explore the Indian use of medicinal plants. As the story goes, a friend introduced him to an old Yaqui Indian who was said to be an expert on the hallucinogen peyote.

The Indian, don Juan Matus, said he was a *brujo*, a term which connotes a sorcerer, or one who cures by means of magical techniques. Born in Sonora, Mexico, in 1891, don Juan spoke Spanish 'remarkably well' but appeared at the first meeting to be unimpressed with Castaneda's self-confidence. He indicated, however, that Castaneda could come to see him subsequently, and an increasingly warm relationship developed as the young academic entered into an 'apprenticeship' in shamanic magic.

Carlos Castaneda found many of don Juan's ideas and techniques strange and irrational. The world of the sorcerer contained mysterious, inexplicable forces that he was obliged not to question, but had to accept as a fact of life. The apprentice sorcerer would begin to 'see' whereas previously he had merely 'looked'. Eventually he would become a 'man of knowledge'.

According to Castaneda's exposition of don Juan's ideas, the world that we believe to be 'out there' is only one of a number of worlds. It is in reality a description of the relationship between objects that we have learned to recognize as significant from birth, and which has been reinforced by language and the communication of mutually acceptable concepts. This world is not the same as the world of the sorcerer, for while ours tends to be based on the confidence of perception, the brujo's involves many intangibles. The sorcerer's universe is a vast and continuing mystery which cannot be contained within rational categories and frameworks.

In order to transform one's perception from ordinary to magical reality, an 'unlearning' process has to occur. The apprentice must learn how to 'not do' what he has previously 'done'. He must learn how to transcend his previous frameworks and conceptual categories and for a moment freeze himself between the two universes, the 'real' and the 'magically real'. To use don Juan's expression, he must learn to 'stop the world'. From this point he may begin to *see*, to acquire a knowledge and mastery of the mysterious forces operating in the environment which most people close off from their everyday perception.

'Seeing', said don Juan, was a means of perception which could be brought about often, although not necessarily, by sacred hallucinogenic plants – among them *mescalito* (peyote), *yerba del diablo* (Jimson weed, or datura) and *humito* (psilocybe mushrooms). Through these, the brujo could acquire a magical ally, who could in turn grant further power and the ability to enter more readily into 'states of non-ordinary reality'. The brujo would become able to see the 'fibers of light' and energy patterns emanating from people and other living organisms, encounter the forces within the wind and sacred water-hole, and isolate as visionary experiences – as if on film – the incidents of one's earlier life and their influence on the development of the personality. Such knowledge would enable the brujo to tighten his defenses as a 'warrior'. He would know himself, and have complete command over his physical vehicle. He would also be able to project his consciousness from his body into images of birds and animals, thereby transforming into a myriad of magical forms and shapes while traveling in the spirit-vision.[32]

Although Castaneda succeeded in capturing the popular imagination with his accounts of the magical world of don Juan, he was not alone in bridging the gulf between traditional shamanism and the American counterculture. There were other Native Americans who would also provide this type of fusion. Two in particular would go even further in embracing aspects of the personal growth movement – Sun Bear and Brooke Medicine Eagle.

Sun Bear and Brooke Medicine Eagle

Sun Bear, or Gheezis Mokwa, was born in 1929 on the White Earth Reservation in northern Minnesota, and died in 1992. A medicine-man of Chippewa descent, he headed a communal organization consisting mainly of non-Native Americans, and through his extensive workshops and vision quests went on to become a popular figure in New Age circles.

As a young child Sun Bear had a vision of a large black bear sheathed in a vivid array of rainbow colors. The bear looked steadfastly at him, stood on its hind legs and gently touched him on the head. It was in this way that Sun Bear received his name. Sun Bear learned native medicine ways from his uncles and his brothers on the reservation but didn't practice the medicine path until he was 25 years old.

In 1961 Sun Bear began publishing a magazine called *Many Smokes*, which was intended as a forum for Native American writers and as a means of assisting the ecological cause of Earth awareness. The magazine changed its name to *Wildfire* in 1983 and began publishing a broad range of articles encompassing holistic health, vision quests, wilderness studies, herbalism and New Age philosophy. In this way he became a bridging figure linking Native Americans with urban Americans interested in alternative spiritual paths.

After working for the Intertribal Council of Nevada as an economic development specialist, Sun Bear assisted in a Native Studies program sponsored by the University of California at Davis, north of San Francisco. It was here, in 1970, that he founded the Bear Tribe. Most of the members were his former students from the Davis campus. Sun Bear maintained that he selected the name because the bear is 'one of the few animals that heals its own wounds' and he had in mind an organization whose members 'could join together to help with the healing of the earth'.

For a time the Bear Tribe was based outside Placerville,

California, before relocating to a 100-acre farm close to Vision Mountain, near Spokane in Washington State. The Spokane community soon became self-sufficient, growing its own food, maintaining an extensive range of livestock, and also running an extensive program of workshops.

Sun Bear believed it was no longer appropriate to restrict Native American teachings only to his own people and much of his time was spent spreading this philosophy far afield. To this end he produced several books – among them *The Medicine Wheel*, co-authored with his wife Wabun. He also lectured in a number of countries, including Germany, Holland, England, India and Australia. Whereas Castaneda thrived on secrecy, Sun Bear's message was both publicly expressed and essentially global: we should all learn to 'walk in balance on the Earth Mother'. The following passage from *The Medicine Wheel* captures this feeling very effectively: 'We all share the same Earth Mother, regardless of race or country of origin, so let us learn the ways of love, peace and harmony and seek the good paths in life.'[33]

Drawing strongly on Native American tradition, Sun Bear taught members of his community and visiting group participants how to undertake a vision-quest – which included fasting, prayers and ritual cleansing in a sweat lodge: 'a symbolic act of entering the womb of the Mother to be reborn'. He also explained that by selecting suitable sites for periods of visionary isolation it was possible to draw on the vitality of locations where the Earth Mother seemed strong, and where spirits might appear. For Sun Bear it was the presence of spirits – in dreams or in visions – that would provide an authentic sense of personal direction. As he explained to members of his community: 'Each medicine-man has to follow his own medicine and the dreams and visions that give him power.' Sun Bear told his followers that they would always know intuitively when the spirits were near. 'Sometimes,' he said, 'it is just little whisperings, and sometimes a different energy, a change in the air that you feel. It is very recognizable ...

You feel and experience things as an energy that comes through the spirit forces at the time.'[34]

Like Sun Bear, Brooke Medicine Eagle has similarly become a bridge between two cultures, emphasizing through her work how shamanism can link the old and the new. Her lineage and ancestry point back to the traditional ways of the American Indians but she has also been educated at a Western university and has utilized various holistic health modalities in formulating her contemporary worldview.

Brooke Medicine Eagle is of Sioux and Nez Perce extraction, although she was raised on the Crow reservation in Montana. The great-great-grandniece of Nez Perce holy man Grandfather Joseph, Brooke was brought up in modest circumstances, living 10 miles from the closest reservation village and nearly 60 miles over dirt roads from any major town. She says that the initial desire to be a healer-shaman came substantially from within her own experience.

Brooke took her shamanic vision-quest with an 85-year-old Northern Cheyenne shamaness called The Woman Who Knows. Together with a younger medicine-woman they journeyed to a place called Bear Butte, near the Black Hills of South Dakota. This region had been used for hundreds of years by the Sioux and Cheyenne as a location for the vision-quest. Here Brooke underwent the traditional preparation of fasting and cleansing. She was expecting to spend up to four days and nights alone on a mountain top, without food and water, praying for her initiatory vision.

After preparing a sage-bed, smoking a pipe and offering prayers, the women departed and Brooke was left alone. She recalls that in the evening, as she lay there peacefully, she suddenly became aware of the presence of another woman who had long black braided hair and was dressed in buckskin. She seemed to be imparting some sort of energy into her navel – the communication between them was not in words.

As clouds moved across the sky, allowing the moonlight to filter through, Brooke Medicine Eagle became aware of a 'flurry of rainbows' caused by hundreds of beads on the woman's dress. Now she could also hear drumming, and it seemed then that she was surrounded by two circles of dancing women – 'spirits of the land' – and that these circles were interweaving with each other. One circle included seven old grandmothers, 'women who are significant to me, powerful old women'.[35]

Then the circles disappeared and once again Brooke was alone with the Rainbow Woman. The woman now told her that the land was in trouble – that it needed a new sense of balance and specifically a more feminine, nurturing energy and less male aggression. She also said that all dwellers on the North American continent were 'children of the rainbow' – mixed bloods – and there could be a balancing between the old cultures and the new.

After they had spoken with each other in this way it was time for the Rainbow Woman to leave, and it was now abundantly clear that the Rainbow Woman was a spirit teacher and not a physical human being:

Her feet stayed where they were, but she shot out across the sky in a rainbow arc that covered the heavens, her head at the top of that arc. And then the lights that formed that rainbow began to die out, almost like fireworks in the sky, died out from her feet and died out and died out. And she was gone.[36]

For Brooke Medicine Eagle the impact of the visitation was both personal and profound, for the communication had touched on the crucial distinction between Native American and Western ways. She had also learned how she could be of service:

The Indian people are the people of the heart. When the white man came to this land, what he was to bring was the intellect, that analytic, intellectual way of being. And the Indian people were to develop the heart, the feelings. And those two were to come together to build a new age, in balance, not one or the other ...

[The Rainbow Woman] felt that I would be a carrier of the message between the two cultures, across the rainbow bridge, from the old culture to the new, from the Indian culture to the dominant culture, and back again. And in a sense, all of us in this generation can be that. We can help bridge that gap, build that bridge into the new age of balance.[37]

This has become Brooke Medicine Eagle's particular path in shamanism, and one which she brings to her workshops and writings. It is a path she treads with a special conviction, believing as she does that the Earth will benefit from more feminine energy and more caring. 'We need to allow, to be receptive, to surrender, to serve ... The whole society, men and women, need that balance to bring ourselves into balance.'

Shamanism and the Transpersonal Perspective

In addition to Native American teachers like Sun Bear and Brooke Medicine Eagle who have drawn primarily on their own individual tribal shamanic traditions, one of the most influential figures in the international transpersonal movement is the American anthropologist Dr Michael Harner, a leading exponent of experiential shamanism. A former visiting professor at Columbia, Yale and the University of California, Harner is now Director of the Foundation for Shamanic Studies in Mill Valley, California.

Born in Washington DC in 1929, Harner spent the early years of his childhood in South America. In 1956 he returned to do fieldwork among the Jivaro Indians of the Ecuadorian Andes and between 1960 and 1961 visited the Conibo Indians of the Upper Amazon in Peru. His first period of fieldwork was conducted as 'an outside observer of the world of the shaman', but his second endeavor – which included his psychedelic initiation among the Conibo – led him to pursue shamanism first hand. In 1964 he returned to Ecuador to experience the supernatural world of the Jivaro in a more complete way.

After arriving at the former Spanish settlement of Macas, Harner made contact with his Jivaro guide, Akachu. Two days later he ventured with him northwards, crossing the Rio Upano and entering the forest. It was here that he told his Indian friend that he wished to acquire spirit-helpers, known to the Jivaro as *tsentsak*. Harner offered gifts to Akachu and was told that that the first preparatory task was to bathe in the sacred waterfall. Later he was presented with a magical pole to ward off demons. Then, after an arduous journey to the waterfall, Harner was led into a dark recess behind the wall of spray – a cave known as 'the house of the Grandfathers' – and here he had to call out, attracting the attention of the ancestor spirits. He now had his first magical experiences: the wall of falling water became iridescent, a torrent of liquid prisms. 'As they went by,' says Harner, 'I had the continuous sensation of floating upward, as though they were stable and I was the one in motion ... [It was like] flying inside a mountain.'[38]

Deeper in the jungle, Akachu squeezed the juice of some psychedelic datura plants he had brought with him and asked Harner to drink it that night. Reassuring him, Akachu told him he was not to fear anything he might see, and if anything frightening did appear, he should run up and touch it!

That night was especially dramatic anyway – with intense rain, thunder and flashes of lightning – but after a while the effects of the datura became apparent and it was clear that something quite specific was going to happen.

Suddenly Harner became aware of a luminous, multicolored serpent writhing towards him. Remembering his advice from Akachu, Harner charged at the visionary serpent with a stick. Suddenly the forest was empty and silent and the monster had gone. Akachu later explained to Harner that this supernatural encounter was an important precursor to acquiring spirit-helpers. And his triumph over the serpent had confirmed that he was now an acceptable candidate for the path of the shaman.

Harner believes, as the Jivaro do, that the energizing force within any human being can be represented by what the Indians call a 'power animal'. One of the most important tasks of the shaman is to summon the power animal while in trance, and undertake visionary journeys with the animal as an ally. It is in such a way that one is able to explore the 'upper' and 'lower' worlds of the magical universe. The shaman also learns techniques of healing which usually entail journeys to the spirit world to obtain sources of 'magical energy'. This energy can then be transferred to sick or *dis*-spirited people in a ceremonial healing rite.[39]

After living with the Conibo and Jivaro, Harner undertook further fieldwork among the Wintun and Pomo Indians in California, the Lakota Sioux of South Dakota, and the Coast Salish in Washington State. The techniques of 'practical applied shamanism' that he now teaches in his workshops, and which are outlined in his important book *The Way of the Shaman*, are a synthesis from many cultures, but they are true to the essence of the native traditions themselves. Harner has gone to great lengths to make his anthropological research accessible to a Western audience interested in exploring trance states and mystical consciousness.

For Michael Harner, shamanism takes the individual 'into the realms of myth and the Dreamtime ... and in these experiences we are able to contact sources of power and use them in daily life'. Harner usually holds his shamanic workshops in city tenement buildings or in large open lecture rooms on different university campus sites, and has also trained numerous shamanic facilitators to continue this work both within the United States and internationally. Most of his workshop participants are familiar with the concept of the shamanic visionary journey and the idea of 'riding' rhythmic drumming into a state of meditative trance.

Harner's sessions begin as he shakes a gourd rattle to the four quarters in nearly total darkness, summoning the 'spirits' to participate in the shamanic working. He also encourages his group members to sing native shamanic chants and to enter into the process of engaging with the mythic world. His techniques include journeying in the mind's eye down the root system of an archetypal 'cosmic tree' or up imaginal smoke tunnels into the sky. As the group participants delve deeper into a state of trance, assisted all the time by the drumming, they enter the 'mythic dreamtime' of their own unconscious minds, frequently having visionary encounters with a variety of animal and humanoid beings and perhaps also exploring unfamiliar locales. They may also make contact with spirit-allies or 'power animals'. Harner's approach is to show his participants that they can discover an authentic mythic universe within the depths of their own being.

In the core shamanic model that Harner utilizes, humanity is said to dwell on Middle Earth, and two other magical domains – the upper and lower universes – may then be accessed through the shamanic trance journey. Often the upper and lower worlds appear to merge into a single 'magical reality' which parallels the familiar world but which also seems invariably to extend beyond it. The shaman seeks his 'power animals' or spirit allies as a way of obtaining new sources of vitality and sacred knowledge. The core intent is one of personal growth and healing, with many individual participants feeling that they have extended the boundaries of their awareness and their being. Sometimes one gains a sense of the extraordinary range of mythological images which become available through the shamanic process.

One woman in a Harner workshop ventured to the upper world and had a remarkable 'rebirth' experience:

I was flying. I went up into black sky – there were so many stars – and then I went into an area that was like a whirlwind. I could still see the stars and I was turning a lot, and my power animals were with me. Then I came up through a layer of clouds and met my teacher – she was a woman I'd seen before. She was dressed in a long, long gown and I wanted to ask her how I could continue with my shamanic work, how to make it more a part of my daily life. Then she took me into her, into her belly. I could feel her get pregnant with me and felt her belly stretching. I felt myself inside her. I also felt her put her hands on top of her belly and how large it was! She told me that I should stop breathing, that I should take my nourishment from her, and I could actually feel myself stop breathing. I felt a lot of warmth in my belly, as if it were coming into me, and then she stretched further and actually broke apart. Her belly broke apart and I came out of her, and I took it to mean that I needed to use less will in my work, and that I needed to trust her more and let that enter into my daily life. That was the end of my journey – the drum stopped and I came back at that point.[40]

Michael Harner believes that mythic experiences of this sort are common during the shamanic journey and he maintains that they reveal a dimension of consciousness rarely accessed in daily life:

Simply by using the technique of drumming, people from time immemorial have been able to pass into these realms which are normally reserved for those approaching death, or for saints. These are the realms of the upper and lower world where one can get information to puzzling questions. This is the Dreamtime of the Australian Aboriginal, the 'mythic time' of the shaman. In this area, a person can obtain knowledge that rarely comes to other people.[41]

This of course begs the question of whether the shaman's journey is just imagination. Is the mythic experience *really* real? Harner's reply is persuasive:

> Imagination is a modern western concept that is outside the realm of shamanism. 'Imagination' already pre-judges what is happening. I don't think it is imagination as we ordinarily understand it. I think we are entering something which, surprisingly, is universal – regardless of culture. Certainly people are influenced by their own history, their cultural and individual history. But we are beginning to discover a map of the upper and lower world, regardless of culture. For the shaman, what one sees – that's *real*. What one reads out of a book is secondhand information. But just like the scientist, the shaman depends upon first-hand observation to decide what's real. If you can't trust what you see yourself, then what can you trust?[42]

In addition to conducting his own experiential workshops Michael Harner is now engaged in training native tribal peoples in shamanic techniques which have disappeared from their own indigenous cultures. Several groups, including the Sami (formerly known as Lapps) and the Inuit (formerly known as Eskimos) have approached him to help restore sacred knowledge lost as a result of missionary activity or Western colonization. Harner and his colleagues at the Foundation for Shamanic Studies have been able to help them with what he calls 'core shamanism' – general methods consistent with those once used by their ancestors. In this way, he believes, members of these tribal societies can elaborate and integrate the practices on their own terms in the context of their traditional cultures.

Chapter 10

Science and Spirituality

When we consider possible connections between science and spirituality the so-called 'Gaia Hypothesis' comes readily to mind. As we have seen in our earlier exploration of the appeal of shamanism within the counterculture and the New Age movement, the primal idea of a holistic bond with Nature flows from the idea that the planet itself is a living system. This is a concept reinforced by the Gaia Hypothesis.

Gaia was the ancient Greek 'Earth Mother', and from a mythic perspective she is one of the many personifications of Mother Nature – an archetype of renewal and abundance. However, the Gaia Hypothesis is not only a spiritual metaphor but also a scientific proposition. It was put forward by the British chemist Dr James Lovelock, a former consultant to the California Institute of Technology, who at one time worked on the scientific investigation of life on Mars.

While Lovelock concluded on the basis of his study of the relatively static Martian atmosphere that no life existed on that planet, he became intrigued by the dynamics of Earth's atmosphere. He found, for example, that Earth's atmosphere differed greatly from the levels anticipated by physical chemistry. The concentration of atmospheric oxygen is around 21 percent, and yet in theory – since oxygen is a very reactive gas – it should be almost completely absorbed, resulting in an atmospheric level close to zero. Lovelock was also fascinated by the fact that Earth's atmosphere was able to retain a composition suitable for the continuation of life on the planet. His conclusion was that the Earth's atmosphere was affected by a wide range of living processes on the Earth itself, all of which helped maintain the atmosphere and the surface temperature: in short, that the Earth was a type of organically interrelated 'whole'. Gaia became a metaphor for Earth's total biosystem, including the atmosphere, oceans and landforms, and all of Earth's plants, animals and fungi. This biosystem contributed to a state of homeostasis appropriate for the conditions of life.

In his influential book *Gaia: A New Look at Life on Earth*, Lovelock presented the Gaia model as a 'self-regulating, self-sustaining system, continually adjusting its chemical, physical and biological processes in order to maintain the optimum conditions for life and its continued evolution'.[1] However, while Lovelock resisted taking the extra step of identifying the biosphere as a single living organism, the Gaia Hypothesis soon became a powerful metaphor for global environmental awareness. For many in the New Age movement, the Earth itself is now seen as having consciousness – *it is fundamentally alive.*

This idea is also reflected in the animistic beliefs of indigenous peoples across the planet. For Native American Indians the planet is the Mother of all living beings – animals, plants, rocks and human beings all have life and are all interrelated – and Mother Earth herself needs to be honored and nourished. As Sun Bear once said, 'The whole earth is sacred ... many parts of the sacred earth are hungry right now. They need people to go to them and feed them with prayers and thanksgiving ...'[2] And as the Aboriginal writer Miriam-Rose Ungunmerr of the Ngangikurungkurr people has expressed it: 'In our view the Earth is sacred. It is a living entity in which other living entities have [their] origin and destiny. It is where our identity comes from, where our spirituality begins, where our Dreaming comes from; it is where our stewardship begins. We are bound to the Earth in our spirit. By means of our involvement in the natural world we can ensure our well-being.'[3]

For the dominant Western cultures, though, Nature is a domain to be exploited and ravaged for her economic resources.

Quite apart from feeling any sense of intrinsic respect or reverence for the natural environment, and failing to see – as indigenous people everywhere see – that to rape and ravage Nature is also to destroy ourselves, it often seems that in the West we are actually at war with Mother Earth. We are everywhere engaged in an ongoing process of exterminating natural species, drastically reducing regions of native forests and grasslands, poisoning the water and making economic decisions for short-term gain, irrespective of our grudging acknowledgment of the finite resources of the planet and the needs of the human generations yet to come. Dr Ralph Metzner calls this process *ecocide* and sees it as arising through the loss of holistic consciousness:

> The metaphor of man against Nature, at war with Nature and the elements, is one that many people have formulated. It has a kind of religious world-view rationale in certain aspects of the Christian technological civilization of Europe and North America. It represents the shadow side of our obsession with individual separateness and power. At the same time there are concepts and attitudes of the mystics, or shamanic cultures and contemporary formulations of ecologically holistic world-views that promise a way out of the self-created dilemmas of humankind.[4]

For Metzner, the Gaia model points us back in the direction of interconnectedness:

> Once we recognize our inescapable embeddedness in the living, organic ecosystem and our mutual interdependence with all other co-existing species, our sense of separate identity, so strenuously acquired and desperately maintained, recedes more into the background, and the *relationships*, whether balanced or imbalanced, become the foreground and

focus of concern. This is the perceptual basis for the new and ancient points of view of the Gaian scientists and artists: It is holistic and comprehensive, and it is inevitably accompanied by a sense of wonder and reverence.[5]

Morphic Resonance

The British biologist and biochemist Dr Rupert Sheldrake has similarly suggested that one of the reasons why conventional scientists remain mechanistic and reductionist in their outlook is that they have not yet absorbed the holistic paradigm as a function in Nature. In recent years Sheldrake has gained international recognition for introducing his concept of 'morphic resonance' to the study of patterns of natural order.

Sheldrake believes that patterns of order in Nature emerge with the passage of time. All biological forms develop from simpler forms through the process of morphogenesis. Mechanistic science uses the hereditary chemical DNA to provide an explanation, but according to Sheldrake this is insufficient. While Sheldrake acknowledges that DNA is undoubtedly an important factor in heredity, it doesn't explain what he calls 'the coming into being of form'. The form of a human leg or arm, for example, is quite different even though the individual's DNA is the same.

Sheldrake does not believe that form happens by chance. He supports the vitalist tradition in biology which maintains that there is a formative principle at work in Nature and that this formative principle directs living processes: 'The mechanistic approach to morphogenesis,' says Sheldrake, 'is challenged by the fact that when we cut a bit off an embryo, very often the embryo manages to grow and to form a complete organism. If a young sea urchin is cut in half, the result is not half a sea urchin, but a complete sea urchin which is about half the normal size. The rest of the cells adjust; although part of the embryo has been removed, the remaining part somehow remains a whole and gives rise to a whole organism.'[6]

Sheldrake believes that the concept which best helps explain this situation is the concept of morphogenetic fields. This concept was first proposed by the Russian scientist Alexander Gurwitsch in 1922. Gurwitsch suggested that morphogenetic fields were fields that gave rise to form, that they directed tissues and cells in such a way that they developed their characteristic shape or form in the embryo. Sheldrake supports this idea: 'If part of an embryo is cut away,' he notes, 'the remaining part still has the morphogenetic field associated with it. This field has a holistic property, because fields are continuous; they are not atomistic, one cannot cut bits out of fields. The complete form is restored because the field remains a whole. ... the field is a causal structure that guides the development of form.'[7]

Expanding on Gurwitsch's original concept Sheldrake believes that, with the passage of time, morphogenetic fields may determine what happens to a particular species so that any given species is influenced by, and connected with, all of its past members. This is the process that Sheldrake calls *morphic resonance* and it is essentially a holistic concept of natural form and development.[8]

Sheldrake maintains that the problem with mechanistic scientists is that they mistake parts for the whole and also forget that they are dealing at a fundamental level with a profound mystery that finally transcends science itself: 'The morphic resonance hypothesis suggests the way patterns and forms are repeated in Nature. It obviously does not explain where the first form, the pattern, or the first creative idea come from ... The nature of creativity is really a philosophical question which does not lie within the realm of natural science.'[9]

As Sheldrake and Metzner have indicated, there is clearly a marked contrast between what we might call a holistic approach to Nature and its mechanistic, reductionist counterpart. Does this mean, then, that the world of science and the world of spirit can never really meet – that the holistic paradigm and the mechanist approach represent fundamentally different ways of responding to the natural world? This is indeed a crucial question, but before an answer can even be attempted we must first explore the fundamental issue of objectivity and the sorts of scientific models we accept as reflections of 'reality'. This in turn leads us to consider some of the paradoxes thrown up by quantum theory and the New Physics.

The Disappearing Universe

For most of us operating in the everyday world, our notion of familiar 'reality' draws substantially on the apparent evidence of our senses, and it is entirely reasonable that this should be so. This has given rise in transpersonal psychology to the idea of the 'consensus reality' – the agreed perceptual basis on which language and cultural norms are constructed. In the West our consensus reality is built primarily on the so-called Newtonian-Cartesian model of the universe, which in turn is based on the ideas of Isaac Newton and René Descartes. In this model the basic elements of the material universe are regarded as solid and ultimately indestructible. The fundamental building blocks of matter – atoms – are subject to gravity and the laws of cause and effect, and matter itself is mediated through the passage of time. Descartes believed that mind and matter were intrinsically separate, that matter was inert, and that the universe was objectively real – independent of the process of observation.

However, this model of the universe was eventually challenged by the scientific analysis of light, when it became evident that light itself appeared at certain times to consist of particles while at other times it displayed the characteristics of waves. Einstein then proposed that perhaps space was not three-dimensional but four-dimensional. Time was not separate from the physical world but was intimately connected with it: together they formed a four-dimensional space/time continuum. Einstein also believed that time was relative, because separate observers would perceive and construct events differently in time if these observers moved with different velocities relative to the events they were observing. This in turn suggests that space and time are mental constructs and not absolutes. As transpersonal psychologist Dr Ronald Valle has observed, 'both are merely elements of the language a particular observer uses for his or her description of phenomena'.[10]

The Newtonian three-dimensional model faced a more fundamental challenge when it was discovered that, at the subatomic level, matter does not exist with certainty in any fixed location but only shows a 'tendency to exist'. Werner Heisenberg's famous Uncertainty Principle affirms that it is not possible to determine with absolute precision both the position and momentum of any given subatomic particle. According to Heisenberg's Uncertainty Principle, the wave and particle descriptions of being preclude one another. While *both* are necessary to get a full grasp of what being is, only *one* is available at any given time. We can never measure an electron's exact position (when it expresses itself as a particle) or its momentum (when it expresses itself as a wave) at the same time.[11] As a consequence of this discovery Heisenberg came to the view that at a fundamental level 'reality' itself was essentially indeterminate: one could no longer rest in the security of a fixed vantage point. The entire universe was characterized by flux and change – by probabilities rather than certainties.

Heisenberg's findings have had an enduring impact on the nature of scientific perception. Indeed, transpersonal psychiatrist Dr Stanislav Grof believes that the very authority of mechanistic science has been eroded because the myth of solid and indestructible matter – its central dogma – soon began to disintegrate once scientists began to understand that atoms, far from being solid, were essentially empty:

Subatomic particles showed the same paradoxical nature as light, manifesting either particle properties or wave properties depending on the arrangement of the experiment. The world of substance was replaced by that of process, event and relation. In subatomic analysis, solid Newtonian matter disappeared. What remained were activity, form, abstract order and pattern. In the words of the famous mathematician and physicist Sir James Jeans, the universe began to look less like a machine and more like a thought system.[12]

Quantum theory has also had a profound influence on the study of consciousness. As transpersonal physicist Dr Fritjof Capra writes in his well-known book *The Tao of Physics*:

Quantum theory has ... demolished the classical concepts of solid objects and of strictly deterministic laws of Nature. At the subatomic level, the solid material objects of classical physics dissolve into wavelike patterns of probabilities, and these patterns, ultimately, do not represent probabilities of things, but rather probabilities of interconnections. A careful analysis of the process of observation in atomic physics has shown that the subatomic particles have no meaning as isolated entities, but can only be understood as interconnections between the preparation of an experiment and the subsequent measurement. Quantum theory thus reveals the basic oneness of the universe. It shows that we cannot decompose the world into independently existing smallest units. As we penetrate into matter, Nature does not show us any isolated 'basic building blocks' but rather appears as a complicated web of relations between the various parts of the whole.[13]

The Holistic Perspective of David Bohm

The American quantum physicist Dr David Bohm (1917–1992) was Professor at Birbeck College in London for over 20 years.

Bohm had worked earlier with Einstein before going on to develop a theory of quantum physics which treated the whole of existence, including matter and consciousness, as an unbroken whole. In his seminal work *Wholeness and the Implicate Order* – a book regarded as a classic in transpersonal circles – Bohm proposed that the 'unbroken wholeness of the totality of existence [could be] seen as an undivided flowing movement without borders'.[14] Bohm conceived of an *implicate order* within which the totality of existence was enfolded. This implicate order included space, time and matter but its presence could only be inferred through observing its manifestations.

In a manner reminiscent of the creation process described in various mystical cosmologies – including the Kabbalah and the emanationist systems in Gnosticism – Bohm maintained that the implicate order 'unfolds' into the explicate order: the world of manifestation. According to Bohm, the reductionist methods used in modern science actually prevent scientific observers from grasping that all things owe their existence to an unbroken wholeness – a wholeness nevertheless subject to the unending process of constant flux he termed the 'holomovement'. Bohm believed that the universe was like a total organism in which the constituent parts only made sense in relation to the whole. He also believed that in the final analysis there could be no distinction between mind and matter:

The mental and the material are two sides of one overall process that are (like form and content) separated only in thought and not in actuality. Rather, there is one energy that is the basis of all reality … There is never any real division between mental and material sides at any stage of the overall process.[15]

American Jungian psychologist Dr June Singer, meanwhile, has compared Bohm's perspective with that of Carl Jung:

We experience the explicate order when we perceive realities with our senses. Our familiar world is one of separate objects subject to various physical forces like gravity etc. We can see that certain things may be in relationship to each other, and in this explicate world of things and thoughts, we can hope to integrate the various disparate parts. Wholeness appears to us as an ideal state of being ... For Jung, the collective uncon-scious was the fundamental reality, with human consciousness deriving from it. In a similar way, Bohm sees the implicate order as the fundamental reality, with the explicate order and all its manifestations as derivative.[16]

The Observer and the Observed

In quantum theory the very act of observation involves a process of interaction with what is observed – and Nature and the observer are not separate and distinct as we have always assumed. Scientific psychology, on the other hand, is based on the principle that if perceptions of the physical world are to be accepted as real, separate observers must be able to agree on, and 'validate', the innate characteristics of what is observed – that there is a clear need for 'objectivity', or an ability to stand apart from what is being observed. Clearly quantum theory and scien-tific psychology reflect two essentially different perspectives – and in this instance quantum physics appears to favor the mystics. Eastern mysticism and quantum theory are essentially holistic while scientific psychology is innately reductionist – focusing on what are taken to be discrete and tangible 'facts'. As transpersonal writers like Fritjof Capra and Gary Zukav have observed, quantum theory supports the position of the Eastern mystical tradition in affirming that the observed and the observer are essentially one. As Zukav notes in his influential book *The Dancing Wu Li Masters: An Overview of the New Physics*: 'According to quantum mechanics there is no such thing as objectivity. We cannot eliminate ourselves from the picture. We are a part of

Nature, and when we study Nature there is no way around the fact that Nature is studying itself.'[17]

However, while quantum theory proposes a holistic view of the physical universe, the entire foundations of Western science still remain grounded in Newtonian-Cartesian thinking. Scientific psychology continues to be strongly influenced by behaviorism which insists that the observer or experimenter be treated as separate and distinct in relation to the behavior being observed and measured. This in turn leaves no room whatever for a spiritual component in life because, as Stanislav Grof points out,

> In the reductionist view, human intelligence, creativity, art, religion, ethics and science itself are all byproducts of material processes in the brain. There is no place for mysticism or religion, and spirituality is seen as a sign of primitive superstition, intellectual and emotional immaturity, or even severe psychopathology that science will one day explain in terms of deviant biochemical processes in the brain.[18]

So is there a way out of the impasse? The answer seems to lie in applying the holistic principles of quantum theory to the study of human consciousness itself.

Quantum Psychology

An important contribution to the emerging field of 'quantum psychology' has been provided by British-based American physicist Danah Zohar, who relates the principles of quantum mechanics to an understanding of the human condition.

Zohar is concerned with issues like the nature of individual identity and its relationship to the universe as a whole. On a physical level our physical being is subject to continual change. It is an intriguing fact, for example, that the neurones in the brain and the cells of the body change over entirely every seven years – so where does this leave our sense of self and individuality? Indeed, Zohar asks, if individual people are 'real', what is it that holds them together? Each of us is an organism made up from billions of cells, with each cell in some sense possessing a life of its own. Within our brains alone some 10,000 million neurones contribute to the rich tapestry of our mental life. And yet if our brains consist of all those myriad neurones, how does the idea of a 'person' actually emerge and how tangible is that person's existence?

Zohar's conclusion is that people, like subatomic matter, exhibit the same wave/particle duality identified in Heisenberg's Uncertainty Principle. Our individuality – our sense of apparent separateness – is equivalent to the specificity of a particle whereas the way we interrelate with others, and with the world as a whole, has more the characteristic of a wave. According to Zohar, if we consider the human being from the perspective of quantum theory – as a *quantum self* – both aspects emerge. Seen this way, 'the quantum self is simply a more fluid self, changing and evolving at every moment, now separating into sub-selves, now reuniting into a larger self. It ebbs and flows, but always in some sense being itself …'[19]

Zohar rejects computer-based models of consciousness because they are essentially impersonal and offer no insights into the continuity of individual identity and the nature of human relationships. All computer models of the brain assume that the brain itself functions like a giant computer but, assuming that to be the case, where do we find the 'central committee of neurones' overseeing the whole process that provides us with our sense of individuality and the will to make spontaneous decisions? Clearly, without a sense of wholeness, as distinct from a myriad variety of brain functions, there is no sense of self. And yet we all know from our own experience that human consciousness is characterized by a sense of unbroken wholeness and continuity which provides cohesion in daily life:

The whole corpus of classical physics and the technology that rests on it (including computer technology) is about the separateness of things, about constituent parts and how they influence each other across their separateness, as the separate neurones in the brain act on one another across the synapses. If there were no other good reasons to reject the computer model of the brain, the argument pointing towards the unity of consciousness would be the most damning.[20]

Zohar believes that in the final analysis, quantum theory leads us towards the realization that all sentient beings are ultimately connected and share a common destiny on the planet:

On a quantum view of the person, it is impossible *not* to love my neighbour as myself, because my neighbour *is* myself ... In a quantum psychology, there are no isolated persons. Individuals do exist, do have an identity, a meaning and a purpose, but, like particles, each of them is a brief manifestation of a particularity. ... Each of us, because of our integral relationship with others, with Nature, and with the world of values, has the capacity to beautify or to taint the waters of eternity.[21]

The implications of the New Physics and the approaches presented by key thinkers like Bohm, Capra, Sheldrake, Grof, Metzner and Zohar are far-reaching. We begin to understand that at a core level everything in the known universe seems to be interconnected, that totally separate and individual identity is ultimately an illusion, and that what we know as 'individual' consciousness contains in essence all the potentials of universal consciousness.

All of this, of course, comes close to the spiritual position which we spoke of earlier in relation to the shamanic perspective of indigenous peoples: they too conceive of a holistic, interconnected universe that is alive with meaning and grounded in a reality far more profound and sacred than reductionist concepts of causality. From an animist view, everything is alive, and consciousness – or spirit – is the very basis of life. For Fritjof Capra, this type of awareness reinforces an ecological perspective which honors both the planet and our place upon the Earth:

The new vision of reality is ecological, but it goes far beyond immediate concerns with environmental protection. It is supported by modern science, but rooted in a perception of reality than reaches beyond the scientific framework to an intuitive awareness of the oneness of all life, the interdependence of its multiple manifestations, and its cycles of change and transformation. When the concept of the human spirit is understood in the transpersonal sense, as the mode of consciousness in which the individual feels connected to the cosmos as a whole, it becomes clear that ecological awareness is truly spiritual.[22]

The Quest for a New Paradigm

Capra, Zohar, Grof and Metzner are not alone in exploring the scientific implications of the New Physics. Indeed, few have tackled the relationship between science and spirituality in more depth than American transpersonal theorist Ken Wilber. Psychologist Daniel Goleman was moved to write in *The New York Times* that Wilber has joined 'the ranks of the grand theorists of human consciousness like Ernst Cassirer, Mircea Eliade and Gregory Bateson', and Dr Roger Walsh of the University of California Medical School at Irvine has called him 'the foremost writer on consciousness and transpersonal psychology in the world today'. Wilber started young, writing his first book, *The Spectrum of Consciousness*, in the winter of 1973 when he was still finishing graduate studies. He has now produced over a dozen substantial volumes on the history and development of consciousness, including *No Boundary, Up from Eden* and *Sex, Ecology and Spirituality.*

Ken Wilber studied at Duke University and later at graduate school in Nebraska, pursuing degrees in chemistry and biology. However, he was also extremely interested in psychotherapy, philosophy and religion. Eventually he began to perceive a major gulf between Freudian psychology, which emphasized the strength of the ego, and the Buddhist concept of surrendering the ego in an act of transcendence. He came gradually to the view that there is a hierarchy, or spectrum, of levels of consciousness, with each part of the spectrum comparatively valid and apparently 'real' on its own level. For Wilber the different levels are rather like boxes within larger boxes, each potentially more all-encompassing than the others. 'Just as Newtonian physics is a subset of Einsteinian physics,' he maintains, 'so existentialism is a smaller box – correct as far as it goes – which is encompassed by the larger box of the transcendentalists.'[23]

Wilber himself has been substantially influenced by Theosophy, by the teachings of Krishnamurti, and by such figures as Philip Kapleau, Eido Roshi and Da Free John. His own meditative practices derive from the Tibetan Vajrayana Buddhist tradition, which consists of oral instructions and secret teachings intended to develop wisdom and compassion; his principal teachers have been Kalu Rinpoche and Trungpa Rinpoche. However, Wilber's spectrum model derives not so much from his meditative experience as from his remarkably far-ranging scholarly review of the 'Perennial Philosophy' – the wisdom tradition of both East and West. According to Wilber:

Human personality is a multi-levelled manifestation or expression of a single Consciousness, just as in physics the electro-magnetic spectrum is viewed as a multi-banded expression of a single, characteristic electro-magnetic wave ... each level of the Spectrum is marked by a different and easily recognized sense of individual identity, which ranges from the Supreme Identity of cosmic-consciousness through several gradations or bands to the drastically narrowed sense of identity associated with egoic consciousness.[24]

Wilber believes that 'man's "innermost" consciousness is identical to the absolute and ultimate reality of the universe known variously as Brahman, Tao, Dharmakaya, Allah, the Godhead – to name but a few'. He refers to these collectively as 'Mind' for, according to the Perennial Philosophy, this is all that exists in the ultimate sense. However, a problem arises because humans usually operate in a dualistic state of consciousness – characterized, for example, by the distinction between 'subject' and 'object' – and each of us tends to lose sight of this overriding One-ness. As Wilber notes in *The Spectrum of Consciousness*, dualism gives rise to psychological boundaries which are perceived as real. 'We divide reality,' he writes, 'forget that we have divided it, and then forget that we have forgotten it.'[25] So each level of mind below the level of Unity Consciousness represents a progressive distortion of Mind's truly unified reality. These levels of consciousness (or illusion) represent the different states of perception which all human beings must pass through in their quest for self-knowledge. According to Wilber's model, the levels below the state of Unity Consciousness are like bands in a spectrum:

The 'lowest' level of Wilber's spectrum is a stage of consciousness he calls the 'Shadow', where individuals identify with an impoverished self-image and have repressed part of their psyche as 'alien', 'evil' or 'undesirable'.

On the next level of 'Ego', the individual identifies with a mental image of himself but perceives himself to exist '*in* his body and not *as* his body'. This, for Wilber, is a substantially intellectual level of reality.

At the next level in Wilber's hierarchy – the existential level –

individuals identify with the 'total psycho-physical organism'. Wilber would say that here there has been a profound development towards individual integration because the person now accepts all facets of his or her total organism. He quotes Gestalt therapist Fritz Perls as embodying this process: 'Lose your mind and come to your senses!'

Wilber recognizes, though, that beyond the individual level of psychophysical awareness, and at a higher existential level, may be found what he calls 'Biosocial Bands' of consciousness. Here we are considering the individual in the context of society. But social patterns filter our capacity for feeling and perceiving into culturally accepted modes, so to this extent cultural patterns distort or restrict consciousness. They do so because all societies consist of people in a web of relationships, and a certain amount of social cohesion and stability is required. However, as a consequence, human consciousness is prevented from attaining complete self-realization.

At the transpersonal levels of the spectrum we arrive at a perceptual domain where consciousness is able to transcend the individual level. However even here, as Wilber puts it, transpersonal awareness may not yet be 'completely identified with the All'. The transpersonal levels of consciousness have been associated by some theorists with Jungian archetypes and the Collective Unconscious – the realm of mythic, primordial consciousness – and Jung himself defined mystical experience as the 'experience of archetypes'.[26] However, Wilber has made it clear, in his somewhat extravagantly titled *A Brief History of Everything*, that he disagrees with Jung on this point. For Wilber, 'the *collective* is not necessarily *transpersonal*. Most of the Jungian archetypes ... are simply archaic images lying in the *magic* and *mythic* structures ... There is nothing transrational or transpersonal about them ... they are not themselves the source of a transpersonal or genuinely spiritual awareness.'[27]

Many commentators though, myself included, would

disagree with Wilber on this point, and such a view demarcates Wilber strongly from those within the personal growth movement – figures like Jean Houston and Jean Shinoda Bolen, among many others – who, in continuing the work of scholars like Joseph Campbell, have sought to enrich the exploration of mystical consciousness with a mix of mythic diversity. In the final analysis, though, it may come down to how one defines magic and myth. For Wilber, magical and mythic dimensions of consciousness are 'pre-rational' and therefore regressive, whereas for others mythic archetypes enliven what would otherwise be a comparatively sterile collective psyche. It is also of interest that in his experiential work Stanislav Grof has confirmed the existence of archetypal levels of mythic awareness at profoundly transpersonal levels of consciousness and he believes they have a defining, rather than regressive role.[28]

For Wilber, nevertheless – and few transpersonal theorists would disagree on this point – the supreme level is reached only when Mind alone exists, when there is no distinction whatsoever between subject and object. Wilber reminds us, for example, that there is still a hint of dualism when the mystic feels he is *witnessing* something beyond himself. The truth of Unity Consciousness is only realized, says Wilber, when 'the witness and the witnessed are one and the same'.[29]

In the final analysis, Wilber's spectrum model embraces the essentially non-dualist position of Vedanta and Vajrayana Buddhism, and the breadth of his study, as I have mentioned, has been widely acclaimed. However, it has to be said that some have found Wilber's tendency to categorize and label different religious, psychological and philosophical traditions – a necessary approach if one is considering 'boxes within boxes' – to be, by its very nature, a limiting process. At times his approach in defining levels of human consciousness seems too cerebral in its construction to be completely convincing, and the dynamism – the sheer awesomeness of metaphysical consciousness and the rich poetic tapestry of archetypal imagery – sometimes seems diminished by highly structured models like this. I myself share some of these concerns, for structures tend to imply their own sense of certainty, and when we embrace them we tend to forget that, after all, models and maps of mystical and visionary consciousness are only that: they draw finally on metaphors, symbols and allusions. Nevertheless, Ken Wilber's spectrum model remains one of the most all-encompassing approaches to spiritual consciousness that has yet been proposed. Together with Stanislav Grof's framework of perinatal and transpersonal levels of consciousness, and John Lilly's model of positive and negative mystical states, the Wilber model has helped define transpersonal concepts of human evolution, bringing science and spirituality closer together within a coherent holistic paradigm.

Meanwhile, if the emergent transpersonal perspective affirms the concept of a holistic universe grounded in a matrix of universal order, mind or consciousness, what does this say to us about the nature of death? We all face the inevitable trauma of our own impending death and there are many deep and profound issues to consider. Does the death of the brain bring with it the extinction of our personal identity, as the reductionist model in science would imply? Is our sense of personal worth and individuality nothing other than a by-product of our human biochemistry? How significant are spiritual and religious beliefs in the dying process? And what actually happens when we die?

Chapter 11

The Challenge of Death

From a transpersonal perspective, exploring the experience of death is perhaps the greatest remaining challenge in the study of human consciousness. Knowing more about death would not only teach us more about what to expect when we die, but also how we should live our lives on the planet *now*. Fortunately, the scientific and medical investigation of the near-death experience is beginning to provide useful insights into the possible nature of death itself. Thanatology – the study of death and the dying process – is now a major realm of enquiry within the international personal growth movement and the emerging perspectives on death may yet challenge current concepts of the mind/body relationship.

Death – 'the Final Stage of Growth'
This phrase was used by Swiss psychiatrist Dr Elisabeth Kubler-Ross (1926–2004) as the title of one of her many books on death and dying, and it conveys a clear sense of optimism. According to Dr Kubler-Ross, although many people associate death with trauma and crisis, it is also possible to regard death as a challenge. Death then becomes just another transitionary state of consciousness. The final stage of growth, yes. The end of identity and awareness? On the basis of the current evidence, probably not...

We usually define death as the absence of all visible signs of life – there is no heartbeat or respiration and all brain-wave activity has ceased (any EEG monitoring of electrical brain impulses would register as zero). To all intents and purposes such a person is clinically dead. The issues we are considering here relate to the experiences of people who have been pronounced medically to be clinically dead and yet revived to recount their often mystical and visionary experiences. Because these people didn't finally die after all, their visionary episodes are referred to as *near-death experiences*, or NDEs. They nevertheless provide us with the best scientifically based data on what may happen to us when we die, and to that extent they represent a potential meeting ground between the worlds of science and spirituality.[1]

Exploring the Near-Death Experience

The term 'near-death experience' was coined in 1975 by the American philosopher and teacher Dr Raymond Moody, author of the bestselling book *Life After Life*. Moody had begun collecting anecdotal accounts of near-death incidents in 1972 and his book was based on 150 accounts from people who contacted him as a result of articles he had written or lectures he had given on this topic.

The NDE by definition involves the return from apparent clinical death to waking consciousness and as such can be considered a substantially contemporary phenomenon because it has been greatly assisted by advances in medical technology.[2] It is only because the techniques of medical resuscitation and life support are now so sophisticated that we have a burgeoning literature which describes the accounts of people who have seemingly 'died' and yet lived to tell the tale. These accounts, and the scientific and medical commentaries accompanying them, provide a new focus for the philosophical issues of mind and body in the debate over the nature of human consciousness and the 'soul'.

Among the first modern accounts anticipating the NDE studies was the work of Swiss geologist Professor Albert Heim, who collected data on the experiences of people who had nearly died in mountain-climbing accidents or warfare. Heim's writings were translated in the 1970s by Russell Noyes and Ray Kletti, and included instances where people faced with the prospect of imminent death experienced a panoramic life-review or heard transcendental music.

Also preceding the more recent NDE literature were the findings of Dr Karlis Osis, a Latvian-born parapsychologist based in New York, who conducted a survey of deathbed visionary experiences. Osis despatched questionnaires to 10,000 physicians and nurses and received 540 responses. On the basis of these he published a book titled *Deathbed Observations by Physicians and Nurses* in 1961 and followed it with a more substantial volume, *At the Hour of Death*, in 1977. In these works Osis noted that terminal subjects often experienced periods of bliss and spiritual peace prior to death. Some also saw apparitions of deceased relatives or friends coming to greet them, and seemed to realize intuitively that these figures were about to help them through the transition of death itself.

However, it was Raymond Moody's book, *Life After Life*, that became the principal catalyst and inspiration for others interested in NDEs, and there have been several systematic research studies of the phenomenon since then – in the United States, Britain, Holland and Australia. Among those who have played a prominent role in this work are Dr Kenneth Ring from the University of Connecticut (co-founder of the International Association for Near-Death Studies – IANDS – in the United States), his British colleague Dr Margot Grey, world-famous thanatologist Dr Elisabeth Kubler-Ross, Australian psychologist Dr Cherie Sutherland, Dr Michael Sabom from Emory University in Atlanta and Dr Bruce Greyson from the University of Virginia, They have been joined in more recent years by the Dutch cardiologist Dr Pim van Lommel and British researchers Dr Sam Parnia and Dr Peter Fenwick – all of whom believe that studying the NDEs of cardiac arrest patients provides us with the most pertinent insights into key aspects of the dying process.

Kenneth Ring's *Life at Death*, published in 1980, was the first scientific study of NDEs and was based on over 100 interviews with medical subjects who had survived near-death. Ring followed it in 1984 with *Heading Toward Omega*, a lucid overview of the spiritual implications of the NDE.

Ring and his international colleagues have described the 'core' NDE in broadly the same way: an 'altered state' of feeling (peace, joy, serenity etc.); a sense of movement or separation from the body (an aerial perspective on the body, generally heightened awareness); a journey through a tunnel towards either a transcendent dimension or some other, more tangible realm (a celestial valley, garden or city); the experience of light and beauty; encounters in the spirit world with deceased relatives, spirits or 'guides' and sometimes religious figures like Jesus or 'God'. They have also sought to evaluate the impact such visionary experiences have had on the lives of the NDE subjects themselves.

Ring, Grey, Greyson, Sutherland and van Lommel have all come to the conclusion that the 'core' NDE is largely *invariant*, that it occurs in much the same form – though not with all the characteristics present in every individual case – irrespective of nationality, social class, age, sex, educational level or occupation. What is highly significant about this finding is that the core aspects of the NDE are comparatively constant irrespective of whether that person is a religious believer, atheist or agnostic: in other words, the NDE seems to be pointing towards character-istics of human consciousness rather than towards a wide variety of disjointed or divergent sensory experiences such as one might expect if the experience was purely hallucinatory. To this extent the NDE seems to be telling us about the process of dying itself and the various stages or transitions of human perception which might occur beyond bodily death.

Once again we have the difficult issue of body, mind and spirit to resolve: during a NDE, is the subject projecting consciousness beyond the confines of the physical body and, if so, how is such a thing possible? In Kenneth Ring's *Life at Death* survey, 97.4 percent of core NDE experiencers felt that their bodies were light or absent; 94.6 percent found their sense of time either expanded or absent; and 81.8 percent experienced space 'as either extended, infinite or absent'. As Ring observes: 'For most respondents, body, time and space simply disappear – or, to put it another way, they are no longer meaningful constructs.'[3]

Such aspects of the NDE, as one would expect, have proved problematic for reductionist researchers keen on explaining away the phenomenon as illusory or hallucinatory. Among the most commonly reported 'explanations' from this camp are that NDEs are delusory experiences which result from temporal lobe seizure or loss of oxygen as one approaches death; that they are simply re-enactments of the birth process; that they are caused by anaesthetic drugs; and that they are the symptoms of psychological factors related to the likely onset of death.

Here is a summary of these explanations, with comments on their relevance in each case:

Hallucinations and delusions: Dr Michael Sabom was particularly impressed in his medical survey by the ability of autoscopic (out-of-the-body/self-observing) NDE subjects to report details of actual events (medical equipment, surgical procedures, real conversations) from a detached and elevated position. 'The details of these perceptions were found to be accurate in all instances where corroborating evidence was available.' Dr Sabom also reported that some NDE subjects experienced hallucinations during their coma states and were able to distinguish clearly between the two categories of perception.[4]

Temporal lobe seizure: Seizures deriving from the temporal lobes (or non-motor portions) of the brain involve sensory distortions of the size or location of objects close by, and sometimes a feeling of detachment from the environment. They are also characterized by feelings of fear and loneliness and visual or auditory hallucinations. On the other hand, many NDE subjects report accurate, undistorted perceptual fields and may feel elated or relaxed about their dissociated condition.

Loss of oxygen in the brain: Under normal circumstances, if the oxygen supply to the brain is reduced, this produces a state of mental confusion and cognitive dysfunction. This is certainly not characteristic of the core NDE, which is often described by subjects as profoundly real and perceptually coherent. Some subjects suffering from brain hypoxia (oxygen loss) – for example, mountain climbers who have trekked in rarefied atmospheres – find they experience an onset of laziness and irritability, and they may also find it difficult to remember what they were thinking or doing at the time. Many NDE subjects, on the other hand, are so awed by the clarity and detail of their experiences that they remember them for many years afterwards.

Reliving the birth process: If NDEs, which are characterized by feelings of passing through a tunnel towards light, are somehow related to the normal birth process, then people born by Caesarian section should not experience them. Dr Susan Blackmore – a well-known skeptic in relation to the NDE data – gave a questionnaire to 254 people, of whom 36 had been born by Caesarian section. 'Both groups reported the same proportion of out-of-the-body and tunnel experiences,' she has written. 'It could be that the experiences are based on the *idea* of birth in general, but this drastically weakens the theory.'[5]

Anaesthetic drugs: There are several cases of NDE subjects who received no anaesthetic drugs during their hospitalization, so this explanation, if indeed it is one at all, would not apply in many instances. While it is true that some dissociative anaesthetics like ketamine hydrochloride (Ketalar) may produce an experience in which one's consciousness appears distinct from the body and there may also be an awareness of journeying through tunnels in space, Ketalar is not widely used in human medical treatment and is now for the most part restricted to veterinary practice. In general, drug-induced hallucinations seem to be markedly different from NDEs. Dr Sabom notes that drug experiences are 'highly variable and idiosyncratic' and 'markedly different from NDEs, which always show a remarkable degree of invariance'.

Psychological factors: One psychological view of NDEs is that the experience derives from 'depersonalization'. This theory, advanced by Noyes and Kletti (who translated the Heim material), argues that the ego has to protect itself from impending death and thus creates a perceptual scenario which supports the feeling of continuing mental integration. As Dr Noyes has said: 'As an adaptive pattern of the nervous system it alerts the organism to its threatening environment while holding potentially disorganizing emotion in check.' Dr Sabom rejects this view as a blanket explanation of the NDE because there were subjects in his survey who had out-of-the-body NDEs without being aware psychologically of any likelihood of imminent death. Some of these were subjects who experienced loss of waking consciousness without warning, due to a stoppage of the heart. Also, as Dr Margot Grey has indicated, 'depersonalization' is unable to account for NDE subjects who have claimed to have had meetings with relatives who had recently died but whom the NDE subject *at the time did not know had died.* Here the NDE subject would learn of the relative's actual death only after recovering from the NDE: the expectation prior to the NDE would be that the person concerned was still alive.

What Happens During a NDE?

It may be worthwhile at this point to quote a few brief but characteristic examples of what NDE subjects actually report, because their testimonies are our starting point and they provide insights into the processes involved:

I felt as though I was looking down at myself, as though I was way out here in space ... I felt sort of separated. It was a wonderful feeling. It was marvelous. I felt very light and didn't know where I was ... And then I thought that something was happening to me ... This wasn't night. I wasn't dreaming ... And then I felt a wonderful feeling as if I was out in space.

I felt myself being separated: my soul, drawing apart from the physical being, was drawn upward seemingly to leave the earth and to go upward where it reached a greater Spirit with whom there was a communion, producing a remarkable new relaxation and deep security.

I went into this kind of feeling of ecstasy and just started moving outward energetically ... and then I experienced a replay of all of my life ... from my birth to the actual operation ... it was like it was on a fast-forward video ... people, places, everything ...

It is not uncommon for NDE subjects to report contact with deceased relatives or friends. In Dr Sabom's survey of 116 NDE subjects, 28 described encounters with other personages. One of Dr Sabom's case studies involved a seriously injured soldier, and his account of his deceased colleagues is intruigingly matter-of-fact:

I came out of my body, and perceived me laying on the ground with three limbs gone ... What makes this so real was that the thirteen guys that had been killed the day before, that I had put in plastic bags, were right there with me. And more than that, during the course of that month of May, my regular company lost forty-two dead. All forty-two of those guys were there. They were not in the form we perceive the human body, and I can't tell you what form they were in because I don't know. But I know they were there. I felt their presence. We communicated without talking with our voices. There was no sympathy, no sorrow. They were already where they were. They didn't want to go back. That was the basic tone of our communication ... that we were all happy right where we were.[6]

NDE Research Among the Blind

In a potentially highly significant research study, Kenneth Ring and his colleague Sharon Cooper have recently explored near-death experiences among the blind. This research is important because if it could be demonstrated that blind people have their sight restored to them during a near-death experience, the entire relationship between body, mind and spirit would obviously have to reassessed.

In 1997 Ring and Cooper approached eleven national and regional American associations for the blind in order to locate individuals who had experienced near-death experiences (NDEs) or out-of-the-body experiences (OOBEs). Forty-six individuals were subsequently screened for the research study, of whom 31 qualified for inclusion. They included 20 females and 11 males, most of them Christian and all of them Caucasian. Nearly half of the participants had been blind from birth. The research study took two years to complete.[7]

One of the subjects in the research study – a 45-year-old woman named Vicki – had been born blind: her optic nerve had been completely destroyed at birth because of excess oxygen received in an incubator. Nevertheless, Vicki appeared to be able to 'see' during her NDE.

Vicki found herself floating above her body in the emergency room of a hospital following an automobile accident. She was aware of being up near the ceiling of the room and she could see a male doctor and female nurse working on her body. At first she thought she must be dead: 'I just briefly saw this body,' she said later, 'and I knew that it was mine because I wasn't in mine.'

She then went on to identify features of her clothing and personal possessions: 'I think I was wearing the plain gold band on my right finger and my father's wedding ring next to it. But my wedding ring I definitely saw ... That was the one I noticed the most because it's most unusual. It has orange blossoms on the corners of it. This was the only time I could ever relate to seeing and to what light was, because I experienced it.'[8]

During her NDE, Vicki also reported visiting a very bright realm 'where everybody ... was made of light'. She saw herself surrounded by trees and flowers and a vast number of people. It was here she became aware of specific people whom she had known in real life but who had since died. Two of them were blind schoolmates who had died some years before. She also encountered her grandmother who had died two years before her accident.[9]

Ring and Cooper's research provides evidence that the blind are indeed able to experience some sort of vision during their NDEs, even though their normal sight organs are not functioning. Ring and Cooper have speculated that this may involve a unique type of telepathic perception they call 'mindsight'. Their research is ongoing and may prove to be of considerable importance because mindsight clearly involves an ability to perceive in a manner beyond the currently known limits of the material brain.

Different Levels of the NDE

Let us now consider the different categories within the NDE. As indicated above, a number of the experiences involve a substantially physical frame of reference. Many subjects perceive themselves to be just slightly dissociated from the physical plane of events – perhaps observing their comatose bodies, before rising into the sky above their house or perhaps observing themselves being resuscitated by a doctor in a hospital. In such instances it is not uncommon for subjects to also hear and accurately report specific conversations which have taken place at that time.

At a more removed level, though – perhaps at a level that brings the subject closer to physical death – a different experiential domain reveals itself: one that the American parapsychologist D. Scott Rogo referred to as 'eschatological'. It is here that the NDE subject may have visionary, religious or spiritual experiences – usually shaped by cultural expectations or by the person's individual belief system. The visionary material itself can be of varying degrees of profundity, ranging from a dreamlike or surreal flow of imagery through to powerful archetypal experiences. In instances like these, subjects report encounters with celestial beings, superhuman beings from classical mythology or encounters with 'God'. And sometimes they even transcend these levels of imagery, experiencing a dissolving of personal boundaries as the ego melts into other beings or forms, or seems to unite with the entire manifested universe.

Implications for an Afterlife

Perhaps more than any other person, Dr Kubler-Ross was associated with the process of death and dying. She acknowledged cultural variations with regard to the visionary episodes different individuals might anticipate after death, but maintained that there was substantial evidence for post-mortem survival. 'For me,' Kubler-Ross once remarked, 'it is no longer a matter of belief, but rather a matter of knowing.'[10]

Kubler-Ross's medical work with dying patients predated scientific research into NDEs – it extended back some 30 years. Much of her original medical work and her earlier publications on the process of death and dying were concerned primarily with the various stages of engaging with death, including denial and self-questioning, the role of grief, and the idea of death as an integral part of human development. It is only comparatively recently that Kubler-Ross expressed her ideas on the afterlife in any detail. A small volume titled *On Life After Death*, published in 1991, brought together Kubler-Ross's principal writings on the afterlife for the first time.

Kubler-Ross maintained that her views were based on a study of more than 20,000 people who have had near-death experiences, although, unlike the Ring and Sabom studies, many of her references were anecdotal. In essence she believed that none of us dies alone, that those of our loved ones who have preceded us in death will be there to assist our transition through death, and that death, like life, is 'a birth into a different existence'.[11] Kubler-Ross claimed that she became convinced about the reality of meeting loved ones after death after researching family car accidents. In particular she was interested in the evidence from accidents where most, but not all, of the people had been killed. Seriously injured children involved in accidents of this sort were generally taken to trauma units in hospitals and Kubler-Ross was able to visit them two or three days before they died. She found that children about to experience death in these circumstances were invariably calm and serene and were always somehow assured that others would be waiting for them after death. These children had not been advised by the medical staff that their parents or siblings had died because usually there was a practice of keeping such information secret. It was thought that children in crisis would give up hope and not fight to stay alive if they knew that other members of their family had died. Nevertheless, said Kubler-Ross, 'In fifteen years I have not had a single child who did not somehow know when a family member had preceded them in death.'[12]

Many dying subjects experience a distinct separation of body and 'consciousness' – sometimes to the extent of looking down on their bodies in a hospital or at the scene of an accident – and Kubler-Ross claimed quite categorically that none of her patients who had ever had an out-of-body experience was ever again afraid to die. In her view, death simply involved discarding one's physical form in transition to a different state of conscious awareness:

> Death is simply a shedding of the physical body like the butterfly shedding its cocoon. It is a transition to a higher state of consciousness where you continue to perceive, to understand, to laugh, and to be able to grow. The only thing you lose is something that you don't need anymore, your physical body. It's like putting away your winter coat when spring comes. You know that the coat is shabby and you don't want to wear it anymore. That's virtually what death is about.[13]

According to Kubler-Ross, this transitionary experience then opens out into a state of cosmic awareness:

> After we pass through this visually very beautiful and individually appropriate form of transition, say the tunnel, we are approaching a source of light that many of our patients describe and that I myself experienced in the form of an incredibly beautiful and unforgettable life-changing experience. This is called cosmic consciousness. In the presence of this light, which most people in our western hemisphere call Christ or God, or love or light, we are surrounded by total and absolute unconditional love, understanding and compassion.[14]

Kubler-Ross's emphasis on the positive and loving aspects of the afterlife transition is also supported by Kenneth Ring's NDE data, although he does not draw the same final conclusion as she does. Ring believes that the almost universal occurrence of *positive* visionary states of consciousness experienced during a NDE (as distinct from negative, hell-like states) may simply be a mapping of one's initial contact with the Inner Light and may by no means represent the total spectrum of visionary after-death encounters. It may well be that works like the *Tibetan Book of the Dead* present a more complete picture, and that what Kubler-Ross describes is simply the first stage of a much more extensive process. Considered in this context, if the *Tibetan Book of the Dead* is in any sense correct, at the point of physical death we will all encounter the Great Light and the positive deities – or archetypes of the psyche – first, and the negative images will emerge later. According to the Tibetan model of post-mortem consciousness, if we are unable to transcend these powerful visionary encounters we may then find ourselves being gradually drawn back into the more tangible dimensions of physical awareness prior to entering a new human incarnation.

Elisabeth Kubler-Ross and her colleagues in the field of near-death research were not alone in sharing their speculations about death and the afterlife. Two other maverick figures on the fringe of the transpersonal movement also played a unique role in the exploration of consciousness states related to death and near-death. The first of these is the Canadian-born medical professor Ian Stevenson (1918–2007), whose systematic international research into claimed cases of reincarnation among young children has attracted widespread respect and attention. The second is American paranormal investigator Robert A. Monroe (1915–1995), whose research into out-of-the-body experiences and the transitional states following death may yet redefine our understanding of what it is like to die. Both Stevenson and Monroe are highly regarded in the New Age movement and their publications continue to attract an ongoing readership. Stevenson's best-known work is *Twenty Cases Suggestive of Reincarnation* (1966, revised edition 1995); Monroe's exploration of out-of-the-body states was documented in his three books: *Journeys out of the Body* (1971), *Far Journeys* (1985) and *Ultimate Journey* (1994).

The Reincarnation Research of Dr Ian Stevenson

For many years reincarnational cases involving young children were a consuming interest of Dr Ian Stevenson, former Alumni Professor of Psychiatry at the University of Virginia's School of Medicine. Professor Stevenson believed that young children – children under the age of five or six years, for example – are less worldly than teenagers or adults, have scant access to information from other regions and localities, and would therefore have little inclination or personal capacity to fabricate evidence. He therefore considered reincarnation evidence in young children to be of special interest, particularly in those instances when it was possible to independently verify the claims these children made.

Over a period spanning several decades Professor Stevenson and his staff traveled to many different countries – including India, Sri Lanka, Brazil, Lebanon, Turkey and Thailand – in their search for evidence of reincarnation. Dr Stevenson and his colleagues also visited Tlingit Indian communities in south-eastern Alaska where several reincarnation cases have been reported. As a consequence, Professor Stevenson and his successor at the University of Virginia, Dr Jim B. Baker, have now documented around 3,000 cases of claimed reincarnational memories in young children and have published their findings in a number of scholarly books and journals.[15] An analysis of these cases suggests that reincarnational memories in the children of different cultures are remarkably similar – even in isolated communities that have had little contact with other cultural groups.

Professor Stevenson did not take all of these cases on face value, and argued that in some instances other factors like telepathy, 'racial memory', and sometimes even fraud could also be involved in the reincarnational memories of young children. However it was not only the reincarnation accounts themselves that attracted him. Towards the end of his professional career Dr

Stevenson began to explore what he called the relationship between biology and reincarnation – especially apparent connections between birthmarks and reincarnational memories. He was particularly interested in the existence of birthmarks that appeared to correspond to bullet or stab wounds inflicted in previous lives, and he explored the issue of whether a violent death was more likely to lead to a hasty reincarnation. The Tlingit Indians, for example, believe it is better to be killed than to die a natural death because they maintain this will result in a rapid rebirth. Members of the Druse sect in Lebanon believe that a dead person's spirit will be reincarnated immediately after death but they maintain that this happens swiftly anyway, regardless of how a person dies.

Birthmark evidence is especially prevalent among the Inuits (or Eskimos) and the Tlingit Indians of Alaska – occurring in approximately half of all reported reincarnation cases. Both the Tlingits and the Inuits are familiar with violent death and with wounds caused by savage attacks from wild animals. They also report frequent injuries inflicted by spears, guns, knives or axes as the result of fights. Dr Stevenson explored several hundred cases where the birthmarks that appear on a person's body are claimed to be linked to surgical procedures or stab and bullet wounds that occurred in previous lives.

One of Dr Stevenson's numerous case studies involved a man known as Victor Vincent.[16] Victor was a full-blooded Tlingit Indian who lived on an island in southern Alaska. In 1946, towards the end of his life, he became very close to his niece, Mrs Corliss Chotkin – the daughter of his sister – and told her that after he died he would be reborn as her next son. Vincent also maintained that she would know it was him because her newborn son would bear two birthmarks related to scars that Vincent had on his body. Vincent had a very distinctive scar on his back and another on the right side of his nose near its base. He told Mrs Chotkin that he would imprint these scars onto the body of his next incarnation to prove that he had indeed been reborn.

In December 1947, fifteen months after her uncle Victor died, Mrs Chotkin gave birth to a son, whom she named Corliss Junior, and the baby was born with birthmarks in exactly the same location as Victor Vincent's scars. The scar near the boy's nose became less noticeable as he grew older but the mark on his back became even more distinctive and had all the characteristics of a surgical incision that had healed over. It was raised and pigmented and also itched like a wound that was on the mend.

When the boy was just over a year old he began to utter his first words, and around the age of 13 months he said to his mother, 'Don't you know me? I'm Kahkody.' This was Victor Vincent's tribal name, and Mrs Chotkin was amazed that her son seemed to speak with the same accent as her deceased uncle. Later, when he was two and being wheeled along the street in the town of Sitka, where the family lived, Corliss Junior spontaneously recognized one of Victor Vincent's stepdaughters and called her correctly by her name, Susie. Later that year he recognized Victor Vincent's son William, who was visiting Sitka unannounced, and said to his mother, 'There is William, my son.'[17]

At the age of three Corliss Junior identified Victor Vincent's widow, Rose, in a large crowd – spotting her even before Mrs Chotkin had noticed her – and on another occasion he recognized a close family friend of Victor's who happened to be in Sitka at the time. Later he identified other friends of Victor's, referring to them correctly by their tribal names. By the age of nine, however, Corliss was able to recall fewer and fewer memories of his former life and by the age of 15 he could recall nothing whatever from his previous incarnation. Indeed, in most cases like this the memories of past lives seem to disappear with the passage of the time. It is with good reason that Dr Stevenson sought to document the evidence of reincarnational memories in young children before the evidence itself was lost.

Over the years Dr Stevenson was always somewhat circumspect when asked whether he believed his research had established the existence of reincarnation. He finally came to the view that reincarnation was difficult to prove scientifically but that the evidence tended to support it. 'Of the cases we know now,' he told his biographer Tom Shroder, 'at least for some, reincarnation is the best explanation we have been able to come up with. There is an impressive body of evidence, and I think it is getting stronger all the time.'[18]

Robert Monroe: Journeys out of the Body

Robert A. Monroe went further than Ian Stevenson in supporting the reality of reincarnation – he claimed it as a 'known' rather than a belief. And it has to be emphasized that Monroe was by no means a natural mystic. Of all the pioneers of altered states of consciousness, Monroe stands out as a surprising and atypical example because he stumbled upon the paranormal almost by accident. Monroe's research into out-of-the-body experiences was an unexpected consequence of his use of sleep-learning techniques.

Monroe studied engineering and journalism at Ohio State University and in 1939 went to New York, where he eventually created and produced some 400 radio and television programs over a period of 21 years. Later he formed his own production company, generating 28 radio network shows weekly. He subsequently became a director and Vice-President of Mutual Broadcasting Inc., a position he held until 1956.

In the spring of 1958 Monroe had the first of what would become a series of out-of-the body experiences. He had been experimenting with techniques of absorbing data while asleep, using a tape recorder. One afternoon he was lying quietly on his couch at home when he felt a 'warm light' on his body and began to 'vibrate' quite strongly. At the same time he found himself unable to move, as if he had been trapped in a metal vice.

During the following months the same condition recurred several times. Monroe gradually discovered, however, that he could move his fingertips during the onset of the vibrations, and he was surprised to find that he could 'extend' them to feel things beyond his normal reach. It also became apparent that his fingers were not feeling in the physical sense because they were able to penetrate through normally solid surfaces.

Shortly afterwards he again had a similar experience except that he now found himself extended and floating in his entirety, just below the surface of the ceiling in his room. Beneath him lay his immobile body, clearly visible on the bed. Monroe panicked, thinking he had died, and in desperation sought hurriedly to return to his body. These initial fears proved groundless, however, and gradually Monroe acquired more confidence. He subsequently began to explore the new dimensions of awareness made available to him in an out-of-the-body state.

On several occasions Monroe would 'travel' to see his friends – sometimes at unscheduled times. He was able to set up a number of double blind experiments with friends and colleagues where he could later confirm what he had seen, checking such details as the time of his encounters, the clothes his friends had been wearing, and their specific movements and activities.

Monroe gradually identified different 'locales' that he was able to visit while journeying out-of-the-body. Locale I was the familiar realm of everyday experience, viewed simply from a new perspective. This was where he encountered his everyday colleagues while out-of-the-body, and as a perceptual realm it contained no strange beings, environments or imagery. However Monroe soon became aware of a dimension that he called Locale II. This was a realm described in esoteric literature as the 'astral plane'. It encompassed regions one might associate with Heaven and Hell and included imagery associated with fantasies and raw emotions. It also seemed to be home to various discarnate beings, some of whom were unaware that they had died. Monroe noted that beings in Locale I could not normally detect beings resident in Locale II. A further domain which Monroe visited, and which he called Locale III, seemed to be some kind of 'anti-matter duplicate of our physical world'.[19]

Robert Monroe's personal quest to explore altered states continued after the publication of his first book, *Journeys out of the Body*, in 1971. Encouraged by the enthusiastic reception he had received for his work internationally, Monroe decided to establish a laboratory to research the out-of-the-body experience (OOBE) more systematically. Located in the foothills of Virginia's Blue Ridge Mountains, the center eventually became known as the Monroe Institute of Applied Sciences. Drawing on his experience as a sound engineer, Monroe was soon able to establish that certain sound frequencies could assist in inducing the out-of-the-body experience.

When sounds of different wavelengths are played into opposite ears through stereo headphones, the brain assimilates the two pulses and 'hears' the difference between them. For example, if one were to feed 100 cycles per second (100 Hz) into one ear and 110 cycles (110 Hz) into the other, the difference would be a 10 Hz wave. This corresponds to a low alpha-wave frequency in the brain – a pattern associated with meditative states. Monroe was able to establish that OOBEs were primarily associated with the theta wave frequency which ranges from 4 to 7 Hz, although other frequencies were also involved. He subsequently developed a sound system known as the Hemi-Sync process to feed identical wave forms into both brain hemispheres, making it possible for research participants to fully utilize the potential in the right side of their brains as well as the left.[20] In *Ultimate Journey*, Monroe describes the right brain as 'that portion of our mind-consciousness that emanates from our Core Self which was present when we began the human experience'.[21]

Monroe then established the Gateway Program at the Institute where individuals could experience altered states for themselves – including the possibility of the OOBE. Monroe and his colleagues built a number of specially designed isolation booths with individual headphones – these were then wired to allow participants to receive audio and electromagnetic signals from a central location. Each individual could be monitored for EEG (brain waves), EMG (muscle tone), pulse rate and body voltage. Wearing their headphones and relaxing in a state of total darkness, participants would then progress from meditation and visualization exercises through to out-of-the body journeys, in a series of carefully graded steps. By the mid-1990s over 8,000 people had attended the Institute's programs, among them Dr Elisabeth Kubler-Ross, Dr Rupert Sheldrake, and psychologist Joseph Chilton Pearce.

It was perhaps inevitable that a specific cosmology would emerge as a result of the Institute's research programs. As one might expect, the Monroe Institute cosmology is one in which post-mortem states are associated with different vibratory levels of awareness, strongly suggesting that after death human consciousness functions on an entirely different vibratory frequency. According to Robert Monroe the world is surrounded by 'rings' of discarnate entities, reflecting varying levels of spiritual evolution. Many of these beings remain in an intermediate state, unaware that they are dead, while others appear to envelop themselves in 'emotionally based fears and drives which they attempt to act out but never conclude'. These discarnate beings are very much in need of psychic assistance to help them avoid remaining in a 'locked-in state' – a situation which experienced researchers at the Institute have sought to remedy through what is known as the Lifeline Program. Lifeline helpers have been trained to journey out-of-the-body into experiential realms where their assistance is most needed. By the mid-1990s Monroe claimed to have trained hundreds of people at his Institute to help guide the souls of the dead.[22]

As mentioned earlier, in addition to identifying three out-of-the-body Locales, Robert Monroe also identified different vibrationary levels associated with the after-death state and he maintained that one should approach these realms carefully, by gradually becoming acclimatized to a specific range of altered states. Monroe identified the basic levels of modified awareness, which he labeled Focus 1 through to Focus 10, as levels where the mind remained awake while the body gradually fell asleep – a basic precondition for inducing an out-of-the-body state. He associated Focus 12 with a state of 'expanded awareness' and Focus 15 with a level of awareness where there was no sense of time. Focus 21, meanwhile, was identified as a place to explore one's true inner nature, and Focus 22 as a place where 'humans still in physical existence [had] only partial consciousness ... remembered as dreams or hallucinations'.

In his third book, *Ultimate Journey*, Monroe went on to describe Focus 23, a level where the confused spirits of those who had recently died came together to try to make sense of their recent life-experiences. Monroe describes Focus 23 as a 'level inhabited by those who have recently left physical existence but who either have not been able to recognize and accept this or are unable to free themselves from the Earth Life System.'[23] It was here that some research participants made direct contact with deceased family members and loved ones, in some cases concluding unfinished business that had been interrupted by the process of death. But there were further levels still... Monroe identified Focus 24, 25 and 26 as levels associated with various religious belief systems and it was clear to him that many discarnate beings would choose to immerse themselves after death in imagery associated with their personal religious beliefs. However Monroe maintained that one could pass through these 'belief system territories' and then enter what he called Focus 27. Here one would come to a place he called the

Park – a place where discarnate spirits were taken for rest and renewal.

Monroe's associate F. Holmes Atwater, who has published his own account of out-of-the body research, describes Focus 27 as a type of spiritual 'way station' intended to 'ease the trauma and shock of the transition out of physical reality and assist in evaluating options for the next steps in growth and development'.[24] The Park is a visionary construct that Monroe says has been intentionally created by discarnate human intelligence to provide a comforting psychic environment for those in a state of spiritual transition. Interestingly, many near-death subjects completely unconnected with the research at the Monroe Institute have reported entering paradisiacal gardens that provided a profound sense of solace and peace. Sometimes, too, these NDE subjects report that they have encountered deceased relatives in such settings.[25] Meanwhile, some Monroe Institute researchers now say they have begun to explore the realms beyond Focus 27, entering uncharted territory where 'it is nearly impossible to relate experiences in human terms'.[26] Their future reports will no doubt be received with considerable interest.

Six years before his death in 1995 I interviewed Robert Monroe at his Institute in Virginia with the specific purpose of asking him about his own conception of the afterlife.[27] Monroe told me that one of the most important challenges we all face as human beings is to convert our religious beliefs into 'knowns' – so that our ideas and concepts can then be based on personal experience. He told me he had been able to establish reincarnation as one of his personal 'knowns' – for him a knowledge of past lives was no longer a matter of faith or belief but the result of direct experience. However he also said that those who did not embrace a belief in rebirth would not reincarnate in the future – electing to be reborn was very much a matter of choice. Monroe also spoke of spiritual freedom, describing it as the ability to step outside the hologram of the known physical universe. 'All previous knowledge and information relating to the lifetimes is within the hologram,' he told me. '*All* of our belief systems are within the hologram. When you step out of the hologram, as an intelligent energy that is nevertheless separate and apart from it, you are no longer human, and you are no longer part of time and space. Then you can have an experience of all your lifetimes – it is like a dream of all the things that happened within the hologram.'[28]

A Celebratory View of Death

In May 1997 a satellite-bearing Pegasus rocket was launched above the Atlantic Ocean with a number of small containers strapped to one its booster engines. Inside the containers were the cremated remains of Dr Timothy Leary, Gene Roddenberry – creator of *Star Trek* – and 22 other posthumous space travelers. In what was to become the world's first space funeral, Pegasus soared into space and then jettisoned both its engines and the ashes, allowing them to fall into orbit in a blaze of light.

Carol Rosin, a close personal friend of Leary's, had helped coordinate the mission to place his ashes into orbit. Rosin said that Leary's message to her during the last phase of his life was that all of us are 'free to ride the light' on earth and into space. It was an optimistic message, and Leary both believed it and put it into practice. His approach to death was essentially celebratory. After being told by his doctors in January 1995 that he was terminally ill with an advanced cancer in his prostate gland, Leary decided to gather his friends around him, 'to reflect on the past, help plan and design my future death, and just plain hang out and have a good time'. For Leary there could be no morbidity – he simply wanted his friends around him in a spirit of joy and friendship. 'Instead of treating the last act in your life in terms of fear, weakness and helplessness,' wrote Leary in his posthumously published book *Design for Dying*, 'think of it as a triumphant graduation.'[29]

Forever a showman and always intently hostile to the dictums of the status quo, Leary believed in the idea that you should live fully and joyously until you die. 'The house party is a wonderful way to deal with your divinity as you approach death,' said Leary. 'I can't recommend it enough ... Invite people to your house party who share your celestial ambitions.' No stranger to controversy, Leary was happy to flout contemporary taboos around death by maintaining a running commentary about his dying process on a home website.

Leary always maintained that death is a trip to higher realms of consciousness and he also emphasized that it is 'the single transcendent experience that *every* person will undergo'.[30] This makes death special. If we are to follow Timothy Leary's advice, it is something we should all plan for, and hope to do well when our time comes.

Chapter 12

The Future of the New Age

A crucial question – one that has been raised both by enthusiasts and critics alike – is whether the New Age movement is likely to endure for some time to come. My own view is that the immediate future of the New Age movement seems assured because at the deepest level of this movement – the transpersonal level – the New Age perspective draws our attention to issues that are of global spiritual concern.

Central among these issues is the important point, widely held among members of the transpersonal movement, that the scientific thinking which currently governs our definitions of 'reality' should be supplemented by a spiritual or holistic dimension. It is also generally agreed in transpersonal circles that this should be an authentic and well-informed spirituality, one based not on narrow definitions of doctrinal religion but instead on frameworks that explore universal aspects of the spiritual experience and transcend cultural differences. Transpersonal psychologist Frances Vaughan, addressing an international conference aimed at integrating ancient wisdom and modern science, expressed it well when she said: 'Science without wisdom can destroy the world; wisdom without science remains ineffectual. The transpersonal perspective sees the eastern and western approaches as complementary, and recognizes the transcendental mystical unity of all religions.'[1]

A Receptive Spirituality
One especially positive aspect of the New Age movement is its sense of spiritual open-endedness and receptivity. The fact that it has no dominant or entrenched doctrinal position and is willing

to absorb perennial wisdom teachings from both East and West, while also accommodating insights based on new scientific discoveries, seems to me to be very much in its favor. In Orthodox Judaism, Christianity and Islam, by way of contrast, it is much more difficult to maintain the same degree of intellectual and spiritual flexibility. Historically, these religions are based on unique spiritual revelations from founder-prophets, and these revelations have in turn determined that these religions would subsequently become grounded in specific doctrinal frameworks. This explains the otherwise puzzling contradiction, for example, that even now, in the 21st century, Christian Creationists should choose to ignore the presence of the fossil record, reverting instead to a fundamentalist interpretation of the Book of Genesis that is clearly at odds with scientific discoveries. The lack of a consolidated doctrinal position within the transpersonal movement, on the other hand, means that the New Age remains potentially much more open to incorporating transformative concepts and progressive scientific ideas. To this extent, what some Christian critics of the New Age, like Dr David Tacey, have seen as a weakness of the New Age – namely, the absence of a formal religious tradition – may yet emerge as a strength.[2]

Another positive aspect of the New Age perspective is its willingness to subject personal spiritual beliefs to the test of experience – a willingness, as consciousness researcher Robert Monroe expressed it, to convert 'beliefs' into 'knowns'.[3] New Agers are undoubtedly eclectic and discursive in their spiritual tastes but their eclecticism is generally based on what feels true – on what measures up as 'real'. And, clearly, evaluations based on broad-based human experience provide us with a useful yardstick for measuring spiritual 'reality'. Gautama Buddha made the same point over 2,000 years ago:

Do not believe in what you have heard. Do not believe in traditions because they have been handed down for many generations. Do not believe anything because it is rumored and spoken of by many. Do not believe merely because the written statement of some old sage is produced. Do not believe in conjectures. Do not believe merely in the authority of your teachers and elders. After observation and analysis, when it agrees with reason and it is conducive to the good and benefit of one and all, then accept it, and live up to it.[4]

As in the Buddhist teachings, the New Age credo emphasizes that all individuals need to take responsibility for both their own lives and their own personal spiritual beliefs. At the same time it is necessary to remain mindful of the fact that all belief systems are themselves metaphors or constructs that seek, in their own limited and incomplete way, to describe what we believe to be true. Spiritual beliefs – especially those which seek to explain 'God' or concepts of ultimate spiritual causality – need to remain as open-ended as possible. As transpersonal neurophysiologist Dr John C. Lilly observed in his influential book *Simulations of God*, when we refer to the awesome and transcendental nature of God our concept of God 'must be huge – in order to include one's ignorance, the unknown, the ineffable. Instead of God as the Belief, the Simulation, the Model, one adheres to God as Mystery, God as the Unknown. The explorer of inner spaces cannot afford the baggage of fixed beliefs. This baggage is too heavy, too limited and too limiting to allow further exploration.'[5] As Lilly points out, religious dogmas arise when followers assert the exclusiveness and 'truth' of a specific belief system – when they narrow the options and assert that their interpretation alone is valid.

Transpersonal perspectives tend to avoid references to exclusive sources of spiritual authority. Similarly, New Agers orientate somewhat eclectically towards body, mind and spirit practices that are experientially effective in the 'here-and-now' – which accounts for the widespread popularity of meditation and yoga. From the New Age perspective there is little value in retaining religious teachings conceived for another time and place if their orientation and function has become no longer relevant. To this extent, no one can afford the complacency of allowing their spiritual horizons to become frozen in time.

The New Age and Fundamentalism

In the future we may well find an increasing polarization across the spectrum of contemporary spiritual beliefs – with a clear division between those who embrace an eclectic form of non-institutionalized spirituality and those who turn instead in the opposite direction towards religious fundamentalism, with its promise of doctrinal certainty. Religious fundamentalism has an undoubted appeal in uncertain and troubled times, with its clear distinction between good and evil and its emphatic demarcation between supporters and disbelievers. However, fundamentalist religions of all kinds invariably signal a return to the authority of the past. The fundamentalist position resists doctrinal change. The very authority of any religious institution is grounded in orthodoxy – and any move for fundamental change is likely to be branded as deviance or heresy and fiercely resisted. Indeed, religious institutions are obliged, by their very nature and innate conservatism, to become substantially inflexible. Heresy, on the other hand, is openly welcomed in the New Age movement – as long as it is heresy that works.

Paradoxically, something akin to religious fundamentalism is also found in some scientific circles. When supporters of particular scientific models become so closely aligned with specific interpretations of scientific data that they adopt a closed mind with regard to any new information that might challenge their current position, this changes science into what transpersonal psychologist Dr Charles Tart has referred to as 'scientism'. Scientism arises when science itself is converted into a belief system. Dr Tart, a distinguished scientist in his own right, notes that when science acts like a belief system it ossifies instead of providing a continual challenge to further thought.[6]

The transpersonal movement has itself been subject to attack from those who practice a form of scientism. As we have already seen, the transpersonal perspective promotes a holistic concept of Nature and the universe and a corresponding movement away from more limited mechanistic models. But there are many who cling to the old mechanistic paradigm, despite the findings of quantum theory and the New Physics. As is becoming increasingly obvious, prevailing paradigms often take some time to change – even when the scientific evidence points in a new direction.

Paradigm Shifts

Transpersonal perspectives have so far made little impact on reductionist scientific models of reality and perception. An influential but entirely reductionist work by American philosopher Daniel C. Dennett titled *Consciousness Explained* makes no mention of any of these thinkers and neglects the transpersonal perspective altogether. But Dennett – who is himself an exponent of computer-based models of consciousness – has at least been bold and honest enough to assert: 'The prevailing wisdom is *materialism*: there is only one sort of stuff, namely matter – the physical stuff of physics, chemistry and physiology – and the mind is somehow nothing but a physical phenomenon. In short, the mind is the brain.'[7]

Nevertheless, for many in the transpersonal movement it is just a matter of time before a sense of the larger perspective makes its presence felt. The groundswell supporting the new paradigm in physics is already underway and a change of perspective now seems inevitable. As Dr Stanislav Grof has noted:

One of the most important achievements of the Western

philosophy of science is the recognition that scientific theories are but conceptual models organizing the data about reality available at the time. As useful approximations to reality, they should not be mistaken for correct descriptions of reality itself. The relationship between theory and the reality which it describes is like that between a map and territory ... to confuse the two represents a violation of scientific thinking.[8]

As we have already mentioned, while it purports to be empirical, scientific enquiry is often highly subjective and value-laden and at times becomes more akin to a belief system itself. Paradigm shifts affect science in the same way they affect the social and philosophical impact of religious beliefs. In his influential book *The Structure of Scientific Revolutions*, philosopher Thomas Kuhn explains the dynamics which arise as one paradigm replaces another. Initially the dominant paradigm consolidates a body of scientific data, helps define various areas of research, provides methodology for experiments and also proposes acceptable criteria for evaluating the data collected. For a time the dominant paradigm will go unchallenged – and vocal critics may even be denounced as scientific heretics – but with time new data emerges which is incompatible with the prevailing view. Eventually an accumulation of such data challenges the prevailing paradigm and forces a revision of the dominant perspective. And so the process continues.

According to Kuhn, all scientific revolutions are paradigm shifts. In relation to the scientific study of human consciousness the quantum/transpersonal model, with its holistic implications, presents a clear challenge to the model of reductionist materialism which continues to prevail. Yet who can predict when a point of critical mass will be reached enabling the emergent paradigm to gain widespread currency? It is also true, as Ian Barbour points out in his interesting book *Myths, Models and Paradigms*, that while paradigms may help determine the way a scientist sees the world, it is also the case that scientists with rival paradigms may gather quite dissimilar sorts of data in order to support their own personal cause.[9] Hopefully, in the name of true science, the most complete ideas will triumph in the end.

Global Spirituality

Transpersonal and New Age approaches to the spiritual life extend beyond the familiar social context to the idea of the mythic or 'noetic' self – towards the idea that everyday life can encompass mythic and sacred realities. Today many sense a feeling of profound existential crisis, a fragmentation of both self and society, as the world's political situation becomes increasingly unstable. Many also feel that our inner core, the deep inner self of our being, is becoming ever harder to sustain. In shamanic terms it is as if we have become collectively 'dis-spirited' – we are suffering increasingly from a collective withdrawal of the human spirit – and our fractured world has begun to reflect this reality. As shamanic counselor and author Sandra Ingerman has observed: 'The planet is mirroring back to us our own soul loss'.[10]

The transpersonal solution to this global problem is to seek progress in incremental stages, from personal self-transformation through to the transformation of communities and whole societies, thereby moving gradually towards a broader international context. Aimed squarely against this holistic vision of human development are the enormous forces of wealthy transnational corporations and the maneuvering of long-established, self-interested organizations and economic blocs whose power impacts on human and global resources everywhere. Nevertheless the transpersonal movement encourages the personal drive towards physical, mental and spiritual self-empowerment despite the widespread feeling that the odds are increasingly stacked up in opposition.

A deep sense of the sacred and the mythic takes us, in human terms, beyond the realms of secular power towards the very ground of our being. As Jean Houston has written: 'When myths are actively pursued ... they can lead us from the personal-particular concerns and frustrations of our everyday lives to the personal-universal, with its capacity to broaden the context of our lives and our vision.'[11] In effect the transpersonal movement and the New Age are calling for a collective drive towards re-sacralizing the world and towards reaffirming the perennial wisdom principle that there is a spiritual basis to our human existence – a unifying mystical purpose which transcends the ebb and flow of secular power and influence. This is undoubtedly a global interpretation of spirituality, a necessary perspective if we are to embrace a holistic vision of our place and purpose on the planet. As Jean Houston affirms, and she says it as eloquently as anyone else in the international transpersonal movement,

This shift from the personal-particular to the personal-universal may well be a deep and essential requirement for an emerging planetary society. Otherwise, locked into our own experience and culture, we will have neither the passion for the possible nor the moral energy to co-create with others of different cultures and beliefs a world that works. We are now in the process of learning to see with our souls – combining our life's experience with our deepest archetypal knowings.[12]

It seems to me that the rise of the transpersonal movement and its New Age counterpart has lasting and challenging implications for religious belief and doctrinal orthodoxy in the West. The key message that emerges collectively from these movements is that we should all seek, in our own individual way, to become vision-aries ourselves, to explore every way possible of expanding our spiritual horizons. From the New Age perspective, each of us will find that sacred source in different ways. Some will embrace the sacred through the guidance of a guru, spiritual teacher or religious organization; others through meditation, shamanic practice or devotional prayer. Still others will tap that sacred source by wandering in wilderness regions, mountains or rainforests – thereby opening their hearts and souls to the rhythms and spirit of Nature.

In embracing the idea that there are many different, but nonetheless valid and authentic, paths to spiritual self-realization, the New Spirituality recognizes that teachings and practices which may open one person to the sacred and infinite may seem inappropriate to another. Nevertheless, the aim of attaining a state of Oneness with the sacred and unifying ground of being remains the ultimate goal of all mystical paths. The New Spirituality seeks to call all metaphysical and religious paths to account by urging us to ask questions like the following: Is the path I am following broad enough to embrace all aspects of body, mind and spirit that are part of my spiritual quest? Are my frameworks of 'reality' sufficiently broad and open-ended to allow the transcendent dimension to enter my life? Are the practices and teachings I am following essentially liberating or restrictive? Do they encourage inner personal growth and connectedness with others – thereby leading to powerful possibilities for social transformation – or do they perpetuate an outdated and restrictive belief system? These are questions that each of us will have to answer and resolve by ourselves.

We stand at a very interesting crossroads in spiritual history. The New Spirituality affirms that we should all have the opportunity to embrace the many and diverse approaches that lead towards spiritual self-realization and that this will lead inevitably towards new paradigms for human development. The main alternative is to retreat into the security of formal doctrinal belief systems that have persisted for centuries as explanations of the perceived relationship between humanity and God. A continuing problem with the latter solution is that many of these doctrinal concepts of God exclude the rights of outsiders and non-conformists – including those who have chosen to embrace the sacred in other ways or through other belief systems. Many doctrinal definitions of God are essentially tribal in nature, defining God in anthropomorphic terms as a deity who protects his chosen people and their territorial and religious borders, to the exclusion of others. However on this point we could well heed the insights of the Buddhist tradition which rejects any concept of a god who protects only one people and whose power stops at certain frontiers. As the Dalai Lama has observed, 'Whoever excludes others will find himself excluded in turn. Those who affirm that their god is the only God are doing something dangerous and pernicious because they are on the way to imposing their beliefs on others, by any means possible. And proclaiming themselves to be the chosen people is the worst of all.'[13]

Transpersonal perspectives emphasize that our belief systems should be reinforced by the ongoing personal experience of the deeper, inner realities. At the same time it is important to remember that any particular spiritual path is but one of many possibilities – an essential attitude if we are to have any hope of engendering feelings of religious tolerance in an increasingly polarized world. It is also crucial to translate beliefs and spiritual insights into practice. As Frances Vaughan has explained: 'We cannot just talk about spirituality; it needs to be an experiential realization. Enlightenment does not come simply from following the wisdom teachings. It comes from direct experience ... This work is also important in our emphasis on community, which translates intellectual work and personal transformation into community service.'[14]

In this present phase of our cultural history, perhaps for the first time on a wide scale in contemporary Western society, it has become possible to formulate our spiritual and developmental paradigms on the basis of what we have collectively experienced, rather than what we have simply hoped for or have been brought up to believe. Shared knowledge and cumulative experiential wisdom are likely to be the crucial determinants of the spiritual quest in the years that lie ahead.

Notes

Introduction

1. The Theosophical Society was founded in New York in 1875 by Madame Helena Blavatsky and Colonel Henry Olcott. One of its main objectives was to study world religions in order to understand the universal truths underlying all of the major spiritual traditions. It was also concerned with the development of the latent divine powers present in all human beings – see Chapter 1.

2. The term 'transpersonal' was adopted by Abraham Maslow and Stanislav Grof in 1967 as the most suitable name for the new 'fourth force' psychology then emerging from humanistic psychology. However the term itself had been used earlier by the Jungian philosopher Erich Neumann, as well as by Ira Progoff and Dane Rudhyar.

Chapter 1: Wisdom from the East, Wisdom from the West

1. Swedenborg, *Docs*.1, pp.35–36.
2. Swedenborg, *Arcana Coelestia*, para.68.
3. Swedenborg, TCR, para.202.
4. Wilson Van Dusen, *The Presence of Other Worlds*, Harper & Row, New York 1974, p.16.
5. See *Arcana Coelestia*, paras.904, 5470, 5848, 6189.
6. This observation anticipates the findings of many contemporary near-death experience (NDE) researchers. See Chapter 11.
7. Swedenborg, *Heaven and Hell*, para.495.
8. Swedenborg, TCR, para.763.
9. Swedenborg, AC, para.1285.
10. Swedenborg, AE, para.20.
11. Wilson Van Dusen, op. cit., p.222.
12. In a paper published in 1779 Mesmer stated that all the

heavenly bodies, the Earth and life on it, were interconnected. He believed that the common medium uniting these
natural forms was a magnetic fluid that was 'so continuous
as not to admit of a vacuum and incomparably subtle'.

13. For further details see Nevill Drury, *The Healing Power*,
Muller, London 1981, p.92.

14. Nandor Fodor, *An Encyclopaedia of Psychic Science*, Citadel
Press, New York 1974, p.240.

15. *The Memoirs of Count Witte*, translated from the original MS
and edited by A. Yarmolisky, London 1921.

16. John Symonds, 'Madame Blavatsky', *Man, Myth and Magic*,
vol.10, BPC Publishing, London 1970, p.286.

17. Colonel Olcott produced fifteen articles on the Eddy
brothers and the psychic phenomena at Chittenden and
these were subsequently published in book form as *People
from the Other World*, Tuttle, Boston 1972.

18. According to Peter Washington, Madame Blavatsky and
Colonel Olcott were never lovers but regarded each other as
'chums' – see Washington's fascinating and informative book
Madame Blavatsky's Baboon, Secker & Warburg, London 1993,
p.43.

19. Quoted in Jill Roe, *Beyond Belief: Theosophy in Australia
1879–1939*, University of New South Wales Press, Sydney
1986, p.1.

20. *Isis Unveiled*, 1972 edition, Theosophical Publishing House,
Wheaton, Illinois, vol. 1, p.xi.

21. See Jill Roe, *Beyond Belief: Theosophy in Australia 1879–1939*,
p.4.

22. Robert S. Ellwood points out in his book *Alternative Altars*
(1979, p.131) that Olcott is honored in Sri Lanka for his
contribution to Buddhism and has even been featured on a
local postage stamp.

23. Jill Roe, loc. cit., pp.4–5

24. Ibid, p.18.

25. This statement was published in the *Australian Herald*, October 1890, p.21. The newspaper itself was published by an eclectic, broad-based organization called the Australian Church which was sympathetic to Theosophy.

26. Christmas Humphreys, 'Helena Petrovna Blavatsky' in Colin Wilson (ed.), *Men of Mystery*, W.H. Allen, London 1977, p.58.

27. Vivekananda said of Ramakrishna, 'I learnt from my Master ... that the religions of the world ... are but various phases of one eternal religion.' See *Collected Works*, vol.4, p.180 – quoted in Andrew Rawlinson, *The Book of Enlightened Masters*, Open Court, Chicago and La Salle, Illinois 1997, p.596.

28. James Webb, *The Flight from Reason*, Macdonald, London 1971, p.40.

29. See Steven F. Walker, 'Vivekananda and American Occultism' in H. Kerr and C.L. Crow (eds.) *The Occult in America*, University of Illinois Press, Urbana and Chicago 1983, p.165.

30. Hal Bridges, *American Mysticism: From William James to Zen*, Harper & Row, New York 1971, p.73.

31. See Christopher Isherwood (ed.), *Vedanta for Modern Man*, Collier Books, New York 1962, p.442.

32. Hal Bridges, *American Mysticism: From William James to Zen*, op. cit., p.86.

33. Gerald Heard actively encouraged Esalen co-founders Michael Murphy and Richard Price to establish their new personal growth center.

34. Louis Pauwels, *Gurdjieff*, Samuel Weiser, New York 1972.

35. Quoted in P. Travers, 'Gurdjieff', *Man, Myth and Magic*, BPC Publishing, London 1970, vol. 42, p.1168.

36. Having separated from Gurdjieff in 1923, Ouspensky would later reject Gurdjieff's theories outright in 1931. Orage also formally rejected Gurdjieff in 1931.

37. Quoted in P.D. Ouspensky, *In Search of the Miraculous*,

Harcourt, Brace, New York 1949, p.297.

38. See P. Travers, op. cit., p.1189.

39. Ibid.

40. For further information on the enneagram, readers are referred to Kathleen Riordan's chapter, 'Gurdjieff', in Charles Tart (ed.), *Transpersonal Psychologies*, Harper & Row, New York 1975.

41. For further information on the enneagram, readers are referred to Kathleen Riordan's chapter, 'Gurdjieff', in Charles Tart (ed.), *Transpersonal Psychologies*, Harper & Row, New York 1975.

Chapter 2: Pioneers of the Psyche

1. William James, *Psychology: The Briefer Course*, Holt, New York 1892, p.1.

2. William James, *The Variety of Religious Experience*, New American Library, New York 1958, p.298 (first published 1902).

3. James always denied that he was himself a mystic and claimed he had never had a mystical experience. Nevertheless on 9 July 1898 he wrote a letter to his wife after hiking in the Adirondack Mountains. It was a clear, still night and while his companions lay sleeping, James entered a state of 'spiritual alertness' and then spent much of the night 'in the woods, where the streaming moonlight lit up things in a magical checkered play, and it seemed as if the Gods of all the nature-mythologies were holding an indescribable meeting in my breast with the moral Gods of the inner life ... It was one of the happiest lonesome nights of my existence, and I understand now what a poet is.' See Hal Bridges, *American Mysticism*, Harper & Row, New York 1971, p.13.

4. Quoted in Gardner Murphy and Robert Ballou (eds.), *William James on Psychical Research*, Viking, New York 1960,

p.324.

5. See Robert Galbreath, 'Explaining Modern Occultism' in H. Kerr and C.L. Crow (eds.), *The Occult in America*, University of Illinois Press, Urbana and Chicago 1983, p.317.

6. See Gardner Murphy and Robert O. Ballou (eds.), *William James on Psychical Research*, op. cit., pp. 44–45 and 46–47.

7. William James, *The Will to Believe and Other Essays in Popular Philosophy*, Longmans, Green & Co., New York 1902, p.232.

8. William James, *The Principles of Psychology*, vol.2, Dover, New York 1950, p.560 (first published 1890).

9. William James, *Talks to Teachers on Psychology and to Students on Some of Life's Ideals*, Holt, New York 1899, p.100 (republished by Dover, New York 1962) .

10. See J. Fadiman and R. Frager, *Personality and Personal Growth*, Harper & Row, New York 1976, p.201.

11. William James, *The Varieties of Religious Experience*, op. cit., p.391.

12. Carl Jung, *Memories, Dreams, Reflections*, Random House, New York 1989, pp. 168–169.

13. Ilham Dilman, *Freud and the Mind*, Blackwell, Oxford 1986, p.7.

14. See J. Fadiman and R. Frager, *Personality and Personal Growth*, op. cit., p.14.

15. Sigmund Freud, *New Introductory Lectures on Psychoanalysis*, vol.22, Norton, New York 1949, p.80.

16. J. Fadiman and R. Frager, *Personality and Personal Growth*, op. cit., p.20.

17. Ilham Dilman, *Freud and the Mind*, op. cit., p.125.

18. Frank J. Sulloway, *Freud: Biologist of the Mind*, Basic Books, New York 1979, p.338.

19. Sigmund Freud, *The Interpretation of Dreams*, standard edition, quoted in J. Fadiman and R. Frager, op. cit., p.21.

20. Carl Jung, *Memories, Dreams, Reflections*, Vintage Books, New York 1989, pp.155–156.

21. Ibid., pp.150–151.
22. Carl Jung, *Man and his Symbols*, Dell, New York 1968, p.13.
23. Ibid., pp.41–42.
24. Carl Jung, *Two Essays on Analytical Psychology*, Routledge & Kegan Paul, London 1928, p.68.
25. Quoted in William McGuire and R.F.C. Hull (eds.), *C.G. Jung Speaking*, Thames & Hudson, London 1978, p.348.
26. Carl Jung, *Memories, Dreams, Reflections*, op. cit., p.340.
27. Carl Jung, *Two Essays in Analytical Psychology*, op. cit., p.70
28. Ibid., pp.65–66.
29. Carl Jung, 'The Relations Between the Ego and the Unconscious', in *Two Essays on Analytical Psychology: Collected Works*, vol.7, 1928, p.175.
30. Carl Jung, 'The Relations Between the Ego and the Unconscious', op. cit., p.176.
31. David Tacey, *Jung and the New Age*, Brunner-Routledge, Hove, East Sussex 2000.
32. Readers are referred to Robert A. Johnson, *Owning Your Own Shadow: Understanding the Dark Side of the Psyche* and Susan Jeffers, *Face the Fear and Do it Anyway* (see Bibliography).
33. *Letters*, 1973, p.203.
34. Carl Jung, 'Spirit and Life' in *Contributions to Analytical Psychology*, Kegan Paul, Trench Trubner & Co., London 1928, p.78.
35. Quoted in Claire Dunne, *Carl Jung: Wounded Healer of the Soul*, Parabola Books, New York 2000, p.200.
36. Robert A. Segal, *The Gnostic Jung*, Routledge, London 1992, p.48.
37. Stephen Segaller and Merrill Berger, *Jung and the Wisdom of the Dream*, Weidenfeld and Nicolson, London 1989, p.179.
38. H.L. Ansbacher and R. Ansbacher (eds.), *The Individual Psychology of Alfred Adler*, Harper, New York 1956, p.104.
39. J. Fadiman and R. Frager, *Personality and Personal Growth*, op. cit., p.99.

40. H.L. Ansbacher and R. Ansbacher (eds.), *The Individual Psychology of Alfred Adler*, op. cit. p.177.

41. See J. Fadiman and R. Frager, *Personality and Personal Growth*, op. cit., p.99.

42. H.L. Ansbacher and R. Ansbacher (eds.), *Alfred Adler: Superiority and Social Interest: A Collection of Later Writings*, Viking, New York 1964, p.69.

Chapter 3: Towards the Transpersonal

1. J.B. Watson, 'Psychology as the behaviorist views it', *Psychological Review*, vol.20, New York 1913, p.158 et seq.

2. B.F. Skinner, *About Behaviorism*, Knopf, New York 1974, p.225.

3. Abraham Maslow, *Motivation and Personality*, Harper & Row, New York 1970, p.150.

4. Abraham Maslow, *The Further Reaches of Human Nature*, Viking, New York 1971, p.47.

5. Quoted in Anthony J. Sutich, 'The Emergence of the Transpersonal Orientation: A Personal Account', *Journal of Transpersonal Psychology*, vol.8, no.1, 1976, p.6.

6. Anthony J. Sutich, 'The Founding of Humanistic and Transpersonal Psychology: A Personal Account', PhD dissertation presented to the Humanistic Psycholology Institute, April 1976, p.22.

7. Ibid., p.23.

8. Ibid., p.29.

9. Ibid., p.35.

10. Ibid., p.45.

11. Ibid., pp.59–60.

12. Ibid., p.114.

13. Ibid., p.115.

14. Ibid., p.148.

15. Ibid., p.150.

16. Ibid., p.155.

17. Ibid., p.167.
18. Ibid., p.172.
19. Edward Hoffman, *The Right to be Human: A Biography of Abraham Maslow*, Tarcher, Los Angeles 1988, p.266.

Chapter 4: Esalen, Gestalt and Encounter

1. Edward Hoffman, *The Right to be Human: A Biography of Abraham Maslow*, Tarcher, Los Angeles 1988, pp.289–290.
2. Frederick S. Perls, *In and Out of the Garbage Pail*, The Real People Press, Moab, Utah 1969, p.115.
3. Quoted in Martin Shepard, *Fritz*, Saturday Review Press/E.P. Dutton, New York 1975, pp.8–9.
4. Frederick S. Perls, *In and Out of the Garbage Pail*, op. cit., p.272.
5. Quoted in M. Shepard, *Fritz*, op. cit., p.214.
6. Frederick S. Perls, *Gestalt Therapy Verbatim*, The Real People Press, Moab, Utah 1969, p.4.
7. Ibid., p.68.
8. William Schutz, *Joy: Expanding Human Awareness*, Grove Press, New York 1967, p.15.
9. The popular party drug 'ecstasy' is related to MDA.

Chapter 5: The Psychedelic Years

1. Aldous Huxley, 'Wings that Shape Men's Minds', *Saturday Evening Post*, New York, 18 October 1958, pp.111–113.
2. Alan Watts, *The Joyous Cosmology*, Vintage Books, New York 1962, p.1.
3. See Monica Furlong, *Genuine Fake: A Biography of Alan Watts*, Unwin Hyman, London 1987, pp.115–116.
4. Timothy Leary, *Flashbacks*, Tarcher, Los Angeles 1983, p.29.
5. Timothy Leary, *High Priest*, World Publishing, New York 1968, p.25.
6. Timothy Leary, *The Politics of Ecstasy*, Paladin, London 1970, p.112.

7. Ibid., p.131.
8. See W.T. Stace, *Mysticism and Philosophy*, Macmillan, London 1960.
9. Timothy Leary, *The Politics of Ecstasy*, op. cit., p.15.
10. Quoted in Gene Anthony, *The Summer of Love*, 1980, p.29.
11. Hunter S.Thompson, 'The "Hashbury" is the Capital of the Hippies' in *The Great Shark Hunt: Strange Tales from a Strange Time*, Summit Books, New York 1979, p.385.
12. Joe David Brown (ed.), *The Hippies*, Time-Life Books, New York 1967, pp.39–40.
13. See Peter O. Whitmer and Bruce Van Wyngarden, *Aquarius Revisited*, Macmillan, New York 1987, p.201.
14. The best-known and most vivid account of the Merry Pranksters is Tom Wolfe's bestselling book *The Electric Kool-Aid Acid Test* (see Bibliography).
15. Quoted in *The High Times Encyclopedia of Recreational Drugs*, Stonehill, New York 1978, p.145.
16. Quoted in Gene Anthony, *The Summer of Love*, op. cit., p.129.
17. Ibid., p.155
18. Ibid., p.156
19. Quoted in James Webb, *The Occult Establishment*, Richard Drew Publishing, Glasgow 1981, p 462.

Chapter 6: Maps for Inner Space

1. The *Bardo Thodol* is a Tibetan Buddhist text from the Nyingma or 'Old School', one of the four principal schools of Tibetan Buddhism. It was first committed to writing in the time of Padma Sambhava (8th century CE). Sambhava was the founder of Lamaism, or Tantric Buddhism – a form of Mahayana Buddhism.
2. Timothy Leary et al., *The Psychedelic Experience*, University Books, New York 1964, pp.47–49.
3. W.Y. Evans-Wentz (ed.), *The Tibetan Book of the Dead*, Oxford University Press, New York 1960, p.32.

4. For additional background information see John Lilly, *The Centre of the Cyclone*, Calder & Boyars, London 1973, and *The Human Biocomputer*, Abacus, London 1974.

5. Ichazo's *Psychology Today* interview is included in Sam Keen's anthology *Voices and Visions*, Harper & Row, New York 1976.

6. The Lilly/Ichazo model allows for comparisons with the *chakras* in Kundalini yoga and the *sephiroth* in the Jewish mystical Kabbalah, both of these latter systems conceiving of various symbolic 'energy' levels between normal waking consciousness and transcendental states of being.

7. See Francis Jeffrey and John C. Lilly, *John Lilly, So Far...*, Tarcher, Los Angeles 1990, p.172.

8. Ibid., p.272.

9. Interview with the author at the Esalen Institute, Big, Sur, California, December 1984.

10. See Stanislav Grof, *Realms of the Human Unconscious*, Viking, New York 1975, p.49 et seq.

11. Richard T. Tarnas, *LSD, Psychoanalysis and Spiritual Rebirth*, unpublished manuscript, Esalen Institute, Big Sur, California 1976, p.37.

12. Stanislav Grof, *Realms of the Human Unconscious*, op. cit., p.107.

13. See Stanislav Grof, *LSD Psychotherapy*, Hunter House, Pomona, California 1980, p.76 and also Stanislav Grof, *The Holotropic Mind*, HarperCollins, San Francisco 1992, pp.45–56.

14. See Grof, *Realms of the Human Unconscious*, op. cit., p.132.

15. Ibid., p.142.

16. See Stanislav Grof, 'Modern Consciousness Research and the Quest for a New Paradigm', *Re-Vision*, vol.2, no.1, Winter/Spring 1979, pp.42–43.

17. See Grof, 1992, loc. cit., p.83.

18. Ibid., p.84.

19. Interview with the author at Esalen Institute, Big Sur, December 1984.

Chapter 7: The Holistic Perspective

1. For interesting insights into the counterculture transition from psychedelics to Zen meditation see Rick Fields, 'A High History of Buddhism in America', in A.H. Badiner and A. Grey (eds.), *Zig Zag Zen: Buddhism and Psychedelics*, Chronicle Books, San Francisco 2002.

2. S. Miller et al., *Dimensions of Humanistic Medicine*, Institute for the Study of Humanistic Medicine, San Francisco 1975.

3. For further information readers are referred to multi-authored *The Holistic Health Lifebook*, compiled by the Berkeley Holistic Health Center, Stephen Greene Press, Lexington, Massachusetts 1984, and Shepherd Bliss (ed.), *The New Holistic Health Handbook*, Stephen Greene Press, Lexington, Massachusetts 1985. These sourcebooks provide an excellent overview of the holistic health paradigm that began to emerge during the 1970s.

4. See Hans Selye, 'Stress: The Basis of Illness', in Elliott M. Goldwag (ed.), *Inner Balance: The Power of Holistic Healing*, Prentice-Hall, Englewood Cliffs, New Jersey 1979 and Hans Selye, *The Stress of Life* (revised edition), McGraw-Hill, New York 1976.

5. Meyer Friedman and Ray H. Rosenman, *Type A Behavior and Your Heart*, Knopf, New York 1974.

6. Lawrence LeShan, *You Can Fight for Your Life*, Evans, New York 1977.

7. Carl Simonton and Stephanie Matthews-Simonton, 'Belief Systems and Management of the Emotional Aspects of Malignancy', in Shepherd Bliss (ed.), *The New Holistic Health Handbook*, Stephen Greene Press, Lexington, Massachusetts 1985, p. 210.

8. Carl and Stephanie Simonton, 'The Role of the Mind in

Cancer Therapy' in R.J. Carlson (ed.), *The Frontiers of Medicine*, Regnery, New York 1975. See also O.C. Simonton, S.M. Simonton and J. Creighton, *Getting Well Again*, Tarcher, Los Angeles 1978.

9. Candace Pert, *Molecules of Emotion*, Fireside/Simon & Schuster, New York 1997.

10. R. Wechsler, 'A New Paradigm: Mind Over Malady', *Discover* magazine, February 1987, p.59.

11. Quoted in W.W. Bartley, *Werner Erhard*, Clarkson Potter, New York 1978, p.74.

12. Reprinted in *New Age News*, vol.2, no.1, April 1988.

13. Ibid.

14. Interview with the author, Sydney, November 1988.

15. Ibid.

Chapter 8: Mystics and Metaphysicians

1. Reported in an article by Deborah Cameron, 'Satan and the Showgirl· The New Age under Fire', *Good Weekend*, Sydney, 11 March 1989, p.20.

2. Ibid.

3. In my capacity as the former manager of a leading New Age bookshop in Sydney, I was involved in arranging several in-store author promotions for a range of New Age writers, including Doreen Virtue. Dr Virtue recounted her tale of the interceding angel both in our bookshop, and later at a large public seminar. During the period when I worked in this New Age bookshop (December 2000–September 2002), Doreen Virtue shared equal billing with the Dalai Lama as the shop's two bestselling authors.

4. *Interface*, Boston, Fall 1997.

5. Readers interested in spiritual responses to our current global crisis may wish to peruse *A Way Forward: Spiritual Guidance for our Troubled Times*, which I co-authored with Anna Voigt, Red Wheel, Boston 2003.

6. Arthur C. Hastings, 'Channeling and Spiritual Teachings', in Charles T. Tart (ed.), *Body Mind Spirit: Exploring the Parapsychology of Spirituality*, Hampton Roads, Virginia 1997 and also Hastings' definitive study of channeling, *With the Tongues of Men and Angels* (1991) – see Bibliography.

7. Interview by Rachael Kohn, *The Spirit of Things*, ABC Radio National, Sydney, 19 January 2003.

8. *Southern Crossings*, Sydney, August 1985, p.7.

9. Mark Chipperfield, 'New Age Inc.', *The Australian Magazine*, Sydney, 10 December 1988.

10. Quoted in C. William Henderson, *Awakening: Ways to Psycho-spiritual Growth*, Prentice-Hall, Englewood Cliffs, New Jersey 1975, p.113.

11. Jacob Needleman, *The New Religions*, Pocket Books/Simon & Schuster, New York 1972, p.130.

12. Ibid., p.129.

13. See Daniel Cohen, *The New Believers: Young Religion in America*, Ballantine, New York 1976, p.78.

14. Christopher Magarey, 'Meditation: The Essence of Health', in Nevill Drury (ed.), *Inner Health*, Harper & Row, Sydney 1985, p.141.

15. Ibid., p.143.

16. John Cooper, 'Swami Muktananda and the Yoga of Power', in Nevill Drury (ed.), *Frontiers of Consciousness*, Greenhouse Publications, Melbourne 1975, p.138.

17. Interested readers are referred to the articles 'O Guru, Guru, Guru' by Lis Harris and 'The Secret Life of Swami Muktananda' by William Rodarmor, published on the website http://cyberpass.net/truth/secret.html. Rodarmor says wryly in his article that 'when crowds saw Muktananda step from a black limousine to a waiting Lear jet, it was clear that the diminutive, orange-robed Indian was an American-style success'.

18. Originally both Swami Chidvilasananda (Gurumayai) and

her brother Swami Nityananada were nominated to succeed Swami Muktananda after his death. After admitting to sexual transgressions and breaking his vow of celibacy, Swami Nityananada withdrew from the Siddha Yoga Foundation and it is now headed by Gurumayi alone.

19. Included in the media press-kit for Sri Chinmoy's tour of Australia and New Zealand, November–December 1987.
20. Ibid.
21. 'Ma Anand Sheela interview on Cable News Network', *The Rajneesh Times*, vol.3, no.5, 9 August 1985, p.4.
22. Krishnamurti was very much a figure of his times and was not averse to the material benefits of the Western lifestyle. He liked well-cut Savile Row suits and expensive shoes, and was also a very accomplished golfer – playing at a standard close to that of a professional.
23. Pupul Jayakar, *Krishnamurti: A Biography*, Harper & Row, San Francisco 1986, p.26.
24. See Nevill Drury and Gregory Tillett, *Other Temples, Other Gods: The Occult in Australia*, Methuen, Sydney 1980, p.24. The amphitheater was demolished in 1951.
25. Ibid.
26. Pupul Jayakar, *Krishnamurti: A Biography*, op. cit., p.85.
27. Ibid., p.88.
28. Ibid., pp.403–404.

Chapter 9: Spirit, Myth and Cosmos

1. Interview with Joseph Campbell (1971) included in Sam Keen (ed.), *Voices and Visions*, Harper & Row, New York 1976, p.73.
2. Ibid., p.72.
3. Sam Keen (ed.), *Voices and Visions*, op. cit., p.76.
4. Stephen and Robin Larsen, *A Fire in the Mind: The Life of Joseph Campbell*, Doubleday, New York 1991, pp.xix–xx.
5. Diane K. Osbon (ed.), *A Joseph Campbell Companion*,

HarperCollins, New York 1991, p.40.

6. Campbell was a close friend of Alan Watts and also encouraged Michael Murphy and Richard Price to establish the Esalen Institute. Watts and Campbell both lectured at Esalen on numerous occasions.

7. Richard Daab and Silma Smith, 'Midwife of the Possible: An Interview with Jean Houston', part 3, *Magical Blend*, Fall 1988, p.22.

8. Ibid., p.10.

9. Jean Houston, *The Hero and the Goddess*, Ballantine, New York 1992, p.7.

10. Ibid., p.13.

11. Jean Houston, *The Search for the Beloved: Journeys in Sacred Psychology*, Crucible, Wellingborough, UK 1990, p.13.

12. Jean Houston, *The Passion of Isis and Osiris: A Union of Two Souls*, Ballantine, New York 1995, p.6.

13. See Mirka Knaster, 'The Goddesses in Jean Shinoda Bolen', *East West*, March 1989, p.45. An interesting interview with Bolen is also included in Alexander Blair-Ewart, *Mindfire: Dialogues in the Other Future*, Somerville House, Toronto 1995.

14. Ibid., p.44

15. Jean Shinoda Bolen, *Gods in Everyman*, HarperCollins, New York 1989, p.287.

16. Interview with Mirka Knaster, loc. cit., p.73.

17. David Feinstein and Stanley Krippner, *Personal Mythology: The Psychology of Your Evolving Self*, Tarcher, Los Angeles 1988, p.231.

18. Joseph Campbell, *Myths to Live By*, Viking Press, New York 1972, p.104.

19. I have described the emergence of modern Western magic, Wicca and neo-shamanism in my book *Stealing Fire from Heaven: The Rise of Modern Western Magic*, Oxford University Press, New York 2011.

20. Naomi Goldenberg, *Changing of the Gods: Feminism and the End of Traditional Religions*, Beacon Press, Boston 1979.

21. See Mary Daly, *Gyn/Ecology: The Metaethics of Radical Feminism*, Beacon Press, Boston 1978, p.190.

22. See Mary Farrell Bednarowski and Barbara Starret, 'Women in Occult America', in Howard Kerr and Charles L. Crow (eds.), *The Occult in America: New Historical Perspectives*, University of Illinois Press, Urbana and Chicago 1983, p.190.

23. Judy Davis and Juanita Weaver, 'Dimensions of Spirituality', *Quest*, 1, 1975, p.2.

24. Starhawk, *The Spiral Dance*, Harper & Row, New York 1979.

25. Alexander Blair-Ewart, *Mindfire: Dialogues in the Other Future*, Somerville House, Toronto 1995, p.127.

26. Ibid., p.128.

27. Starhawk, 'The Goddess', in Roger S. Gottlieb (ed.), *A New Creation: America's Contemporary Spiritual Voices*, Crossroad, New York 1990, p.213.

28. For details of this intriguing situation see Andrei Znamenski, *The Beauty of the Primitive: Shamanism and the Western Imagination*, Oxford University Press, New York 2007.

29. Republished in S. Keen (ed.), *Voices and Visions*, Harper & Row, New York 1976.

30. See Znamenski, loc. cit., and also Richard de Mille's *Don Juan Papers: Further Castaneda Controversies*, Ross-Erikson, Santa Barbara 1980, for details of what many writers continue to believe was an academic scandal.

31. Andrei A. Znamenski, *The Beauty of the Primitive: Shamanism and the Western Imagination*, loc. cit., p.193.

32. Castaneda's first four books were his most influential: *The Teachings of Don Juan* (1968), *A Separate Reality* (1971), *Journey to Ixtlan* (1972) and *Tales of Power* (1974).

33. Sun Bear and Wabun, *The Medicine Wheel*, Prentice-Hall, Englewood Cliffs, New Jersey 1980, p.xiii.

34. Ron Boyer, 'The Vision Quest', *The Laughing Man*, vol.2, no.4, p.63.
35. Quoted in Joan Halifax (ed.), *Shamanic Voices*, Arkana, New York and London 1991, p. 68.
36. Quoted in Michele Jamal, *Shape Shifters*, Arkana, New York and London 1987, pp.89–90.
37. Ibid.
38. M. Harner, *The Way of the Shaman*, Harper & Row, San Francisco 1980, p.14.
39. According to shamanic tradition, when a person is 'dis-spirited' their animating force, or spirit, has departed. The role of the shaman is to retrieve it.
40. Personal communication during filming for the Cinetel Productions documentary *The Occult Experience*, New York, November 1984 – in which I was involved as interviewer. This documentary was screened in Australia by Channel 10 and released in the United States through Sony Home Video.
41. Quoted in Nevill Drury, *The Occult Experience*, Robert Hale, London 1987, p.145.
42. Ibid.

Chapter 10: Science and Spirituality

1. Peter Russell, *The Awakening Earth*, Ark Books, London 1982, p.12.
2. Sun Bear, 'Honoring Sacred Places', in Fredric Lehrman (ed.), *The Sacred Landscape*, Celestial Arts Publishing, Berkeley, California 1988, pp.139–140.
3. Anna Voigt and Nevill Drury, *Wisdom from the Earth: The Living Legacy of the Aboriginal Dreamtime*, Shambhala Publications, Boston 1998, p.66.
4. Ralph Metzner, 'Gaia's Alchemy: Ruin and Renewal of the Elements', in Fredric Lehrman (ed.), *The Sacred Landscape*, loc. cit., pp.118–119.
5. Ibid.

6. Rupert Sheldrake, 'Morphic Resonance', in Stanislav Grof (ed.), *Ancient Wisdom and Modern Science*, State University Press of New York, Albany 1984, p.49. See also Rupert Sheldrake, *A New Science of Life*, Tarcher, Los Angeles 1981, p.151.

7. Ibid.

8. Ibid., p.156.

9. Ibid., p.166.

10. Ronald Valle, 'Relativistic Quantum Psychology', in Ronald S.Valle and Rolf von Eckartsberg (eds.), *The Metaphors of Consciousness*, Plenum Press, New York 1981, p.424.

11. Danah Zohar, *The Quantum Self*, Flamingo/HarperCollins, London 1991, p.5.

12. Stanislav Grof (ed.), *Ancient Wisdom and Modern Science*, State University of New York Press, Albany 1984, p 10.

13. Fritjof Capra, *The Tao of Physics*, Shambhala Publications, Boulder, Colorado 1975, pp.56–57.

14. David Bohm, *Wholeness and the Implicate Order*, Routledge & Kegan Paul, London 1980, p.172.

15. David Bohm, 'A New Theory of the Relationship of Mind and Matter', in *The Journal of the American Society of Psychical Research*, 1986, vol.80, no.2, p.126.

16. June Singer, *Seeing Through the Visible World: Jung, Gnosis and Chaos*, HarperCollins, San Francisco 1980, p.66.

17. Gary Zukav, *The Dancing Wu Li Masters: An Overview of the New Physics*, Flamingo, London 1980, p.55.

18. Stanislav Grof (ed.), *Ancient Wisdom and Modern Science*, op. cit., p.9.

19. Danah Zohar, *The Quantum Self*, loc. cit., p.106.

20. Ibid., p.51.

21. Ibid., p.151.

22. Fritjof Capra, 'The New Vision of Reality', in S. Grof, *Ancient Wisdom and Modern Science*, op. cit., p.136.

23. See Catherine Ingram, 'Ken Wilber: The Pundit of

Transpersonal Psychology', *Yoga Journal*, September/October 1987, p.44.

24. Ken Wilber, 'Psychologia Perennis: The Spectrum of Consciousness', in Roger N. Walsh and Frances Vaughan (eds.), *Beyond Ego*, Tarcher, Los Angeles 1980, pp.74–75.

25. Ken Wilber, *The Spectrum of Consciousness*, Quest Books, Wheaton, Illinois 1977, p.241.

26. C.G. Jung, *Analytical Psychology: Its Theory and Practice*, Vintage Books, New York 1968, p.110.

27. Ken Wilber, *A Brief History of Everything*, Gill & Macmillan, Dublin 1996, p.214. See also Wilber's chapter, 'The Pre/Trans Fallacy', in his collection *Eye to Eye: The Quest for the New Paradigm*, Shambhala Publications, Boston 1988.

28. For further insights into this debate, readers are referred to the multi-authored volume *Ken Wilber in Dialogue*, edited by Donald Rothberg and Sean Kelly (Quest Books, Wheaton, Illinois 1998) – where both Wilber and Grof present their differing positions.

29. Ken Wilber, 'Psychologia Perennis: The Spectrum of Consciousness', in Roger N. Walsh and Frances Vaughan (eds.), *Beyond Ego*, loc. cit., p.83.

Chapter 11: The Challenge of Death

1. For well-written accounts of recent research into near-death experiences see Janice Miner Holden et al., *The Handbook of Near-Death Experiences: Thirty Years of Investigation*, Praeger, Santa Barbara, California 2009, Sam Parnia, *What Happens When We Die?*, Hay House, London 2008 and Pim van Lommel, *Consciousness Beyond Life: The Science of the Near-Death Experience*, HarperCollins, New York 2010..

2. Nevertheless, there are a significant number of historical cases that could also be considered as NDEs. Readers are referred to Carol Zaleski's fascinating book *Otherworld Journeys: Accounts of Near-Death Experience in Medieval and*

Modern Times, Oxford University Press, New York 1987.

3. Kenneth Ring, *Life at Death*, Coward McCann and Geoghegan, New York 1980, pp.96–97.
4. Michael Sabom, *Recollections of Death*, Corgi Books, London 1982, pp.70–71.
5. Susan Blackmore, 'Visions of the World Beyond', *The Australian*, 14 May 1988 (reprinted from *The New Scientist*).
6. Michael Sabom, op. cit., pp.70–71.
7. Kenneth Ring and Sharon Cooper, *Mindsight: Near-Death and Out-of-Body Experiences in the Blind*, William James Center for Consciousness Studies/Institute of Transpersonal Studies, Palo Alto, California 1999.
8. Kenneth Ring and Sharon Cooper, 'Mindsight: How the Blind can "see" during Near-Death Experiences', *The Anomalist*, no.5, Summer 1997, p.1.
9. Ibid., p.2.
10. Elisabeth Kubler-Ross, *On Life After Death*, Celestial Arts, Berkeley, California 1991, p.10
11. Ibid.
12. See interview with Elisabeth Kubler-Ross in Alexander Blair-Ewart (ed.), *Mindfire: Dialogues in the Other Future*, Somerville House, Toronto 1995, p.223.
13. Elisabeth Kubler-Ross, *On Life After Death*, loc. cit., pp.30–31.
14. Ibid., pp.60–61.
15. In addition to writing several scientific journal articles, which are posted on the University of Virginia website, Dr Baker is also the author of *Life Before Life: Children's Memories of Previous Lives*, St Martin's Press, New York 2005.
16. See Ian Stevenson, *Twenty Cases Suggestive of Reincarnation*, American Society for Psychical Research, New York 1966, pp.231–240 (reprinted by University of Virginia Press, Charlottesville, third edition 1995).
17. Ibid., p.233.
18. Tom Shroder, *Old Souls*, Simon & Schuster, New York 1999, p.33.

19. Jean-Noel Bassior, 'Astral Travel: An Interview with Robert Monroe', *New Age Journal*, November/December 1988, p.47.

20. Monroe felt at the time that too much emphasis had been placed in modern society on 'left hemisphere' brain functions like rational, verbal and analytic skills and not enough on 'right hemisphere' skills like non-verbal holistic learning.

21. Robert A. Monroe, *Ultimate Journey*, Doubleday, New York 1994, p.275.

22. For further information on ways of assisting the 'earth-bound spirits of the dead', readers are also referred to Terry and Natalia O'Sullivan, *Soul Rescuers*, Thorsons, London 1999.

23. Ibid., p.249.

24. F. Holmes Atwater, *Captain of My Ship, Master of My Soul*, Hampton Roads, Charlottesville, Virginia 2001, p.167.

25. See Kenneth Ring, *Heading Toward Omega*, Morrow, New York 1984, Cherie Sutherland, *Within the Light*, Bantam Books, Sydney and New York 1993, and Craig R. Lundahl and Harold A. Widdison, *The Eternal Journey*, Warner Books, New York 1997 – among many other books on near-death experiences.

26. Ibid., p.169.

27. See 'Journeys Beyond the Body: An Interview with Robert Monroe', in N. Drury, *The Visionary Human*, Element Books, Shaftesbury, Dorset 1991 (republished by Chrysalis/Vega Books, London 2002), p.127 et seq.

28. Ibid., p.129.

29. See Timothy Leary and R.U. Sirius, *Design for Dying*, HarperCollins, San Francisco 1997, p.99.

30. Ibid., p.132.

Chapter 12: The Future of the New Age

1. Frances Vaughan, 'The Transpersonal Perspective', in Stanislav Grof (ed.), *Ancient Wisdom and Modern Science*, State

University Press of New York, Albany 1984, p.25.

2. For a recent example of a largely dismissive Christian response to the New Age, readers are referred to David Tacey, *Jung and the New Age*, Brunner-Routledge, Hove, East Sussex 2001.

3. In his recent book *The End of Materialism*, psychologist Dr Charles Tart also emphasizes this idea, referring to the need for what he calls 'evidence-based' spirituality (Noetic Books/New Harbinger Publications, Oakland, California 2009).

4. From the *Kalamas Sutra*, cited in Seymour Boorstein (ed.), *Transpersonal Psychotherapy*, Science and Behavior Books, Palo Alto, California 1980, p.5.

5. John C. Lilly, *Simulations of God*, Simon and Schuster, New York 1975, p.157.

6. Charles T. Tart, *Open Mind, Discriminating Mind*, HarperCollins, San Francisco 1989, p.219.

7. Daniel C. Dennett, *Consciousness Explained*, Penguin Books, London 1993, p.33.

8. See Stanislav Grof (ed.), *Ancient Wisdom and Modern Science*, loc. cit., p.5.

9. Ian G. Barbour, *Myths, Models and Paradigms*, Harper & Row, New York 1976, p. 105.

10. Interview between Lynn Siprelle and Sandra Ingerman, *Grandmother Spider's Spirit Web*, published on the Internet on http://www.grandmother-spider.com/bookstore/ingerman.html

11. Jean Houston, *The Hero and the Goddess*, Ballantine, New York 1992, p.15.

12. Ibid., p.23.

13. Anna Voigt and Nevill Drury, *A Way Forward*, Red Wheel/Weiser, Boston 2003, p.120.

14. Frances Vaughan, 'The Transpersonal Perspective', in Stanislav Grof (ed.), *Ancient Wisdom and Modern Science*, op. cit., p.30.

Bibliography

Abdullah, S., 'Meditation: Achieving Internal Balance', in E. Goldwag (ed.), *Inner Balance*, Prentice-Hall, Englewood Cliffs, New Jersey 1979

Abraham, R., McKenna, T., and Sheldrake, R., *Trialogues at the Edge of the West: Chaos, Creativity and the Resacralization of the World*, Bear & Co., Santa Fe, New Mexico 1992

Achterberg, J., *Imagery in Healing*, Shambhala, Boston 1985

Anderson, W.T., *The Upstart Spring: Esalen and the American Awakening*, Addison Wesley, Reading, Massachusetts 1983

Ansbacher H.L., and Ansbacher, R., *The Individual Psychology of Alfred Adler*, Harper, New York 1956

Ansbacher, H.L., and Ansbacher, R. (eds.), *Alfred Adler: Superiority and Social Interest, a Collection of Later Writings*, Viking, New York 1964

Anthony, D., Ecker, B., and Wilber, K., *Spiritual Choices*, Paragon House, New York 1987

Anthony, G., *The Summer of Love: Haight-Ashbury at its Highest*, Celestial Arts, Berkeley, California 1980

Badiner, A.H., and Grey, A. (eds.), *Zig Zag Zen: Buddhism and Psychedelics*, Chronicle Books, San Francisco 2002

Barbour, I.G., *Myths, Models and Paradigms*, Harper & Row, New York 1976

Bartley, W.W., *Werner Erhard*, Clarkson Potter, New York 1978

Bays, B., *The Journey*, Fireside/Simon & Schuster, New York 2002

Bassior, J-N., 'Astral Travel: An Interview with Robert Monroe', *New Age Journal*, November/December 1988

Bednarowski, M.F., and Starret, B., 'Women in Occult America', in H. Kerr and C.L. Crow (eds.), *The Occult in America: New Historical Perspectives*, University of Illinois Press, Urbana and Chicago 1983

Benz, E., *Emanuel Swedenborg: Visionary Savant in the Age of Reason*,

Swedenborg Foundation, New York 2002

Bergquist, L., *Swedenborg's Secret: A Biography*, Swedenborg Society, London 2005

Berkeley Holistic Health Center, *The Holistic Health Lifebook*, Stephen Greene Press, Lexington, Massachusetts 1984

Bharati, A., *Light at the Center*, Ross-Erikson, Santa Barbara 1976

Blackmore, S., *Dying to Live: Science and the Near-Death Experience*, Grafton, London 1993

Blackmore, S., 'Visions of the World Beyond', *The Australian*, Sydney, 14 May 1988

Blair-Ewart, A. (ed.), *Mindfire: Dialogues in the Other Future*, Somerville House, Toronto 1995

Blavatsky, H.P., *Isis Unveiled*, Theosophical Publishing House, Wheaton, Illinois 1972 (first published: New York 1877)

Blavatsky, H.P., *The Key to Theosophy*, Theosophy Company, Bombay 1931 (first published: London 1889)

Blavatsky, H.P., *The Secret Doctrine* (vols.1 and 2), Theosophical University Press, Point Loma, California 1999 (first published: London 1888)

Bliss, S. (ed.), *The New Holistic Health Handbook*, Stephen Greene Press, Lexington, Massachusetts 1985

Boadella, D., *Wilhelm Reich: The Evolution of his Work*, Arkana, London 1985

Bohm, D., 'A New Theory of the Relationship of Mind and Matter', in *The Journal of the American Society of Psychical Research*, vol.80, no.2, 1986

Bohm, D., *Wholeness and the Implicate Order*, Routledge & Kegan Paul, London 1980

Bolen, J.S., *Goddesses in Everywoman*, Harper & Row, New York 1985

Bolen, J.S., *Gods in Everyman*, Harper & Row, New York 1989

Bolen, J.S., *The Tao of Psychology*, Harper & Row, New York 1979

Boorstein, S. (ed.), *Transpersonal Psychotherapy*, Science and Behavior Books, Palo Alto, California 1980

Boyer, R., 'The Vision Quest', *The Laughing Man*, vol.2, no.4

Bridges, H., *American Mysticism: From William James to Zen*, Harper & Row, New York 1970

Brown, J.D. (ed.), *The Hippies*, Time-Life Books, New York 1967

Brown, M., *The Spiritual Tourist: A Personal Odyssey through the Outer Reaches of Belief*, Bloomsbury, London 1998

Cameron, D., 'Satan and the Showgirl: The New Age Under Fire', in *Good Weekend*, Sydney, 11 March 1989

Campbell, J., *Myths to Live By*, Viking Press, New York 1972

Campbell, J., *The Hero with a Thousand Faces*, Princeton University Press, New Jersey 1972 (first published: Pantheon Books, New York 1949)

Campbell, J., *The Inner Reaches of Outer Space: Metaphor as Myth and as Religion*, Harper & Row, New York 1988

Capra, F., *The Tao of Physics*, Shambhala, Boulder, Colorado 1975

Capra, F., *The Turning Point*, Wildwood House, London 1982

Capra, F., *Uncommon Wisdom*, Simon & Schuster, New York 1988

Carlson, R.J. (ed.), *The Frontiers of Science and Medicine*, Regnery, New York 1975

Castaneda, C., *A Separate Reality*, Simon & Schuster, New York 1971

Castaneda, C., *Journey to Ixtlan*, Simon & Schuster, New York 1972

Castaneda, C., *Tales of Power*, Simon & Schuster, New York 1974

Castaneda, C., *The Active Side of Infinity*, HarperCollins, New York 1998

Castaneda, C., *The Teachings of Don Juan*, University of California Press, Berkeley 1968

Castaneda, C., *The Wheel of Time*, LA Eidolona Press, Los Angeles 1998

Chipperfield, M., 'New Age Inc.', *The Australian Magazine*, Sydney, 10 December 1988

Chopra, D., *How to Know God*, Rider, London 2000

Chopra, D., *The Seven Spiritual Laws of Success*, Amber-Allen Publishing, Novato, California 1995

Cohen, D., *The New Believers: Young Religion in America*, Ballantine, New York 1976

Combs, A., *The Radiance of Being: Complexity, Chaos and the Evolution of Consciousness*, Floris Books, Edinburgh 1995

Cooper, J., 'Swami Muktananda and the Yoga of Power', in N. Drury (ed.), *Frontiers of Consciousness*, Greenhouse Publications, Melbourne 1975

Daab, R., 'An Interview with Jean Houston', *Magical Blend*, issues 18, 19 and 20, Berkeley, California 1988

Daly, M., *Gyn/Ecology: The Metaethics of Radical Feminism*, Beacon Press, Boston 1978

Davis, J., and Weaver, J., 'Dimensions of Spirituality', *Quest*, 1:1975

Dennett, D.C., *Consciousness Explained*, Penguin Books, London 1993

Dilman, I., *Freud and the Mind*, Basil Blackwell, Oxford 1986

Drury, N., *Stealing Fire from Heaven: The Rise of Modern Western Magic*, Oxford University Press, New York 2011

Drury, N., *The Elements of Shamanism*, Element, Dorset 1989

Drury, N., *The Healing Power*, Muller, London 1981

Drury, N., *The Occult Experience*, Robert Hale, London 1987

Drury, N., *The Visionary Human: Mystical Consciousness and Paranormal Perspectives*, Chrysalis/Vega, London 2002

Drury, N., and Tillett, G., *Other Temples, Other Gods: The Occult in Australia*, Methuen, Sydney 1980

Drury, N. (ed.), *Frontiers of Consciousness*, Greenhouse Publications, Melbourne 1975

Drury, N. (ed.), *Inner Health*, Harper & Row, Sydney 1985

Drury, N. (ed.), *The Bodywork Book*, Harper & Row, Sydney 1984

Dunne, C., *Carl Jung: Wounded Healer of the Soul*, Parabola Books, New York 2000

Dyer, W., *Manifest Your Destiny*, HarperCollins, New York 1997

Dyer, W., *There's a Spiritual Solution to Every Problem*, HarperCollins, New York 2001

Dyer, W., *Your Sacred Self*, HarperCollins, New York 1995

Edinger, E., *Ego and Archetype*, Penguin, London 1973

Editors of *High Times* magazine, *The High Times Encyclopedia of Recreational Drugs*, Stonehill, New York 1978

Eliade, M., *Shamanism*, Princeton University Press, New Jersey 1972

Ellwood, R.S., *Alternative Altars: Unconventional and Eastern Spirituality in America*, University of Chicago Press, Chicago 1979

Evans-Wentz, W.Y. (ed.), *The Tibetan Book of the Dead*, Oxford University Press, New York 1960 (first published 1927)

Everett, A., interview with Alexander Everett, *Nature & Health*, Sydney September 1989

Fadiman, J., and Frager, R., *Personality and Personal Growth*, Harper & Row, New York 1976

Farrar, J. and S., *The Witches' Way*, Robert Hale, London 1987

Feinstein, D., and Krippner, S., *Personal Mythology: The Psychology of Your Evolving Self*, Tarcher, Los Angeles 1988

Fenwick, P. and E., *The Art of Dying*, Continuum, London and New York 2008

Ferguson, D.S. (ed.), *New Age Spirituality*, Westminster/John Knox Press, Louisville, Kentucky 1993

Ferguson, M., *The Aquarian Conspiracy*, Putnam, New York 1987

Fields, R., 'A High History of Buddhism in America', in A.H. Badiner and A. Grey (eds.), *Zig Zag Zen: Buddhism and Psychedelics*, Chronicle Books, San Francisco 2002

Fodor, N., *An Enyclopaedia of Psychic Science*, Citadel Press, Secaucus, New Jersey 1974 (first published 1934)

Freud, S., *New Introductory Lectures on Psychoanalysis*, Norton, New York 1949

Freud. S., *The Interpretation of Dreams*, Avon, New York 1967

Friedman, M., and Rosenman, R.H., *Type A Behavior and Your Heart*, Knopf, New York 1974

Furlong, M., *Genuine Fake: A Biography of Alan Watts*, Unwin

Hyman, London 1987

Gawain, S., *Creative Visualization*, Whatever Publishing, Mill Valley, California 1978

Getty, A., *A Sense of the Sacred*, Taylor Publishing, Dallas 1997

Glock, C.Y., and Bellah, R.N. (eds.), *The New Religious Consciousness*, University of California Press, Berkeley 1976

Goldenberg, N., *Changing of the Gods*, Beacon Press, Boston 1979

Goldwag, E. (ed.), *Inner Balance*, Prentice-Hall, Englewood Cliffs, New Jersey 1979

Goleman, D., *The Meditative Mind*, Tarcher, Los Angeles 1988

Goleman, D. (ed.), *Consciousness: Brain, States of Awareness and Mysticism*, Harper & Row, New York 1979

Gottlieb, R.S., *A New Creation: America's Contemporary Spiritual Voices*, Crossroad, New York 1990

Grey, M., *Return from Death: An Exploration of the Near-Death Experience*, Arkana, London 1985

Grof, S., *Beyond the Brain*, State University of New York Press, Albany 1985

Grof, S., *LSD Psychotherapy*, Hunter House, Pomona, California 1980

Grof, S., 'Modern Consciousness Research and the Quest for a New Paradigm', *Re-Vision*, vol.2, no.1, Winter/Spring 1979

Grof, S., *Realms of the Human Unconscious*, Viking, New York 1975

Grof, S., *The Cosmic Game*, State University of New York Press, Albany 1998

Grof, S., *The Holotropic Mind*, HarperCollins, San Francisco 1992

Grof. S., and Halifax, J., *The Human Encounter with Death*, Dutton, New York 1979

Grof, S. (ed.), *Ancient Wisdom and Modern Science*, State University Press of New York, Albany 1984

Grof, S. (ed.), *The Adventure of Self-Discovery*, State University of New York Press, Albany 1988

Grof. S., and Valier, M.L. (eds.), *Human Survival and Consciousness Evolution*, State University of New York Press, Albany 1988

Guiley, R.E., *Encyclopedia of Mystical and Paranormal Experience*, HarperCollins, New York 1991

Gurdjieff, G.I., *Beelzebub's Tales to his Grandson*, Dutton, New York 1973

Gurdjieff, G.I., *Life is Real Only Then, When 'I Am'*, Dutton, New York 1981

Gurdjieff, G.I., *Meetings with Remarkable Men*, Dutton, New York 1969

Hagon, Z., *Channelling*, Prism Press, Dorset 1989

Halifax, J. (ed.), *Shamanic Voices*, Arkana, New York and London 1991

Hanegraaff, W.J., *New Age Religion and Western Culture*, State University Press of New York, Albany 1998

Harner, M., *The Way of the Shaman*, Harper & Row, San Francisco 1980

Hastings, A., *With the Tongues of Men and Angels: A Study of Channeling*, Holt,

Hastings, A. (ed.), *Health for the Whole Person*, Bantam, New York 1981Rinehart and Winston, Fort Worth, Texas 1991

Haule, J.R., *Perils of the Soul: Ancient Wisdom and the New Age*, Weiser, York Beach, Maine 1999

Hay, L., *Heal Your Body*, Hay House, Carlsbad, California 1988

Hay, L., *You Can Heal Your Life*, Hay House, Carlsbad, California 1999

Heelas, P., *The New Age Movement*, Blackwell, Oxford 1996

Henderson, C.W., *Awakening: Ways to Psycho-spiritual Growth*, Prentice-Hall, Englewood Cliffs, New Jersey 1975

Hoffman, E., *The Right to be Human: A Biography of Abraham Maslow*, Tarcher, Los Angeles 1988

Holden, J.E., et al. (eds.), *The Handbook of Near-Death Experiences: Thirty Years of Investigation*, Praeger, Santa Barbara, California 2009

Houston, J., *A Mythic Life*, HarperCollins, San Francisco 1996

Houston, J., *A Passion for the Possible*, HarperCollins, San

Francisco 1997

Houston, J., 'Myth and Pathos in Sacred Psychology', *Dromenon*, vol.3, no.2, Spring 1981

Houston, J., *The Hero and the Goddess*, Ballantine, New York 1992

Houston, J., *The Passion of Isis and Osiris: A Union of Two Souls*, Ballantine, New York 1995

Houston, J., *The Possible Human*, Tarcher, Los Angeles 1986

Houston, J., *The Search for the Beloved: Journeys in Sacred Psychology*, Tarcher, Los Angeles 1987; Crucible, Wellingborough, UK 1990

Humphreys, C., 'Helena Petrovna Blavatsky', in C. Wilson (ed.), *Men of Mystery*, W.H. Allen, London 1977

Huxley, A., *Moksha: Writings on Psychedelics and the Visionary Experience*, Stonehill, New York 1977

Huxley, A., *The Doors of Perception/Heaven and Hell*, Penguin, London 1963

Huxley, A., *The Perennial Philosophy*, Chatto & Windus, London 1946

Huxley, A., 'Wings that Shape Men's Minds', *Saturday Evening Post*, New York, 18 October 1958

Ingerman, S., *Soul Retrieval*, HarperCollins, San Francisco 1991

Inglis, B., *Natural and Supernatural*, Prism Press, Dorset 1992

Inglis, B., *Trance: A Natural History of Altered States of Mind*, Grafton, London 1989

Ingram, C., 'Ken Wilber: The Pundit of Transpersonal Psychology', *Yoga Journal*, September/October 1987

Isherwood, C. (ed.), *Vedanta for Modern Man*, Collier Books, New York 1962

Jamal, M., *Shape Shifters*, Arkana, New York and London 1987

James, W., *Psychology: The Briefer Course*, Holt, New York 1892

James, W., *Talks to Teachers on Psychology and to Students on Some of Life's Ideals*, Holt, New York 1899 (republished by Dover, New York 1962)

James, W., *The Principles of Psychology*, vol.2, Dover, New York

1950 (first published 1890)

James, W., *The Variety of Religious Experience*, New American Library, New York 1958 (first published 1902)

James, W., *The Will to Believe and Other Essays in Popular Philosophy*, Longmans, Green & Co., New York 1902

Jayakar, P., *Krishnamurti: A Biography*, Harper & Row, San Francisco 1986

Jeffers, S., *Feel the Fear and Do it Anyway*, Fawcett, New York 1996

Jeffrey, F., and Lilly, J.C., *John Lilly, So Far...*, Tarcher, Los Angeles 1990

Johnson, R.A., *Owning Your Own Shadow: Understanding the Dark Side of the Psyche*, HarperCollins, New York 1992

Jung, C.G., *Analytical Psychology: Its Theory and Practice*, Vintage Books, New York 1968

Jung, C.G., *Man and his Symbols*, Dell, New York 1968

Jung, C.G., *Memories, Dreams, Reflections*, Random House, New York 1989 (first published 1961)

Jung, C.G., 'Spirit and Life', in *Contributions to Analytical Psychology*, Kegan Paul, Trench Trubner & Co., London 1928

Jung, C.G., *Symbols of Transformation*, Bollingen Foundation, New Jersey 1956

Jung, C.G., 'The Relations Between the Ego and the Unconscious', in *Two Essays on Analytical Psychology*, Routledge & Kegan Paul, London 1928

Jung, C.G., *Two Essays on Analytical Psychology*, Routledge & Kegan Paul, London 1928

Kalweit, H., *Dreamtime and Inner Space*, Shambhala, Boston 1988

Keen, S. (ed.), *Voices and Visions*, Harper & Row, New York 1976

Kelly, E.F., and Kelly, E.W. (eds.), *Irreducible Mind: Toward a Psychology for the 21st Century*, Rowman & Littlefield, Lanham, Maryland 2007

Kerr, H., and Crow, C.L. (eds.), *The Occult in America: New Historical Perspectives*, University of Illinois Press, Urbana and Chicago 1983

Knaster, M., 'The Goddesses in Jean Shinoda Bolen', *East West*, March 1989

Knight, J.Z., *A State of Mind*, Warner Books, New York 1987

Knight, J.Z., *Ramtha: The Mystery of Birth and Death*, JZK Inc., Yelm, Washington 2001

Koestler, A., and Smythies, J.R., *Beyond Reductionism*, Beacon Press, Boston 1969

Kripal, J.J., *Esalen: America and the Religion of No Religion*, University of Chicago Press, Chicago 2007

Krishnamurti, J., and Bohm, D., *The Ending of Time: Thirteen Dialogues*, Gollancz, London 1985

Kubler-Ross, E., *Death: The Final Stage of Growth*, Prentice-Hall, Englewood Cliffs, New Jersey 1975

Kubler-Ross, E., interview in A. Blair-Ewart (ed.), *Mindfire: Dialogues in the Other Future*, Somerville House, Toronto 1995

Kubler-Ross, E., *On Life After Death*, Celestial Arts, Berkeley, California 1991

Kuhn, T., *The Structure of Scientific Revolutions*, second edition, University of Chicago Press, Chicago 1970

Langley, N., *Edgar Cayce on Reincarnation*, Warner Books, New York 1988

Larsen, R. (ed.), *Emanuel Swedenborg: A Continuing Vision*, Swedenborg Foundation, New York 1988

Larsen, S., *The Shaman's Doorway*, Harper & Row, New York 1976

Larsen, S. and R., *A Fire in the Mind: The Life of Joseph Campbell*, Doubleday, New York 1991

Le Shan, L., *The Medium, the Mystic and the Physicist*, Viking, New York 1974

Le Shan, L., *You Can Fight for Your Life*, Evans, New York 1977

Leary, T., *Flashbacks*, Tarcher, Los Angeles 1983

Leary, T., *High Priest*, World Publishing, New York 1968

Leary, T., *The Politics of Ecstasy*, Paladin, London 1970

Leary, T., et al., *The Psychedelic Experience*, University Books, New York 1964

Leary, T., and Sirius, R.U., *Design for Dying*, HarperCollins, San Francisco 1997

Lehrman, F. (ed.), *The Sacred Landscape*, Celestial Arts, Berkeley, California 1988

Lewis, J.R., and Melton, J.G. (eds.), *Perspectives on the New Age*, State University Press of New York, Albany 1992

Lilly, J.C., *Simulations of God*, Simon and Schuster, New York 1975

Lilly, J.C., *The Centre of the Cyclone*, Calder and Boyars, London 1973

Lilly, J.C., *The Human Biocomputer*, Abacus, London 1974

Lovelock, J., *Gaia: A New Look at Life on Earth*, Oxford University Press, London and New York 1979

Lowrey, R., *Dominance, Self-esteem, Self-actualization*, Brooks Cole, Monterey, California 1973

Lundahl C.R., and Widdison, H.A., *The Eternal Journey*, Warner Books, New York 1997

Luton, L., 'Reichian and Neo-Reichian Therapy', in N. Drury (ed.), *The Bodywork Book*, Harper & Row, Sydney 1984

MacLaine, S., *Don't Fall off the Mountain*, Vintage, New York 1971

MacLaine, S., *Going Within*, Bantam, New York 1991

MacLaine, S., *You Can Get There From Here*, Bantam, New York 1976

Magarey, C., 'Meditation: The Essence of Health', in N. Drury (ed.), *Inner Health*, Harper & Row, Sydney 1985

Maltz, M., *Psycho-Cybernetics*, Pocket Books, New York 1966

Maslow, A., *Motivation and Personality*, Harper & Row, New York 1970

Maslow, A., *The Further Reaches of Human Nature*, Viking, New York 1971

Maslow, A., *Toward a Psychology of Being*, Van Nostrand, New York 1968

Masters, R., and Houston J., *The Varieties of Psychedelic Experience*, Holt Rinehart and Winston, New York 1966

McGuire, W., and Hull, R.F.C. (eds.), *C.G. Jung Speaking*, Thames

& Hudson, London 1978

Meade, M., *Madame Blavatsky: The Woman Behind the Myth*, Putnam, New York 1980

Medicine Eagle, B., *The Last Ghost Dance: A Guide for Earth Mages*, Ballantine, New York 2000

Medicine Eagle, B., *Buffalo Woman Comes Singing*, Ballantine, New York 1991

Mehta, G., *Karma Cola: Marketing the Mystic East*, Jonathan Cape, London 1980

Metzner, R., 'Gaia's Alchemy: Ruin and Renewal of the Elements', in F. Lehrman (ed.), *The Sacred Landscape*, Celestial Arts, Berkeley, California 1988

Metzner, R., *Maps of Consciousness*, Collier Macmillan, New York 1971

Metzner, R., *Opening to Inner Light*, Century, London 1987

Metzner, R., *The Ecstatic Adventure*, Macmillan, New York 1968

Metzner, R., *The Unfolding Self: Varieties of Transformative Experience*, Origin Press, Novato, California 1998

Miller S., et al., *Dimensions of Humanistic Medicine*, Institute for the Study of Humanistic Medicine, San Francisco 1975

Millikan, D., and Drury, N., *Worlds Apart? Christianity and the New Age*, Australian Broadcasting Corporation, Sydney 1991

Monroe, R.A., *Far Journeys*, Doubleday, New York 1985

Monroe, R.A., *Journeys out of the Body*, Doubleday, New York 1971

Monroe, R.A., *Ultimate Journey*, Doubleday, New York 1994

Moody, R., *Life After Life*, Bantam Books, New York 1978

Mumford, J., *Ecstasy Through Tantra*, Llewellyn, St Paul, Minnesota 1988

Mumford, J., *A Chakra and Kundalini Workbook*, Llewellyn, St Paul, Minnesota 1994

Murphy, G., and Ballou, R. (eds.), *William James on Psychical Research*, Viking, New York 1960

Murphy, G., *An Historical Introduction to Modern Psychology*, Routledge & Kegan Paul, London 1967

Myss, C., *Anatomy of the Spirit*, Random House, New York 1997

Naranjo, C., *The One Quest*, Wildwood House, London 1974

Needleman, J., *The New Religions*, Pocket Books/Simon & Schuster, New York 1972

Neher, A., *The Psychology of Transcendence*, Prentice-Hall, Englewood Cliffs, New Jersey 1980

Olcott, H.S., *People from the Other World*, Tuttle, Boston 1972

Ornstein, R., *The Psychology of Consciousness*, Jonathan Cape, London 1975

Osbon, D.K. (ed.), *A Joseph Campbell Companion*, HarperCollins, New York 1991

Osis, K., *Deathbed Observations of Physicians and Nurses*, Parapsychology Foundation, New York 1961

Osis, K., and Haraldsson, E., *At the Hour of Death*, Avon, New York 1977

O'Sullivan, T. and N., *Soul Rescuers*, Thorsons, London 1999

Ouspensky, P.D., *In Search of the Miraculous*, Harcourt, Brace, New York 1949

Parnia, S., *What Happens When We Die?* Hay House, London 2008

Pauwels, L., *Gurdjieff*, Weiser, New York 1972

Pelletier, K., *Holistic Medicine*, Delta Books, New York 1979

Perls, F.S., *Gestalt Therapy Verbatim*, Real People Press, Moab, Utah 1969

Perls, F.S., *In and Out of the Garbage Pail*, Real People Press, Moab, Utah 1969

Pert, C., *Molecules of Emotion*, Simon & Schuster, New York 1997

Peters, T., *The Cosmic Self*, HarperCollins, San Francisco 1991

Ram Dass, *Be Here Now*, Lama Foundation/Crown, New York 1971

Ram Dass, *Doing Your Own Being*, Spearman, London 1973

Ram Dass, *Grist for the Mill*, Bantam, New York 1979

Ram Dass, *Still Here*, Riverhead, New York 2000

Ram Dass, *The Only Dance There Is*, Doubleday, New York 1974

Rawlinson, A., *The Book of Enlightened Masters: Western Teachers in*

Eastern Traditions, Open Court, La Salle and Chicago 1997

Robbins, A., *Awakening the Giant Within*, Fireside/Simon & Schuster, New York 1992

Robbins, A., *Notes from a Friend*, Fireside/Simon & Schuster, New York 1995

Ring, K., *Heading Toward Omega*, Morrow, New York 1984

Ring, K., *Life at Death: A Scientific Investigation of the Near-Death Experience*, Coward McCann & Geoghegan, New York 1980

Ring, K., and Cooper, S., 'Mindsight: How the Blind can "see" during Near-Death Experiences', *The Anomalist*, no.5, Summer 1997

Ring, K., and Cooper, S., *Mindsight: Near-Death and Out-of-Body Experiences in the Blind*, William James Center for Consciousness Studies/Institute of Transpersonal Studies, Palo Alto, California 1999

Ring, K., and Valarino, E.E., *Lessons from the Light: What We Can Learn from the Near-Death Experience*, Plenum, New York 1998

Riordan, K., 'Gurdjieff', in C. Tart (ed.), *Transpersonal Psychologies*, Harper & Row, New York 1975

Roberts, J., *Seth Speaks*, Amber-Allen, Novato, California 1994

Roe, J., *Beyond Belief: Theosophy in Australia 1879–1939*, University of New South Wales Press, Sydney 1986

Rogers, C., *Carl Rogers on Encounter Groups*, Harper & Row, New York 1970

Rogo, D.S., *The Return from Silence: A Study of the Near-Death Experience*, Aquarian Press, Wellingborough, UK 1989

Rosen, E.J. (ed.), *Experiencing the Soul*, Hay House, Carlsbad, California 1998

Rossman, M., *New Age Blues: On the Politics of Consciousness*, Dutton, New York 1979

Roszak, T., *The Making of a Counter Culture*, Faber, London 1970

Roszak, T., *Unfinished Animal: The Aquarian Frontier and the Evolution of Consciousness*, Harper & Row, New York 1975

Rothberg, D., and Kelly, S. (eds.), *Ken Wilber in Dialogue*, Quest

Books, Wheaton, Illinois 1998

Russell, P., *The Awakening Earth*, Ark/Routledge & Kegan Paul, London 1982

Schucman, H., *A Course in Miracles*, Foundation for Inner Peace, second edition, New York 1976

Schutz, W., *Here Comes Everybody*, Harper & Row, New York 1971

Schutz, W., *Joy: Expanding Human Awareness*, Grove Press, New York 1967

Segal, R.A., *Joseph Campbell: An Introduction*, revised edition, Mentor Books, New York 1990

Segal, R.A., *The Gnostic Jung*, Routledge, London 1992

Segaller, S., and Berger, M., *Jung and the Wisdom of the Dream*, Weidenfeld and Nicolson, London 1989

Selye, H., 'Stress: The Basis of Illness', in E.M. Goldwag (ed.), *Inner Balance: The Power of Holistic Healing*, Prentice-Hall, Englewood Cliffs, New Jersey 1979

Selye, H., *Stress Without Distress*, Dutton, New York 1974

Selye, H., *The Stress of Life*, revised edition, McGraw-Hill, New York 1976

Shapiro, E. and D. (eds.), *The Way Ahead: How Will We Live in the New Millennium?* Element Books, Shaftesbury, Dorset 1992

Sheldrake, R., *A New Science of Life*, Tarcher, Los Angeles 1981

Sheldrake, R., 'Morphic Resonance', in S. Grof (ed.), *Ancient Wisdom and Modern Science*, State University Press of New York, Albany 1984

Sheldrake, R., *The Presence of the Past*, Park Street Press, Rochester, Vermont 1995

Shepard, M., *Fritz*, Dutton/Saturday Review Press, New York 1975

Shroder, T., *Old Souls*, Simon & Schuster, New York 1999

Simonton, C., and Matthews-Simonton, S., 'Belief Systems and Management of the Emotional Aspects of Malignancy', in S. Bliss (ed.), *The New Holistic Health Handbook*, Stephen Greene Press, Lexington, Massachusetts 1985

Simonton, C. and S., *Getting Well Again*, Tarcher, Los Angeles 1978

Simonton, C. and S., 'The Role of the Mind in Cancer Therapy', in R.J. Carlson (ed.), *The Frontiers of Science and Medicine*, Regnery, New York 1975

Singer, J., *Seeing Through the Visible World: Jung, Gnosis and Chaos*, HarperCollins, San Francisco 1990

Skinner, B.F., *About Behaviorism*, Knopf, New York 1974

Spangler, D., 'The New Age: The Movement Towards the Divine', in Ferguson, D.S. (ed.), *New Age Spirituality*, Westminster/John Knox Press, Louisville, Kentucky 1993

Spence, L., *An Enyclopaedia of Occultism*, University Books, New York 1960 (first edition London 1920)

Stace, W.T., *Mysticism and Philosophy*, Macmillan, London 1960

Starhawk, 'The Goddess', in R.S. Gottlieb (ed.), *A New Creation: America's Contemporary Spiritual Voices*, Crossroad, New York 1990

Starhawk, *The Spiral Dance*, Harper & Row, New York 1979

Stevens, J., *Storming Heaven: LSD and the American Dream*, Atlantic Monthly Press, New York 1987

Stevenson, I., *Twenty Cases Suggestive of Reincarnation*, American Society for Psychical Research, New York 1966 (reprinted by University of Virginia Press, Charlottesville, third edition 1995)

Stockton, E., *The Aboriginal Gift*, Millennium Books, Sydney 1996

Storm, R., *The Search for Heaven on Earth*, Bloomsbury, London 1991

Strelley, K., *The Ultimate Game: The Rise and Fall of Bhagwan Shree Rajneesh*, Harper & Row, San Francisco 1987

Sulloway, F.J., *Freud: Biologist of the Mind*, Basic Books, New York 1979

Sun Bear, 'Honoring Sacred Places', in F. Lehrman (ed.), *The Sacred Landscape*, Celestial Arts Publishing, Berkeley, California 1988

Sun Bear and Wabun, *The Medicine Wheel*, Prentice-Hall, Englewood Cliffs, New Jersey 1980

Sutherland, C., *Transformed by the Light: Life After Near-Death Experiences*, Bantam Books, Sydney and New York 1992

Sutherland, C., *Within the Light*, Bantam Books, Sydney and New York 1993

Sutich, A.J., 'The Emergence of the Transpersonal Orientation: A Personal Account', *Journal of Transpersonal Psychology*, vol.8, no.1, 1976

Sutich, A.J., 'The Founding of Humanistic and Transpersonal Psychology: A Personal Account', doctoral dissertation presented to the Humanistic Psycholology Institute, San Francisco, April 1976

Swedenborg, E., *Apocalypse Explained*, Swedenborg Foundation, New York 1996 (first published 1785–89)

Swedenborg, E., *Arcana Coelestia, The Heavenly Arcana*, Swedenborg Foundation, New York 1995 (first published 1749–56)

Swedenborg, E., *Heaven and Hell*, Swedenborg Foundation, New York 1976 (first published 1758)

Swedenborg, E., *True Christian Religion*, Swedenborg Foundation, New York 1997 (first published 1771)

Symonds, J., *In the Astral Light: The Life of Madame Blavatsky – Medium and Magician*, Panther, London 1965

Symonds, J., 'Madame Blavatsky', *Man, Myth and Magic*, vol. 10, BPC Publishing, London 1970

Tacey, D., *Jung and the New Age*, Brunner-Routledge, Hove, East Sussex 2001

Tafel, R.L., *Documents Concerning the Life and Character of Emanuel Swedenborg* (three vols.), Swedenborg Society, London 1890

Talbot, M., *The Holographic Universe*, HarperCollins, New York 1991

Tarnas, R.T., *LSD, Psychoanalysis and Spiritual Rebirth*, unpublished manuscript, Esalen Institute, Big Sur, California 1976

Tart, C., *Open Mind, Discriminating Mind*, HarperCollins, San Francisco 1989

Tart, C., *The End of Materialism: How Evidence of the Paranormal is Bringing Science and Spirit Together*, Noetic Books/New Harbinger Publications, Oakland, California 2009

Tart, C. (ed.), *Altered States of Consciousness*, Wiley, New York 1969

Tart, C. (ed.), *Body Mind Spirit: Exploring the Parapsychology of Spirituality*, Hampton Roads, Charlottesville, Virginia 1997

Tart, C. (ed.), *Transpersonal Psychologies*, Harper & Row, New York 1975

Thompson, G., *Mind Body Spirit Internet Guide*, Thorsons, London 2001

Thompson, H.S., 'The "Hashbury" is the Capital of the Hippies', in *The Great Shark Hunt: Strange Tales from a Strange Time*, Summit Books, New York 1979

Tillett, G., *The Elder Brother: A Biography of Charles Webster Leadbeater*, Routledge & Kegan Paul, London 1982

Travers, P., 'Gurdjieff', *Man, Myth and Magic*, vol.42, BPC Publishing, London 1970

Trenoweth, S., *The Future of God: Personal Adventures in Spirituality with Thirteen of Today's Eminent Thinkers*, Millennium, Sydney 1995

Tucker, J.B., *Life Before Life: Children's Memories of Previous Lives*, St Martin's Press, New York 2005

Valarino, E.E., *On the Other Side of Life: Exploring the Phenomenon of the Near-Death Experience*, Plenum, New York 1997

Valle, R.S., 'Relativistic Quantum Psychology', in R.S. Valle and R. von Eckartsberg (eds.), *The Metaphors of Consciousness*, Plenum, New York 1981

Valle, R.S., and von Eckartsberg, R. (eds.), *The Metaphors of Consciousness*, Plenum, New York 1981

Van Dusen, W., *The Presence of Other Worlds*, Harper & Row, New York 1974

Van Dusen, W., *The Presence of Spirits in Madness*, Swedenborg Foundation, New York 1983

Van Lommel, P., *Consciousness Beyond Life: The Science of the Near-Death Experience*, HarperCollins, New York 2010

Vaughan, F., 'The Transpersonal Perspective', in S. Grof (ed.), *Ancient Wisdom and Modern Science*, State University Press of New York, Albany 1984

Vernon, R., *Star in the East: Krishnamurti, the Invention of a Messiah*, St Martin's Press, New York 2001

Virtue, D., *Angel Visions*, Hay House, Carlsbad, California 2000

Virtue, D., *Divine Guidance*, Renaissance Books, Los Angeles 1999

Virtue, D., *Healing with the Angels*, Hay House, Carlsbad, California 1999

Voigt, A., and Drury, N., *A Way Forward: Spiritual Guidance for our Troubled Times*, Red Wheel/Weiser, Boston 2003

Voigt, A., and Drury, N., *Wisdom from the Earth: The Living Legacy of the Aboriginal Dreamtime*, Shambhala, Boston 1998

Walsch, N.D., *Communion with God*, Berkley, New York 2000

Walsch, N.D., *Conversations with God (Book One)*, Putnam, New York 1999

Walsh, R.N., and Vaughan, F. (eds.), *Beyond Ego*, Tarcher, Los Angeles 1980

Washington, P., *Madame Blavatsky's Baboon*, Secker & Warburg, London 1993 (American edition: Schocken Books, New York 1995)

Watson, J.B., 'Psychology as the Behaviorist views it', *Psychological Review*, vol.20, New York 1913

Watts, A., *The Joyous Cosmology*, Vintage Books, New York 1962

Watts, A., *This is It and Other Essays on Zen and Spiritual Experience*, Pantheon, New York 1960

Webb, J., *The Flight from Reason*, Macdonald, London 1971

Webb, J., *The Harmonious Circle: The Lives and Work of G.I. Gurdjieff, P.D. Ouspensky, and their Followers*, Thames & Hudson, London 1980 (American edition: Putnam, New York

1980)

Webb, J., *The Occult Establishment*, Richard Drew Publishing, Glasgow 1981 (American edition: Open Court, La Salle, Illinois 1976)

Wechsler, R., 'A New Paradigm: Mind over Malady', *Discover* magazine, February 1987

White, J. (ed.), *What is Enlightenment?*, Paragon House, New York 1995

White, J. (ed.), *The Highest State of Consciousness*, Doubleday Anchor, New York 1972

Whitmer, P.O., and Van Wyngarden, B., *Aquarius Revisited*, Macmillan, New York 1987

Wilber, K., *A Brief History of Everything*, Gill & Macmillan, Dublin 1996

Wilber, K., *No Boundary*, Center Publications, Los Angeles 1979

Wilber, K., 'Psychologia Perennis: The Spectrum of Consciousness', in R.N. Walsh, and F. Vaughan (eds.), *Beyond Ego*, Tarcher, Los Angeles 1980

Wilber, K., *The Atman Project*, Quest Books, Wheaton, Illinois 1980

Wilber, K., *The Spectrum of Consciousness*, Quest Books, Wheaton, Illinois 1977

Wilber, K., *Up from Eden*, Doubleday Anchor, New York 1981

Wilber, K. (ed.), *The Holographic Paradigm and Other Paradoxes*, Shambhala, Boston 1985

Wilson, C. (ed.), *Men of Mystery*, W.H. Allen, London 1977

Wolfe, T., *The Electric Kool-Aid Acid Test*, Farrar, Straus & Giroux, New York 1968

Woods, R. (ed.), *Understanding Mysticism*, Image Books/Doubleday, New York 1980

Zaleski, C., *Otherworld Journeys*, Oxford University Press, New York 1987

Zaretsky, I.I., and Leone, M.P. (eds.), *Religious Movements in Contemporary America*, Princeton University Press, New

Jersey 1974

Znamenski, A.A., *The Beauty of the Primitive: Shamanism and the Western Imagination*, Oxford University Press, New York 2007

Zohar, D., *The Quantum Self*, Flamingo/HarperCollins, London 1991

Zohar, D., and Marshall, I., *SQ: Spiritual Intelligence*, Bloomsbury, London 2000

Zukav, G., *The Dancing Wu Li Masters: An Overview of the New Physics*, Morrow, New York 1979

Index

A Course in Miracles, 156
Adler, Alfred, 61-64
Alpert, Richard, 97,117, 121-122
altered states of consciousness, 181
angel therapy (Virtue), 154
anti-Vietnam War demonstrators, 107
archetypes, 56-57, 58, 60, 174, 176, 177, 178, 179-180, 215
AricaTraining, 43,126-127, 129
Arya Samaj, 27
Atlantis, 159
'attention' (Krishnamurti), 173
Atwater, F Holmes, 249
ayurvedic medicine, 153

Bailly, Jean-Sylvain, 19
Baker, Jim, 232
Bays, Brandon, 152
Bear Tribe, 189-190
Beatles, The, 163, 165
Beat Poets, 96
Bednarowski, Mary, Farrell, 183
Behaviorism, 69, 74
belief systems, 239, 241, 244, 245, 246-247, 248, 252
Bennett, J. G., 35
Bertrand, Alexandre, 21-22
Besant, Annie, 172

birthmarks, significance of, 233-234
Blackmore, Susan, 223
Blair-Ewart, Alexander, 184
Blavatsky, H. P., 7, 22-32, 171
blind near-death subjects, 226-227
body armor (Reich), 64
bodywork, Reichian, 65-67
Bohm, David, 206-207
Bolen, Jean Shinoda, 4, 179-180, 216
Braun, Gerhart, 98
Bridges, Hal, 34
Browne, Sylvia, 156
Buddha consciousness, 128
Buddha, Gautama, 244-245
Buddhism, 27, 32, 92
Buddhism, Tibetan, 213
Buddhism, Zen, 95-96
Burroughs, William, 102

Campbell, Joseph, 3, 7, 174-176, 182, 216
Cannon, Dolores, 156
Capra, Fritjof, 4, 206, 208, 212
Castaneda, Carlos, 90, 186-188
Cayce, Edgar, 157, 158-160
Channeling, 156-157
Chidvilasananda, Swami, 168
Chinmoy, Sri, 168-169

Chipperfield, Mark, 162
Chopra, Deepak, 152-153
Christ, Jesus, 178, 221
Christ consciousness,128, 132
Christianity, 1, 8
collective unconscious (Jung),
    54, 55, 56, 208, 215
Communications with God
    (Walsch), 152, 157
Cooper, John, 167
Cooper, Sharon, 226, 227
core shamanism (Harner), 198
Coulomb, Emma, 29
Creationism, 8, 244
Creative Visualization (Gawain),
    147-148
creative visualisation, 47
crystals, healing with, 161-162
cybernetics (Wiener), 145

D' Eslon, Charles, 18, 19, 21
Dalai Lama, 252
Daly, Mary, 183
Danforth, William H., 144
Dass, Ram, 121-122, 125
David Greenwood case
    (Cayce), 159
death, 217, 218-219, 220, 224,
    229-231, 239, 241-242
death-bed experiences, 220
Deleuze, Jean Philippe, 21
Dennett, Daniel C., 247
depersonalization (Noyes and
    Kletti), 224

Descartes, René, 204
Dilman, Ilham, 51
dreams, 51, 52, 53, 54, 56,181
dream-work, 52
drugs, anaesthetic, 223
Dyer, Wayne, 152,154

ecocide, 201
Eddy, Horatio, 23
Eddy, William, 23
Edward, John, 156
encounter groups, 43, 87
enlightenment, 165, 252
Esalen Institute, 35, 76, 79, 80,
    81-93
est (Erhard Seminars Training),
    39, 43
Everett, Alexander, 148-150,
    151

Fadiman, James, 4
Faria, Abbé J. C., 22
Farrar, Janet, 184
Feinstein, David, 180-181
feminism, 182, 183
Fenwick, Peter, 220
Fourth Force Psychology, 78
Fourth Way, The, (Gurdjieff),
    42
Freud, Sigmund, 48-53, 54, 213
fundamentalism, 2, 8, 252

Gaia Hypothesis (Lovelock),
    199-200, 201

Gawain, Shakti, 147-148
Ginsberg, Allen, 114
Gnosticism, 60, 61
God, 60, 61,150,157,166, 174,
    214, 221, 228, 230, 245, 251,
    252
Goddess, The, 182, 183, 184, 185
Goldenberg, Naomi, 183
Goleman, Daniel, 212
Good Friday Experiment, 102-
    106
Grey, Margot, 220, 224
Greyson, Bruce, 220
Grof, Stanislav, 4, 79, 129-136,
    205, 209, 216, 217, 247-248
Gurdjieff, George, 6, 8, 9, 35-43,
    126, 127, 129
Gurumayı
    (ChidvilasanandaSwami),
    168
guru, role of the, 168, 170, 172-
    173
gurus, Indian, 162-173
Gurwitsch, Alexander, 203

hallucinations, 222
Harner, Michael, 193-198
Hay, Louise, 152
healing, spiritual, 16
Heard, Gerald, 34, 35, 172
Hehl, Maximilian, 17
Heim, Albert, 219-220, 224
Hemi-Sync process (Monroe),
    237

Hierarchy of needs (Maslow),
    71
Hill, Napoloeon, 144-145, 146
Hinduism, 27, 34
hippies, 108-115
Hodgson, Richard, 30
holism.16, 63-64, 137-139, 201,
    202, 204, 209, 211, 217, 243
Holism and Evolution (Smuts),
    63
holistic health, 137-150
Hollingshead, Michael, 101
holotropic breath therapy
    (Grof), 135-136
Houston, Jean, 4, 176-179, 216,
    250
human potential movement, 69
Humphreys, Christmas, 32
Huxley, Aldous, 3, 7, 34, 35, 90,
    94-95, 172
hypnotherapy, 7, 16, 22
hypnotism, 31

Ichazo, Oscar, 43, 126-127
id (Freud), 49, 50, 51
individuation (Jung), 58, 59
Ingerman, Sandra, 249
In Search of the Miraculous
    (Ouspensky), 40
Isherwood, Christopher, 34
Isis, 178
Isis Unveiled (Blavatsky), 26

James, William, 34, 44-48

Jayakar, Pupul, 172
Jeans, Sir James, 206
journey of the hero, Joseph
    Campbell's, 175
Jung, Carl, 3, 51, 53-61, 174,
    207, 208, 215

karma, 158
karma-burning, 126
Keen, Sam, 186
Kesey, Ken, 110-111
Ketamine, 223-224
Kletti, Ray, 220-224
Knight, J. Z., 156, 160-161
Krippner, Stanley, 180, 181
Krishnamurti, Jiddu, 3, 73, 170-
    173, 213
Kubler-Ross, Elisabeth, 218,
    220, 228-231, 238
Kuhn, Thomas, 248
Kundalini yoga, 166, 167-168

Lammers, Arthur, 158
Law of Seven (Gurdjieff), 41
Law of Three (Gurdjieff), 40-41
Leadbeater, C.W., 170, 171, 172
Leary, Timothy, 97-103,105-106,
    114, 117, 241-242
Le Shan, Lawrence, 140-141
libido (Freud), 49, 50
life-goals (Adler), 62
Lifeline Program (Monroe), 238
life-readings (Cayce), 158, 159,
    160

Lilly, John, 122-129, 217, 245
Lovelock, James, 199-200
Lowen, Alexander, 50
LSD, 95, 96, 97, 101, 112, 124,
    129, 130-135, 136, 165

MacLaine, Shirley, 152, 156
Magarey, Christopher, 167
magnetism, animal, 18, 19, 21
Maharishi Mahesh Yogi, 163-
    164
Mahatmas, 25, 27, 29
Maltz, Maxwell, 145-146
mantras, personal, 165
Maslow, Abraham, 3, 70-80
Mayblom, Lynette, 162
Medicine Eagle, Brooke, 191-193
meditation, 166, 245
mediumism, 29
Merry Pranksters, 111
Mesmer, Anton, 7, 16-22, 31
Metzner, Ralph, 97, 100, 117,
    120, 121, 201
Mind Dynamics (Everett), 148-
    149
Monroe, Robert A., 231, 235-
    241, 244
Moody, Raymond, 219,220
morphic resonance, 202-204
morphogenetic fields, 203
Muktananda, Swami, 166-168
Murphy, Michael, 76, 80, 90, 92
mushrooms, sacred, 98-99
Myss, Carolyn, 152

mystical experience, 215
mysticism, 45, 73, 77, 99
mythology, personal, 180-182
mythology, relevance of, 174-176, 177, 178, 179-180, 182, 197, 250
myths, origin of, 175

near-death experiences, 219-228
neuropeptides, 141
neurosis, 48
New Age movement, 31-32
Newtonian-Cartesian model of the universe, 204, 209
Newton, Isaac, 204
Ngangikrungkurr, Miriam-RoseUngunmerr, 200
Nirvana, 164
Noyes Russell, 220, 224

Odysseus, 178
Olcott, Henry Steel, 24-25, 27, 28, 29,171
Orage, A.P., 37
Order of the Star in the East, 171
orgone energy (Reich), 65
Osho, 169
Osiris, 178
Osis, Karlis, 220
Ouspensky, Peter D., 36, 37, 39, 40
out-of-the-body experiences, 226, 229, 235-241

Pace, Bianca, 162
Pahnke, Walter, 102-105
paradigms, birth of new, 248-249
Parliament of Religions, 33
Parnia, Sam, 220
Parsifal, 178
Patricia Farrier case (Cayce), 160
peak experience,79
Pearce, Joseph Chilton, 238
perennial philosophy, 213
Perls, Fritz, 43, 83-87, 215
personal growth, 69, 71, 74
Pert, Candace, 141-144
plants, sacred, 188
power animals, shamanic, 196
Power of Myth, The (Campbell), 174
precognition, 53
Price, Richard, 80
prosperity consciousness, 153
psychedelic drugs, 94-116
psychic research, 45, 53
Psycho-cybernetics (Maltz), 145-146
psychology, gestalt, 83-86
psychology, humanistic, 68, 75, 77
psychology, sacred, 176-182
psychology, transpersonal, 47, 68-80
psycho-neuroimmunology (PNI), 141-142

psychosis, 48
psychosomatic disease, 139-142
Puységur, Marquisde, 20-21

quantum physics, 206, 208, 209, 210, 211

Rajneesh, Bhagwan Shree, 47, 169-170
Ramakrishna, 33, 73
Ramtha (spirit guide), 156, 160-161
Rawson, Albert Leighton, 23
rebirth, spiritual, 133
Reich, Wilhelm, 64-67
reincarnation, 232-235, 240
Ring, Kenneth, 4, 220, 221, 222, 226, 230
Robbins, Anthony, 152, 153-154
Roberts, Jane, 156
Roddenberry, Gene, 241
Rogers, Carl, 87, 90
Rogo, D. Scott, 228
Rosin, Carol, 241
Roszak, Theodore, 43
Ryerson, Kevin, 156

Sabom, Michael, 220, 222, 224
Schutz, Will, 87-90
scientism, 246
Secret Doctrine, The (Blavatsky), 32
'seeing' (Castaneda), 188
self-actualization (Maslow), 71, 74, 79
self-awareness, 173
self-help, 155
self-knowledge, 48, 69
self-realization, 215
self-remembering (Gurdjieff), 36, 38
Selye, Hans, 139
sensory isolation, 122-125
Seth (spirit guide), 156
shadow, Jungian, 59
shaktipat, 167
shamanism, 185-198
Sheela, Ma Anand, 169
Sheldrake, Rupert, 202, 238
siddha, 167
Siddha Yoga, 166-167
Simonton, Carl, 141-142
Simos, Miriam (Starhawk), 184
Singer, June, 207
Skinner, B. F., 69
sleep, 51
Smuts, Jan, 63-64
Spiral Dance, The (Starhawk), 184
spirits, discarnate, 23
spiritual illuminati, 151
spiritualism, 24, 29, 34
spirituality, feminist, 182-184
Stace, W. T., 103-104
Starhawk, 184-185
Starret, Barbara, 183
Stevenson, Ian, 231, 232-235
St Francis of Assisi, 178

Sufis, 35, 38
Summer of love (San
    Francisco), 94, 106-114
Sun Bear, 189-191
Sutich, Anthony, 70-78
Swedenborg, Emanuel, 6, 9-15

Tacey, David, 59, 244
Tai Chi, 92
Tao of Physics, The (Capra), 206
Tart, Charles, 4, 246
Teachings of Don Juan, The
    (Castaneda), 186
temporal lobe seizure, 222-223
thanatology, 218
Theosophical Society, 25-26, 31,
    32, 33, 170, 171, 272
Theosophy, 29, 30, 31, 32, 36,
    157
Tibetan Book of the Dead, The,
    117-120, 231
Tibetan Masters, 26, 28, 30, 171
TM (transcendental
    meditation), 164-166
tolerance, religious, 252
trance states, 195
Transpersonal movement, 3,
    244, 249, 250
Type A personality, 140
Type B personality, 140

Uncertainty Principle,
    Heisenberg's, 205, 210
Unity Consciousness, 214, 216

Valiente, Doreen, 184
Valle, Ronald, 205
Van Lommel, Pim, 220
Varieties of Religious Experience,
    The (James), 34, 44, 45
Vaughan, Frances, 4, 243
Vedanta, 33, 34, 35, 216
Virtue, Doreen, 152, 154
vision-quest, shamanic, 191-
    193
visualization, 142, 147-148, 177
Vivekananda, 33-34, 45, 73

Walsch, Neale Donald, 152
Watson, John B., 69
Watts, Alan, 7, 74-75, 90, 95-97,
    102
Way of the Shaman, The
    (Harner), 195
Weiss, Brian, 154
Wiener, Norbert, 145
Wilber, Ken, 4, 7, 212-217
Wilde, Stuart, 154
witchcraft, 184,185

yippies, 115

Zohar, Danah, 4, 209-211
Zukav, Gary, 208

B O O K S

O is a symbol of the world, of oneness and unity. In different cultures it also means the "eye," symbolizing knowledge and insight. We aim to publish books that are accessible, constructive and that challenge accepted opinion, both that of academia and the "moral majority."

Our books are available in all good English language bookstores worldwide. If you don't see the book on the shelves ask the bookstore to order it for you, quoting the ISBN number and title. Alternatively you can order online (all major online retail sites carry our titles) or contact the distributor in the relevant country, listed on the copyright page.

See our website **www.o-books.net** for a full list of over 500 titles, growing by 100 a year.

And tune in to myspiritradio.com for our book review radio show, hosted by June-Elleni Laine, where you can listen to the authors discussing their books.

MySpiritRadio